Noël C

Noël Coward was born in 1899 in Teddington, Middlesex. He made his name as a playwright with *The Vortex* (1924), in which he also appeared. His numerous other successful plays include *Fallen Angels* (1925), *Hay Fever* (1925), *Private Lives* (1930), *Design for Living* (1933), and *Blithe Spirit* (1941). During the war, he wrote screenplays such as *Brief Encounter* (1944) and *In Which We Serve* (1942). In the fifties, he began a new career as a cabaret entertainer. He published volumes of verse and a novel, *Pomp and Circumstance* (1960), two volumes of autobiography and four volumes of short stories: *To Step Aside* (1939), *Star Quality* (1951), *Pretty Polly Barlow* (1964) and *Bon Voyage* (1967). He was knighted in 1970 and died three years later in Jamaica.

Barry Day OBE originally worked in advertising in London and New York, eventually as Worldwide Creative Director and Vice Chairman of the McCann-Erickson agency and Creative Director of the IAA, before retiring in 2000. He has published some twenty-five books – twelve of them on Noël Coward – as well as Dorothy Parker, P.G.Wodehouse, Oscar Wilde, Johnny Mercer and Raymond Chandler. His *The Letters of Noël Coward* won the Book of the Year Award from ASCAP, the music industry's governing body, as well as being a *New York Times* Book of the Year. He also served as Communications Director in Sam Wanamaker's rebuilding of Shakespeare's Globe. Barry Day is the Literary Advisor to the Noël Coward Estate, as well as a Trustee of the Coward Foundation. In 2015, he received an Honorary Doctorate (D.Litt.) from the University of Westminster.

also by Noël Coward

Coward
Collected Plays: One
(Hay Fever, The Vortex, Fallen Angels, Easy Virtue)

Collected Plays: Two
(Private Lives, Bitter-Sweet, The Marquise, Post-Mortem)

Collected Plays: Three
(Design for Living, Cavalcade, Conversation Piece,
and Hands Across the Sea, Still Life, Fumed Oak
from To-night at 8.30)

Collected Plays: Four
(Blithe Spirit, Present Laughter, This Happy Breed,
and Ways and Means, The Astonished Heart, 'Red Peppers'
from To-night at 8.30)

Collected Plays: Five
(Relative Values, Look After Lulu!
Waiting in the Wings, Suite in Three Keys)

Collected Plays: Six
(Semi-Monde, Point Valaine, South Sea Bubble,
Nude With Violin)

Collected Plays: Seven
(Quadrille, 'Peace in Our Time',
and We Were Dancing, Shadow Play, Family Album, Star Chamber
from To-night at 8.30)

Collected Plays: Eight
(I'll Leave It To You, The Young Idea, This Was A Man)

Collected Revue Sketches and Parodies

The Complete Lyrics of Noël Coward

Collected Short Stories

Pomp and Circumstance
A Novel

Autobiography

Present Indicative

Future Indefinite

in the same series

Private Lives

Semi-Monde

Star Quality

Hay Fever

Noël Coward Screenplays

In Which We Serve
Brief Encounter
The Astonished Heart

NOËL COWARD

Edited by Barry Day

Bloomsbury Methuen Drama
An imprint of Bloomsbury Publishing Plc

B L O O M S B U R Y
LONDON · OXFORD · NEW YORK · NEW DELHI · SYDNEY

Bloomsbury Methuen Drama

An imprint of Bloomsbury Publishing Plc

Imprint previously known as Methuen Drama

50 Bedford Square	1385 Broadway
London	New York
WC1B 3DP	NY 10018
UK	USA

www.bloomsbury.com

BLOOMSBURY, METHUEN DRAMA and the Diana logo are trademarks of Bloomsbury Publishing Plc

British Library Cataloguing-in-Publication Data

A catalogue record for this book is available from the British Library.

ISBN:	HB:	978-1-4725-6824-3
	PB:	978-1-4725-6809-0
	ePDF:	978-1-4725-6830-4
	ePub:	978-1-4725-6829-8

Library of Congress Cataloging-in-Publication Data

A catalog record for this book is available from the Library of Congress.

Typeset by Fakenham Prepress Solutions, Fakenham, Norfolk NR21 8NN

Printed and bound in India

Contents

List of Images

1. Poster for *In Which We Serve*, ITV/REX

2. Poster, *Brief Encounter*, ITV/REX

3. Poster, *The Astonished Heart*, Courtesy Everett Collection/ REX

4. *The Astonished Heart*, Margaret Leighton and Celia Johnson, Photofest

5. *The Astonished Heart*, Noël Coward and Margaret Leighton having cocktails together in a restaurant, Photofest

6. *In Which We Serve*, Noël Coward shaking John Mills's hand with men in Customs Warehouse, Photofest

7. *In Which We Serve*, Noël Coward with an injured Richard Attenborough, Photofest

8. *In Which We Serve*, Noël Coward, John Mills and Bernard Miles clinging to the life raft, ITV/REX

9. *Brief Encounter*, Celia Johnson talking out of train window to Trevor Howard, ITV/REX

10. *Brief Encounter*, Celia Johnson and Trevor Howard under railway bridge, ITV/REX

11. *Brief Encounter*, Stanley Holloway and Joyce Carey talking over café counter, ITV/REX

12. AMPAS certificate for *In Which We Serve*, courtesy of Academy of Motion Picture Arts and Sciences

Foreword

Story is the skeletal structure of every narrative film: dialogue adds sinew suggesting an eventual dramatic torque. A shooting script is plot, dialogue and a description of what is to be photographed. It is the Bible of the filmmaking process to which each director and craftsperson refers, and to which he adheres or, much more likely, alters as the contingencies of production demand. It is a rare shooting script that ends up the true and actual screenplay of a completed film, and we have Barry Day to thank for providing the reader with the only three finished screenplays – radiant, quick-witted and emotionally wise – Noël Coward himself wrote for the cinema, *In Which We Serve* (1942, directed by Coward and David Lean), *Brief Encounter* (1945, David Lean) and *The Astonished Heart* (1950, Terence Fisher and Anthony Darnborough).

The first two of these features are seen by critics, scholars, and audiences alike as precise and enthusiastic portraits of British character – resolute, cheeky and understated, the cinema has ever produced. *Brief Encounter* is ranked second on the British Film Institute's list of the Best British Films of All Time (the first – the list being very British, is a film set in Vienna – *The Third Man*). *In Which We Serve* floats in at ninety-two. If ever the British were thought as a people muted in feelings and repressed in the most civilized manner, Coward's chronicle of an unconsummated yet subcutaneously passionate love affair between a married doctor and a suburban mother, confirms and elevates this perception. Coward adapted *Brief Encounter* from *Still Life*, one in his cycle of ten short plays, *Tonight at 8.30*. He expanded and elaborated *Still Life* into a screenplay just as he subsequently re-imagined for the screen another of his plays from the same cycle *The Astonished Heart* whose title derives from Deuteronomy 28.28 – 'The Lord shall smite thee with madness, blindness and astonishment of heart'.

The two screenplays make a neat if contrapuntal comparison. What is sublimated in *Brief Encounter* runs a very decorous amok in *The Astonished Heart*. The blight of astonishment compels a renowned psychiatrist, Dr. Christian Faber (played by Coward) to forsake his perfectly reasonable wife for a very appealing temptress leading to a catastrophic breakdown of domesticity, professional relationships and, most significantly to a diminution of self. As Laura Jesson, the resistant matron of *Brief Encounter* avers, 'It is awfully easy to lie when you know that you're trusted implicitly. So very easy and so very degrading'. Yet Dr. Faber's degradation may explain Coward's popularity today.

In a 2009 interview recorded at the New York Public Library, Barry Day, Coward's indefatigable champion, believes Coward, who was a major celebrity in his day, is regarded with even more popular and critical favour in the new millennium. Day attributes this favour in part to Coward's descriptions of the dark side of life namely the 'impossibility of love', a melancholy that transcends the brittle wit for which the writer/composer/performer is otherwise applauded. The profound difficulty of achieving an ideal relationship may be the experience of a man whose sexuality had to some extent remain covert and constrained but whose desire to love was both overwhelming and irrepressible. In this regard Coward's contemporary success may be likened to that of another artist, the late German filmmaker, Rainer Werner Fassbinder, whose films about passion, either unrequited or disapproved, speak to the angst of recurring generations. This recognition of existential pain is best expressed again by Laura Jesson as, in the heat of her inner conflict, she thinks, 'This can't last. This misery can't last. I must remember to control myself. I must remember that and try to control myself. Nothing lasts really. Neither happiness nor despair. Not even life lasts very long'.

I add another reason for Coward's revival, and that is Barry Day whose British modesty would forbid him to make such a claim himself. Day, who never met Coward, became involved with his estate after a troubling visit to Firefly, the late author's home in Jamaica. Day contacted and befriended Graham Payn, Coward's lifetime companion who appears as Dr. Faber's loyal assistant in *The Astonished Heart*. Payn gave Day, who had been the editor of *The Isis* magazine at Oxford, and who enjoyed a very successful career in advertising where brevity, purpose and humour are allied in the art of persuasion, access to Coward's papers. Day organized these into several revelatory books of selected writings, public and private, including the screenplays in this volume of which two, *The*

Astonished Heart and *In Which We Serve* have not been published previously.

Day's affection for Coward may be traced to *In Which We Serve*. Growing up in Derby, an industrial city in the Midlands, a target for Nazi bombers, he was sustained, as were his fellow citizens, by the rallying spirit of Noël Coward as melodiously expressed in a song like *London Pride*, and or powerfully articulated in a film like *In Which We Serve*, produced, written, co-directed and starring Coward who also wrote the music for the film.

Although *In Which We Serve* did inspire audiences, it is unlikely propaganda. In the opening moments of this 'story of a ship', the ship, the HMS *Torrin*, a naval destroyer, is itself destroyed. As the ship sinks its crew headed by Captain E. V. Kinross (Coward) thinks back to earlier days on land and sea. These flashbacks form the nostalgic narrative of the film. *In Which We Serve* was made in 1942 when the outcome of the war was hardly certain but shortly after the US declared war on the Axis and Hollywood began making films about military victories rather than Allied defeats. Coward's screenplay is not bombastic in the American sense but in its poetic reserve and striking acknowledgment of the casualties of war, it is about sticking together 'beyond all loss'. Coward recognizes Britain's will to resist – indomitable and irresistible. It is supple grace under fire, and, exemplified by the multi-class crew of the HMS *Torrin*, one of the six hundred British warships then on the seas, it unifies a beleaguered people.

It is interesting to note two other strong films about fortress Britain, one made in 1940, *Convoy* (Penn Tennyson), and the second, shot contemporaneously with *In Which We Serve*, *Next of Kin* (Thorold Dickinson), also kept spirits up by acknowledging military failure. *Convoy* and *Next of Kin* were produced by another great purveyor of British character, the producer Michael Balcon, whose post-war comedies made at Ealing Studios would soon charm the world with their eccentric protagonists. Balcon had had a long relationship with Coward. He had brought three of the playwright's early West End successes to the screen, *Easy Virtue* (1927, Alfred Hitchcock), *The Queen Was in the Parlour* (1927, Graham Cutts) and *The Vortex* (1928, Adrian Brunel) before the advent of sound. Deprived of Coward's words, all films failed at the box office. I suspect the reason neither *Convoy* nor *Next of Kin* are remembered with the same passion nor are revived with the same frequency as Coward's *In Which We Serve* is for somewhat the same reason.

Coward's careful words and stirring phrasing distinguish *In Which We Serve* and make it extraordinary so much so that in 1943 Coward was given an Honorary Academy Award for his film and, beating out another famous wartime melodrama, *Casablanca* (1942, Michael Curtiz), *In Which We Serve* was acclaimed Best Picture of the Year Award by the New York Film Critics Circle.

These screenplays indeed provide a literary banquet.

Lawrence Kardish, Senior Curator Emeritus, Film,
New York's Museum of Modern Art

General Introduction

The writing of screenplays was a talent that Noël acquired relatively late in his precocious career. In retrospect it's easy to understand why.

In 1927 Michael Balcon – then the head of Gainsborough Pictures – had bought the film rights to three of Noël's early plays … *The Queen Was in the Parlour*, *Easy Virtue* and *The Vortex* … and filmed them all in that same year.

Anxious to establish credibility for the fledgling British film industry, he had settled on the strategy of buying successful literary properties that would demonstrate artistic integrity. The only flaw in that thinking was that a Coward play depended almost entirely on its sophisticated dialogue – and the movies were still stubbornly silent!

In the film version Noël was not even invited to provide the title cards and the resulting films left him distinctly disenchanted with film as a medium.

In a magazine interview at the time he was quoted as grandly saying …

> You may take it that I am not interested in writing scenarios
> at all. I want to write words, not stage directions. I don't
> want to cast any slur on scenario work, and I readily admit
> that it is a highly expert business. But as a dramatist,
> dialogue and its psychology are practically my sole concern.
> You will notice that in the published version of my plays the
> stage directions are cut down to the absolute minimum … It
> is work which simply does not appeal to me.

In saying that he was telling only part of the truth. At the time he was trying his hand at an original screenplay for Balcon. It was to be called *Concerto* and it was based on one of his short stories.

Balcon turned it down, which must have been humiliating for Noël but was ultimately good news for the theatre, since he ultimately revised the story line and made it the basis for his successful operetta, *Bitter Sweet* two years later.

In that same interview, however, he made a perceptive observation. Film, he noted, 'should not be regarded as an off-shoot of the stage. It is a totally different medium and one which, in its own distinctive way, should have constructive form and the minimum of digression'. His analysis was correct but the key to the medium was to elude him for some time to come.

And his highly-developed sense of three-act play construction may have had a lot to do with it.

***

By the time he began making regular visits to Hollywood in the early 1930s, sound had arrived and transformed the way films were made but even so, while watching his new-found friends at work interested him as an observer, he felt no compulsion to join or compete with them.

He wrote to his mother Violet – 'I'm not very keen on Hollywood … I'd rather have a nice cup of cocoa, really'.

In 1935 he did edge a small step closer when he agreed to star in *The Scoundrel* to be directed by Ben Hecht and Charles MacArthur but that was shot not in Hollywood but in the more informal Astoria Studios in New York, where his friends could join in and turn it into a party as well as a production.

The fee was small ($5,000) and the anticipated bonus from profits never materialized. The real profit for Noël was the experience of seeing up close how a film got made.

Balcon, Hecht and MacArthur may have written the unwitting prologue but it was David Lean and Orson Welles who set the scene for Noël's eventual entry into filmmaking.

***

In 1941 Noël agreed to write, produce, co-direct and act in a propaganda film about the Royal Navy – a subject close to his heart. He prepared a draft screenplay, which he called *White Ensign* and read it enthusiastically aloud to the key production team he had chosen – co-director David Lean, cameraman Ronald Neame and producer Anthony Havelock-Allan.

When he'd finished, there was an embarrassed silence before Lean spoke up and pointed out that, wonderful as it was, it would take up to five hours of screen time.

'Oh, my God!' said Noël – for once somewhat abashed – 'I never thought of that. I thought you could do anything in the movies. I fear this has as many restrictions around it as the stage'.

Lean saved the day by suggesting, rather diffidently, that Noël might go and see the new Orson Welles film, *Citizen Kane*, that was impressing critics and the public alike. Noël promptly saw the film and saw the light. He promised Lean a rewrite within two weeks.

The overlapping time structure, the introduction of characters and then their 'back story' in the eventual *In Which We Serve* were lessons learned from Welles and they would be refined later in *Brief Encounter*.

***

The rest – as they say – is cinema history.

Barry Day

In Which We Serve

Introduction to *In Which We Serve*

World War I had been a personal humiliation for Noël. Invalided out after a pathetically short period of service, the thought that he had not pulled his weight, when so many of his generation lay in the mud of some foreign field, continued to haunt his mature years. He was determined to compensate for it when the time came, as in the mid-1930s it became increasingly obvious that it would.

Noël's role in World War II did not have a promising start, either. Sent to France as war was declared to co-ordinate propaganda, he found the job he had been given to do unfocused and frustrating. His superiors soon detected 'the beating of wings' and sent him on a fact-finding trip to America. By the time he returned, Paris had fallen and he was 'unemployed' again.

Some time later he was approached by a delegation that included film producers Anthony Havelock-Allan and Filipo del Giudice with a *carte blanche* proposal for Noël to make any film he liked.

Clearly, it must be about the war. Just as clearly, it must embody that spirit of cheerful resilience that Britain prides itself on demonstrating in times of crisis. All that was self-evident. But what was to be the subject?

Noël asked for time to think.

Then over dinner with his old friend, Lord Louis Mountbatten, Noël heard the story of the sinking of Mountbatten's own command, H.M.S. *Kelly* in the Battle of Crete. The story was perfect in every way. It even tapped into his own deeply felt passion for the sea.

'The Royal Navy means a great deal to me', he wrote, 'and here, in this Odyssey of one destroyer, was the very essence of it. All the true sentiment, the comedy, the tragedy, the casual valiance, the undaunted heroism, the sadness without tears, and the pride without end. Later on that night, in my bed at the Savoy, I knew this was a story to tell, if only I could tell it without sentimentality but with simplicity and truth'.

While he was writing his first draft later that year (1941) he and Havelock-Allan handpicked the team. David Lean was their first choice. During his initial search Noël had viewed numerous British films of the recent past and found that in the ones he liked best the

Film Editor was almost invariably Lean. Lean agreed to join the team – with the cheeky proviso that he should also be co-director. He had never directed before – but, then, neither had Noël. In fact, he was distinctly relieved to have someone so technically proficient at his side when there was so much at stake.

Although Noël doesn't mention if himself, there is evidence that in choosing Lean, his hand was guided.

When the film was successfully launched John Mills was dining with director Carol Reed, who told him – 'You know, when Noël Coward went around asking for suggestions as to who should help him with this film, I suggested David Lean … It's the most insidious goddam thing I ever did!'

Reed would have to wait another three years to balance his personal books. When Noël declined to make a follow-up film that featured the Army, Reed would be given the brief to make *The Way Ahead*. The film was a success – but on nothing like the scale of *In Which We Serve*.

As cameraman they were all agreed on Ronald Neame. The trio – Havelock-Allan, Lean and Neame – were to work on three other Coward films before they parted company with him in 1945.

After their brief encounter with Coward, his 'little darlings' as he called them, moved to Dickens to make *Great Expectations* and *Oliver Twist*.

***

The project was not without its problems when it came to execution. Many of the then powers-that-be were aghast at the thought of a naval captain in the line of fire being played by some effete actor fellow and, when it was discovered that the storyline involved one of our ships actually being sunk, there was a concerted official move to withdraw support.

(A British ship *sunk*? Whose side is this fellow Coward *on*!!)

It was only Mountbatten's personal intervention – and the support of George VI – who just happened to be his cousin – that kept the door ajar. The King wrote – 'Although the ship is lost, the spirit which animates the Royal Navy is clearly brought out in the men and the procession of ships coming along to take its place at the end demonstrates the power of the Navy'.

Mountbatten, too, had his qualms. He begged Noël to ensure that the character of Captain Kinross was not based too recognisably on him.

Noël did, indeed, make minor modifications to the script. He demoted the Captain from aristocrat to middle class. The resemblance remained obvious to those in the know. Kinross's Lady lost her title and their Rolls shrank to a Ford. They also acquired a Cocker Spaniel called Trafalgar. Nonetheless, the fuss and fury evaporated as it became clear that a remarkable film was under way and a visit to the set by the Royal Family – carefully orchestrated by Noël himself – silenced the voices of discontent.

It was not known until much later that Noël had worn Mountbatten's own cap in the film. And when Captain 'D' addresses the crew he used some of the phrases he had heard his friend use in the same real life circumstances. Production lasted from 5 February to 27 June 1942.

In his diary Noël describes part of the process ...

Hours of casting discussions ... arguments about the budget ... staring at myself on the screen – heavy jowls, no eyes at all ... discussions with experts – naval experts, film experts, shipbuilding experts, gunnery experts.

He had to be very careful with his own performance. 'I act a great deal with my hands – and naval officers do not! I was clasping my hands behind my back, doing anything rather than do a "Noël Coward" gesture ... doing scenes over and over again to try and eliminate Noël Coward mannerisms ... Ronnie Neame has at last discovered what to do about my face, which is to photograph it from above rather than below'.

The filming was not without incident ...

Richard Attenborough – whose film debut this was – recalled the three weeks in which the survivors of the *Torrin* were immersed in a tank representing the open sea. The water didn't improve with keeping and they would lower themselves in gingerly. 'But not The Master. Always dived in. A little flat but *dived* in. On the last day he emerged and gave his verdict – "There's dysentery in every ripple!"'

***

When Noël as Captain 'D' addresses the crew for the first time he explains his philosophy of command. 'A happy ship is an efficient ship'.

After the first take a sound technician whispered to Lean – would someone please tell Mr. Coward to watch his enunciation during that 'fish-and-chips' speech.

***

John Mills had a bawdier recollection. His character (Shorty) is in the water when a German plane strafes the survivors. To create the necessary effect the Props department rigged up a series of condoms which were exploded under water.

Mills claimed to be 'the only actor shot in the arm with a French letter'.

***

The realism Noël and David Lean created was borne out when the Second Sea Lord – their Navy liaison – was invited to see some of the footage.

He was shown the scene in which the character played by John Mills has to tell Bernard Miles that Miles' wife has been killed in an air raid back home.

When the lights came up the Sea Lord was seen to be wiping his eye. 'By Jove, Coward', he said, 'that convinces me you were right to ask for *real* sailors. No *actors* could possibly have done that'.

***

There would be one more discordant note.

Lord Beaverbrook was the proprietor of the *Daily Express* and he took marked exception to the shot of the paper floating in the water proclaiming *No War This Year* when the war was clearly being waged. By this time he was a key member of Churchill's wartime cabinet and a close advisor to the Prime Minister. He became a rabid enemy of Noël and Mountbatten ever after and was almost certainly influential in persuading Churchill to oppose the granting of Noël's knighthood in 1942, despite the fact that the King himself was in favour. It took another thirty years before Noël received the honour.

The irony here was that the newspaper shot had nothing to do with either Noël or Mountbatten. It was put into the script by Havelock-Allan. I hardly need to add that the film received tremendous critical and public acclaim. It even received a Special 'Oscar'.

Dilys Powell in the *Sunday Times* called it 'the best film about the war yet made in this country or in America', while *The Observer's* C. A Lejeune noted that 'His heart has sneaked up on Mr. Coward. *In Which We Serve* never gushes, but there is a subtle warmth in the old astringency. For the first time he seems to be speaking, not to the select but to the simple'. American critic, Herb Sterne went so far as to say that 'He (Coward) might be described as the British Orson Welles, if Orson could write, act, direct, sing, dance, compose songs and be amusing'.

When it premiered on 27 September 1942, the film spoke most eloquently for itself '... I was moved and proud to see the impact of the picture on that distinguished audience. Towards the end there was a great deal of gratifying nose-blowing and one stern-faced Admiral in the row behind me was unashamedly in tears. For me it was a wonderful experience'.

Even today audiences who have heard nothing more than the rumour of war find themselves moved by the understated truth of the film's emotions. And for someone, like myself, brought up in those heightened times out of time, it never fails to bring back the feeling of how proud one felt to be British.

***

There was a PS:

Noël was dining with his little darlings after the film came out. He was the first to leave and as he passed a nearby table, he heard one of the diners say that he'd enjoyed the film but that he didn't think Noël was right as Captain 'D'.

Noël stopped, leaned over the table and said – '*I* thought I was very, *very* good!'

Shooting Script by David Lean
December 1941

> Be pleased to receive into thy Almighty
> and most Gracious protection the persons
> of us thy servants, and the Fleet
> in which we serve.
> (Forms of Prayer to be used at Sea [First Prayer])

This film is dedicated to the Royal Navy.

'Whereon under the good providence of God, the wealth, safety
and strength of the Kingdom chiefly depend'.

This film would not have been possible without the help, guidance
and co-operation of the following –

The Royal Navy
The Royal Air Force
The 5th Battalion the Coldstream Guards

Production Credits

Produced by Two Cities at Denham Studios.

First shown in London at the Gaumont, Haymarket and the Marble
Arch Pavillion simultaneously on 27 September 1942.

A Noël Coward Production.

Producer	Noël Coward
Associate Producer	Anthony Havelock-Allan
Directors	Noël Coward and David Lean
Assistant Director & Unit Manager	Michael Anderson[1]

---

[1] Assistant Director Michael Anderson would crop up again in Noël's professional
life when he directed *Around the World in Eighty Days* (1956) in which Noël played
a scene as Hesketh-Baggott, the proprietor of an employment agency for gentlemen's
gentlemen opposite John Gielgud.

Screenplay	Noël Coward
Photography	Ronald Neame
Art Director	David Rawnsley
Art Supervisor	Gladys Calthrop
Music	Noël Coward

Score conducted by Muir Mathieson and the London Symphony Orchestra

Editors	David Lean and Thelma Myers[2]
Sound Recording	C. C. Stevens
Operating Cameraman	Guy Green
Production Manager	Sydney S. Streeter
Make Up	Tony Sforzini
Set Dressing	Norman Delaney
Special Effects	Douglas Woolsey
Special Effects Cameraman	Derick Williams
Naval Advisors	Able Seaman I. T. Clark OBE, RN Lieutenant C. R. E. Compton RN

Officers On H.M.S. *Torrin*

Lt-Commander Robin Farrell (Number One)	Derek Elphinstone
Lt. Maurice Hadley (Flotilla Gunnery Office Guns)	Robert Sanson
Commander A.B. Gorman (Commander 'E', 'Chief')	Ballard Berkeley
Lt. John Macadoo (Flotilla Torpedo Officer, 'Torps')	Philip Friend
Lt. Hubert Ritchie (Flotilla Navigator, 'Pilot')	Hubert Gregg

---

[2] The original editor was Reginald Beck, who resigned when he found Lean was coming to the editing suite at night and recutting his material

Lt. E. G.Leggett (Flotilla Signal Officer, Flags)	Michael Wilding
Surgeon-Lt. (Flotilla Medical Officer, 'Doc')	James Donald
Alec Carey, Midshipman ('Snotty')	Chimno Branson
Sub-Lt. Arthur Black, R.N.V.R.	Kenneth Carten
Sub-Lt. Peter Williams ('Sub')	Michael Whittaker
Paymaster Lt.-Commander Charles Borrell ('Secco')	John Varley

Ratings On H.M.S. *Torrin*

Torpedo Gunner's Mate, Brodie	Caven Watson
Edgecombe, Captain 'D's Cabin Hand	Frederick Piper
Ordinary Seaman Joey Mackridge	Geoffrey Hibbert
Able Seaman Hollett	John Boxer
Able Seaman Parkinson	Leslie Dwyer
Able Seaman Fisher	Charles Russell[3]
Able Seaman Coombe	Robert Moreton
Coxwain	Johnnie Schofield
Able Seaman Reynolds	Lionel Grose
Leading Seaman Moran	John Singer
A Young Stoker	Richard Attenborough[4]
Adams (Posty)	Kenneth Evans
Colonel Charles Lumsden	Walter Fitzgerald
Captain Jasper Fry	Gerald Case
Commander H. L.Spencer, Commander of the *Tomahawk*	Franklin Bennett
No.1 on Tremayne	Charles Compton
Mrs. Alix Kinross, Captain 'D's wife	Celia Johnson
Bobby, aged 10, their son	Daniel Massey[5]

[3]Charles Russell would be one of Noël's US management representatives in later years but the relationship ended acrimoniously.
[4]Attenborough took his proud parents to the opening night – only to find that he didn't appear in the credits. He more than made up for it later.
[5]Daniel Massey was one of Noël 's several god children. His mother, Adrianne Allen

Lavinia, aged 8, their daughter	Ann Stephens
Trafalgar, their Spaniel	
Emily, servant of the Kinross house	Josie Welford
Mr. Satterthwaite, Manager of the Shipyard	Norman Pierce
Mrs. Kath Hardy, Walter's wife	Joyce Carey
Mrs. Lemon, her mother	Dora Gregory
Freda Lewis, later wife of Shorty Blake	Kay Walsh
Mr. Blake, Shorty's father	George Carney
Mrs. Blake, Shorty's mother	Kathleen Harrison
May Blake, 14, his younger sister	Jill Stephens
Nell Fosdick, his older sister	Lesley Osmond
Albert Fosdick, her husband, a corporal in the Royal Marines	Micky Anderson
Uncle Fred	Wally Patch
Mrs. Farrell	Eileen Peel
Mrs. Macadoo	Barbara Waring
Maureen Fenwick	Penelope Dudley Ward
Photographer	Roddy Hughes
Barmaid	Kay Young
Freda's baby	Juliet Mills
Narrator	Leslie Howard

A Note on the Shooting Script

Directors have their personal way of compiling a shooting script.

Alfred Hitchcock worked from a storyboard which showed each image and rarely strayed from it when it came to shooting.

Lean – with his editor's eye for how the footage he shot would cut together – carefully itemized each shot. The opening sequences could easily be from the kind of documentary with which he was most familiar.

---

had appeared with Noël in the London production of *Private Lives* in 1930, when she played the part of Sybil, Elyot's second wife. It turned out to be a brief marital encounter!

He later reflected – 'I used this method, which I later did with other writers, and put it into what I call a sort of blueprint for a film. As you shoot, you may alter it slightly, but it serves as a blueprint at your back all the time'.

One of the films that impressed Noël in his search for a director was *One of Our Aircraft is Missing*, which Lean had edited. Comparing the two films today, one can see the editor in the fledgling director.

The battle scenes are shot and assembled in the documentary tradition Lean had already done so much to define – montages of action with guns blazing, explosions, planes diving, hands feeding shells into gun muzzles alternating with close up reaction shots of men in action. Conflict defined in its details.

Shooting Script

In Which We Serve

By Noël Coward
December 1941

Characters

Captain Edward Vivian Kinross, R.N. (Captain 'D', commanding 35 Destroyer Flotilla)
Chief Bo's'n's Mate Walter Hardy (Chief Buffer)
Ordinary Seaman A. G. Blake (Shorty)

Officers in H.M.S. *Torrin*

Lieutenant-Commander Robin Farrell (Number One)
Lieutenant Maurice Hadley (Flotilla Gunnery Officer, Guns)
Commander A. E. Gorman (Commander 'E', 'Chief')
Lieutenant John Macadoo (Flotilla Torpedo Officer, 'Torps')
Lieutenant Hubert Ritchie (Flotilla Navigator, 'Pilot')

Lieutenant E. G. Leggatt (Flotilla Signal Officer, Flags)
Surgeon-Lieutenant Roland Fane (Flotilla Medical Officer, 'Doc')
Paymaster Lieutenant-Commander Charles Borrell (Captain's
Secretary 'Secco')
Sub-Lieutenant Peter Williams (Sub)
Sub-Lieutenant Arthur Black, R.N.V.R.
Illumination Officer
Alec Carey, Midshipman (Snotty)

Ratings in H.M.S. *Torrin*

Torpedo Gunner's Mate, Brodie
Chief Yeoman of Signals
Petty Officer Yeoman
Petty Officers Stephens, Hooper and Ridgeway
Ordinary Seamen Joey Mackridge, Jordan and Fisher
Able Seamen Parkinson, Hottell, Coombe and Reynolds
Leading Seamen Moran and Johnson
Chief Stoker
A Young Stoker
Coxswain
Adams (Posty)
Wireless Telegraphist
Sick Berth Attendant

Three Communications Numbers on Gun Mountings
Three Signalmen
Four Searchlight Crew
Four Action Lookouts
Two Torpedo Control Operators
Messenger
Colonel Charles Lumsden and Captain Jasper Fry
Commander H. L. Spencer (Commander of the *Tomahawk*)

Mrs. Kinross – Alix, Captain 'D's wife
Bobby, aged 10 and Lavinia, aged 8 – their children
Trafalgar, their Spaniel
Edgecombe, Captain 'D's Cabin hand

Emily, servant of the Kinross house
Mr. Satterthwaite, Manager of the Shipyard
Mrs. Walter Hardy – Kath
Mrs. Lerman, her Mother
Freda Lewis
Mr. and Mrs. Blake, Shorty's Father and Mother
Nell Fosdick, his older sister
Albert Fosdick, her husband, a Corporal in the Royal Marines
May Blake, aged 14, his young sister
Uncle Fred
Frank Gordon (an Aircraftman)
Mrs. Farrell, Mrs. Macadoo and Maureen Fenwick
Heathcote and Burton, (two Private Soldiers)
Mona Duke
Winnie, Cecil and Vera, three children
Telegraphy Boy and Telegraph Girl
Little Boy in Pub
Barmaid
Girl in Pub
Freda's Baby
A Hospital Nurse
An Ambulance Attendant
etc. etc.

Cast

Captain Edward Vivian Kinross, R.N.	
(Captain 'D', commanding 35 Destroyer	
Flotilla	Noël Coward
Chief Bo's'n's Mate Walter Hardy	
(Chief Buffer)	Bernard Miles
Ordinary Seaman A. G. Blake ('Shorty')	John Mills

Scene 1

EXT. SHIPYARD. DAY.

The voice of the **Comentator** *begins to speak over a LONG SHOT of an empty shipyard. The year is 1937.*

Leslie Howard (voice over)   This is the story of a ship …

A giant crane swings the first section of a Destroyer's keel across the yard.

(*Note: The remainder of this opening sequence consists of a very quick montage showing the birth of a Destroyer from the laying of the keel to its launching speed trials and Ensign Ceremony, finishing on the 'Daily Express' headline. Those not wishing to read the montage in detail should start reading the script at scene 32.*)

Scene 2

EXT. SHIPYARD. DAY.

CLOSE SHOT. Dockyard **mateys** *guiding the section of keel into the blocks.*

DISSOLVE TO

Scene 3

EXT. SHIPYARD. DAY.

MEDIUM SHOT. Camera PANS with another section of the keel as it swings toward the blocks.

DISSOLVE TO

Scene 4

EXT. SHIPYARD. DAY.

CLOSE SHOT men riveting the two sections together.

DISSOLVE TO

Scene 5

EXT. SHIPYARD. DAY.

LONG SHOT. The keel is complete and the first ribs of the ship are being placed into position.

DISSOLVE TO

Scene 6

EXT. SHIPYARD. DAY.

LONG SHOT from the same set-up as previous shot. The ribs are now all in position together with their cross-sections making the ship a perfect skeleton. The cranes are starting to swing in the side plates of the ship.

Scene 7

EXT. SHIPYARD. DAY.

CLOSE SHOT of the side plate as it is swung into position against the ribs of the ship.

DISSOLVE TO

Scene 8

EXT. SHIPYARD. DAY.

MEDIUM SHOT. Group of **riveters**. *Some are knocking bolts into position, others are already riveting.*

DISSOLVE TO

Scene 9

EXT. SHIPYARD. DAY.

MEDIUM SHOT of the cranes as they swing the deck plates into position.

Scene 10

EXT. SHIPYARD. DAY.

MEDIUM SHOT. High angle from forecastle. The decks are beginning to take shape. Looking down from the Fl'o's'le[6] the incomplete lower decks can be seen below.

Scene 11

EXT. SHIPYARD. DAY.
to

Scene 15

Five BIG CLOSE UPS of riveting and welding.

DISSOLVE TO

---

[6] Abbreviation for Forecastle deck on a ship.

Scene 16

EXT. SHIPYARD. DAY

CLOSE UP. The ship's plate. A woman's voice is heard christening the ship.

A champagne bottle is swung into picture and bursts against the plate.

DISSOLVE TO

Scene 17

EXT. SHIPYARD. DAY.

LONG SHOT as the ship slides down the slips into the water.

DISSOLVE TO

Scene 18

EXT. SHIPYARD. DAY.

and

Scene 19

CLOSE UPs of tugs' sirens whistling.

Scene 20

EXT. SHIPYARD. DAY.

and

Scene 21

CLOSE SHOT. Shipyard **mateys** *cheering.*

Scene 22

EXT. SHIPYARD. DAY.

LONG SHOT 'TORRIN'. She is alongside a wharf. Engine room fittings are being lowered down between decks.

Scene 23

EXT. SHIPYARD. DAY.

CLOSE UP. A giant boiler is lowered into the ship.

Scene 24

EXT. SHIPYARD. DAY.

LONG SHOT 'TORRIN'. The upper deck has now been completed and a gun is being swung into position.

Scene 25

EXT. SHIPYARD. DAY.

CLOSE UP. The gun being lowered onto the deck.

Scene 26

EXT. SHIPYARD. DAY.

MEDIUM SHOT the brow (or gangway). The steaming party is filing on board. This is the first appearance of naval uniform, and the party consists of about 130 **men**. *They are carrying their bags, cases and hammocks.*

Scene 27

EXT. SHIPYARD. DAY.

LONG SHOT 'TORRIN' as she leaves the wharf.

Scene 28

EXT. SHIPYARD. DAY.

LONG SHOT. 'TORRIN' at speed doing her trials.

Scene 29

EXT. SHIPYARD. DAY.

MEDIUM SHOT. The wake of the ship at speed.

DISSOLVE TO

Scene 30

STUDIO EXT. PLYMOUTH JETTY. DAY.

LONG SHOT 'TORRIN' alongside the jetty at Plymouth.

Scene 31

STUDIO EXT. PLYMOUTH JETTY. DAY.

High angle on the quarter deck. A flag fills the screen. (This is the maker's flag. Each shipbuilding firm has a different flag.) The flag is lowered out of picture and discloses a group of **Officers** *and*

men *and a few* **civilians** *who are gathered together for the Ensign Ceremony. The* **Bo's'n**'s **Mate** *pipes the 'Still'. The* **Officers** *and* **men** *salute and the* **civilians** *remove their hats. The White Ensign is hoisted into picture and fills the screen.*

DISSOLVE TO

Scene 32

EXT. PLYMOUTH JETTY. (SMALL TANK). DAY.

Floating in the scum of the dock water we see the front page of the Daily Express bearing the headline THERE WILL BE NO WAR 'Daily Express holds canvass in Europe and ten out of twelve say – NO WAR THIS YEAR. Berlin emphatic. Hitler is not ready'.

(R2)

Scene 33

STUDIO EXT. CRETE. NIGHT. (MODEL).

A title fills the screen. 'CRETE – May 23rd, 1940'.
The TITLE FADES and leaves a LONG SHOT of a caique[7].
The scene is very dark and the caique can only just be discerned.
After a pause of a second or two a searchlight beam flashes across the sea and illuminates the white sails, which show up brightly against the darkness.

Scene 34

STUDIO EXT. BRIDGE OF '*TORRIN*'. NIGHT.

---

[7] A caique is a very large schooner of 200 tons or so, wooden, painted white with two masts, sails hoisted. At Crete these caiques were packed with German soldiers – 200 or so.

CLOSE UP, **Captain 'D'.** *Also on the bridge are* **Guns, Pilot, Torps, Flags, Number One, Illumination Officer** *and the following Ratings* **Chief Yeoman of Signals, Petty Officer Yeoman** *and three* **Signalmen,** *four* **Searchlight Crew,** *four* **Action Lookouts** *and two* **Torpedo Control Operators.**

Captain Open fire!

The camera TRACKS BACK in to a MEDIUM SHOT.

Guns Open Fire!

Gunnery Control Officer *(off)* Shoot!

Scene 35

STUDIO EXT. CRETE COAST LINE. NIGHT. (MODEL).

LONG SHOT, the 'Torrin'. The guns fire a salvo. Camera WHIP PANS on to a LONG SHOT of the 'Tomahawk'. A salvo is fired Camera WHIP PANS on to a LONG SHOT of the 'Torrington'. A salvo is fired. Camera WHIP PANS on to a LONG SHOT of the 'Tancred'. A salvo is fired.

Scene 36

STUDIO EXT. BRIDGE. NIGHT.

CLOSE SHOT, **Captain 'D'** *looking off at the caique. A salvo is fired. The flash illuminates his face.*

(Scenes 37–71 out)

Scene 72

STUDIO EXT. CRETE COAST LINE. NIGHT. (MODEL).

LONG SHOT, the caique illuminated by the searchlight. Tracer bullets are seen coming from the Pom-Pom.

Scene 73

STUDIO EXT. BRIDGE. NIGHT.

CLOSE TWO SHOT, **Captain 'D'***, and* **Torps***.*

Torps   Look at the Huns, sir – they're jumping overboard in full marching order.

Captain 'D' *raises his binoculars to his eyes.*

Scene 74

STUDIO EXT. CAIQUE. (TANK). NIGHT.

CLOSE SHOT, the caiques are seen through binoculars. The **German soldiers** *are seen jumping into the water.*

Scene 75

STUDIO EXT. NUMBER ONE GUN MOUNTING. NIGHT.

CLOSE SHOT, **Shorty***.*

Shorty   Coo – look at that 'Come in, the water's lovely!'

Scene 76

STUDIO EXT. CRETE COAST LINE. NIGHT. (MODEL).

LONG SHOT, the caique illuminated by the searchlight. It is now on fire and sinking fast.

Scene 77

STUDIO EXT. BRIDGE. NIGHT.

MEDIUM SHOT, **Captain 'D'**, **Guns**, **Flags**, *and* **Torps**. *They are watching the caique sinking (to cut in, with the model shot).*

Captain   That caique's sinking fast. Shift to the next caique.

Guns   Aye, aye, sire. Check – check – check – shift target right – follow T.B.I. Range – o-three-o.

Scene 78

STUDIO EXT. CRETE COAST LINE. NIGHT. (MODEL).

The first caique is in a sinking condition. The searchlight sweeps off it and illuminates a second caique. Over this we hear

Gunnery control   (*off*) Check – check – check – shift

Officer   Target right – follow T.B.I. Range o-three-o.

Scene 79

STUDIO EXT. NUMBER ONE GUN MOUNTING. NIGHT.

MEDIUM SHOT, gun's **crew** *including* **Shorty**, **Joey** *and* **Coombe**. *The fire gong rings twice. A salvo is fired.*

Scene 80

STUDIO EXT. CRETE COAST LINE. NIGHT. (MODEL).

LONG SHOT, the caique, caught in the searchlight. It receives a direct hit and the mast is carried away.

Scene 81

STUDIO EXT. BRIDGE. NIGHT.

CLOSE UP, **Captain 'D'** *raises his binoculars.*

Scene 82

STUDIO EXT. CAIQUE. (TANK). NIGHT.

CLOSE SHOT, as seen through binoculars. A fire has started and the **German soldiers** *are jumping overboard.*

Scene 83

STUDIO EXT. NUMBER THREE GUN MOUNTING. NIGHT.

CLOSE SHOT, **Walter**.

Walter   Whew! Look at 'em – somebody must have blown a whistle!

Another salvo is fired.

Scene 84

STUDIO EXT. CRETE COAST LINE. NIGHT. (MODEL).

The caique is sinking fast and suddenly blows up.

Scene 85

STUDIO EXT. BRIDGE. NIGHT.

MEDIUM SHOT, **Captain 'D'**, **Torps**, **Flags** *and* **Guns**

Flags   There are a lot more caiques to port and some bigger transports.

Captain   Right – shift to the big transport.

The **Captain** *raises his binoculars.*

Scene 86

STUDIO EXT. CRETE COAST LINE. NIGHT. (MODEL).

LONG SHOT, three transports, as seen through binoculars.

Guns   (*off*) Aye, aye, sir. Check – check – check – shift target right – follow T.B.I Range 0-four-0. Rapid salvoes.

Scene 87

EXT. NUMBER ONE GUN MOUNTING. NIGHT.

CLOSE UP, the gun muzzles. The gong rings twice. A salvo is fired.

Scene 88

STUDIO EXT. NUMBER ONE GUN MOUNTING. NIGHT.

MEDIUM SHOT, **Shorty** *and the gun's* **crew***. The breach opens and the empty cylinder falls out.* **Shorty** *rams the next shell into position.*

Shorty   Take this – it was my mother's.

The fire gong rings twice. Another salvo is fired.

Scene 89

STUDIO EXT. CRETE COAST LINE. NIGHT. (MODEL).

LONG SHOT, the three transports. The first salvo is seen exploding near the transports. Six eighteen foot splashes rise up near them.

Scene 90

STUDIO EXT. BRIDGE. NIGHT.

CLOSE SHOT, **Captain 'D'**, **Torps** *and* **Flags**.

Torps   Can I fire torpedoes at the transport, sir?

Captain   All right, Torps – you can get your damned mouldies off this time – but not more than two at any transport. (*to* **Flags**) Flags, make to the Division 'Train Tubes to port'.

Flags   Aye, aye, Sir. (*down voice pipe*) Main Office – make 'Tommy, Tommy – port'.

Torps (*to* **Tube Telephone Operator**) Ready – port.

Another salvo is fired. There is a brilliant flash and the Bridge vibrates. **Captain 'D'** *raises his binoculars to look at the transports.*

Scene 91

STUDIO EXT. CRETE COAST LINE. NIGHT. (MODEL).

CLOSE SHOT, one of the transports as seen through binoculars. A salvo carries away the funnel.

Scene 92

STUDIO EXT. NUMBER THREE GUN MOUNTING. NIGHT.

MEDIUM SHOT, **Walter Hardy** (**Chief Buffer**) *and the gun's crew.* **Walter** *is sitting at the elevating receiver in the gun layer's position. The gun is being reloaded in preparation for the next salvo.*

Walter   That's got 'em … come on – shoot when you see the whites of their eyes – bingo!

Another salvo is fired.

Scene 93

STUDIO EXT. BRIDGE. NIGHT.

MEDIUM SHOT, **Captain 'D'**, **Flags**, **Torps** *and* **Pilot**. **Torps** *is looking through the torpedo director sights.*

Flags   Pilot – Torps – stand by to turn to starboard to fire torpedoes.

Executive signal.

Pilot   (*down voice pipe*) Starboard twenty.

Cox'n's voice   (*up voice pipe*) Starboard twenty, sir. Twenty of starboard on, sir.

The ship heels over to port. Another salvo is heard and the Bridge is illuminated by the flash.

Pilot   Very good.

Torps   (*to* **Pilot**) Ten degrees to go, Pilot.

Pilot   (*down voice pipe*) Ease to ten.

Cox'n's voice   (*up voice pipe*) Ease to ten, sir. Ten of starboard on, sir.

Pilot   Very good.

Another salvo is heard and the bridge is illuminated by the flash.

Torps   Fire one!

(*Scene 94 out*)

Scene 95

EXT. TORPEDO TUBES. NIGHT.

CLOSE UP, the torpedo leaves the tubes and splashes into the water on the port side.

Scene 96

STUDIO EXT. BRIDGE. NIGHT.

CLOSE UP, **Torps**.

Torps   Fire two!

Scene 97

EXT. TORPEDO TUBES. NIGHT.

CLOSE UP, another torpedo leaves the tubes and splashes into the water to port.

Scene 98

STUDIO EXT. BRIDGE. NIGHT.

CLOSE THREE SHOT, **Captain 'D'**, **Torps** *and* **Flags**.

Torps   (*to* **Captain**) Torpedoes fired, sir.

Illumination Officer   (*off*) Close the shutter!

The searchlight goes out. Another salvo is heard and the Bridge illuminated by the flash.

Flags   The rest of the Division have fired at the other transports, sir.

(*Scenes 99–103 out*)

Scene 104

STUDIO EXT. CRETE COAST LINE. NIGHT. (MODEL).

LONG SHOT, the three transports. One of them blows up as a torpedo hits her.

Scene 105

STUDIO EXT. BRIDGE. NIGHT.

CLOSE SHOT, **Captain 'D'** *and* **Torps**.

Torps   Our fish have hit, sir. One transport has blown up.

Another salvo is heard and the bridge is illuminated by the flash.

Scene 106

STUDIO EXT. CRETE COAST LINE. NIGHT. (MODEL).

LONG SHOT, the three transports. The first transport is on fire. The second receives a hit.

Scene 107

STUDIO EXT. BRIDGE. NIGHT.

MEDIUM SHOT, **Captain 'D'**, **Flags** *and* **Guns**.

Flags   There goes another – big stuff. The rest of the Division are doing well.

The whine of shells is heard.

Guns   There's an enemy destroyer opened fire on us, sir.

Captain   Right – engage her.

There is the sound of the enemy shells exploding as they fall into the water near the ship.

DISSOLVE TO

(*Scenes 108–22 out*)

Scene 123

EXT. NUMBER ONE GUN MOUNTING. NIGHT.

The MONTAGE MUSIC BEGINS. CLOSE UP, the gun trains round.

Scene 124

EXT. NUMBER TWO GUN MOUNTING. NIGHT.

CLOSE UP, the gun trains round.

Scene 125

EXT. NUMBER THREE GUN MOUNTING, NIGHT.

CLOSE UP, the gun trains round.

Scene 126

STUDIO EXT. *TORRIN*. NIGHT. (MODEL).

LONG SHOT. All guns fire a salvo.

DISSOLVE TO

(*Scenes 127–33 out*)

Scene 134

INT. NUMBER THREE GUN MOUNTING. NIGHT.

CLOSE UP, the **Gun Trainer**. *He is training the gun.*

Scene 135

INT. NUMBER THREE GUN MOUNTING. NIGHT.

BIG CLOSE UP, the **Training Receiver**. *The pointers come into line.*

Scene 136

INT. NUMBER THREE GUN MOUNTING. NIGHT.

BIG CLOSE UP, the **Gun Trainer**.

Trainer   (*shouting*) Trainer on!

Scene 137

STUDIO EXT. NUMBER THREE GUN MOUNTING. NIGHT.

CLOSE SHOT, **Walter**. *He is elevating the gun.*

Scene 138

EXT. NUMBER THREE GUN MOUNTING. NIGHT.

BIG CLOSE UP, the **Elevating Receiver**. *The pointers come into line.*

Scene 139

STUDIO EXT. NUMBER THREE GUN MOUNTING. NIGHT.

BIG CLOSE UP, **Walter**.

Walter   (*shouting*) Gun Layer on!

Scene 140

STUDIO EXT. NUMBER THREE GUN MOUNTING. NIGHT.

CLOSE UP, **Number Two** *at the breach. He makes the interceptor.*

Number Two   (*shouting*) Ready!

Scene 142

STUDIO EXT. FIRE GONG. NIGHT.

BIG CLOSE UP. The hammer strikes twice.

Scene 142

STUDIO EXT. *TORRIN.* NIGHT. (MODEL).

LONG SHOT. All guns fire a salvo.

DISSOLVE TO

(*Scenes 143–5 out*)

Scene 146

STUDIO EXT. BRIDGE. NIGHT.

CLOSE UP, **Captain 'D'** *watching the action. A salvo is fired. The flash illuminates his face.*

DISSOLVE TO

(*Scene 147 out*)

Scene 148

STUDIO EXT. SEA. (TANK). NIGHT.

The sea is swept by the searchlight which illuminates a mass of **men** *swimming among the wreckage.*

The MONTAGE MUSIC dies away.

Scene 149

STUDIO EXT. NUMBER ONE GUN MOUNTING. NIGHT.

CLOSE SHOT, **Shorty** *to cover above montage.*

Scene 150

STUDIO EXT. NUMBER THREE GUN MOUNTING. NIGHT.

CLOSE SHOT, **Walter** *to cover above montage.*

DISSOLVE TO

(*Scenes 151–2 out*)

Scene 153

STUDIO EXT. BRIDGE. NIGHT.

MEDIUM SHOT, **Captain 'D'**, **Guns**, **Flags**.

Captain   I think we've mopped them all up. Can anyone see any more enemy?

Guns   Only some survivors in the water.

Captain   We can't stop to pick them up. We've stirred up a hornet's nest and we'd better clear out at full speed. Flags, make thirty-two knots to the Division.

Flags   Aye, aye, Sir. (*down voice pipe*) Main Office – make to the Division 'George Thirty-two'.

Captain   Are the rest of the Division all right?

Flags *raises his binoculars.*

Scene 154

STUDIO EXT. BRIDGE. NIGHT.

CLOSE SHOT, to cover above scene.

(R2)

Scene 155

STUDIO EXT. CRETE COAST LINE. NIGHT. (MODEL).

The three other destroyers of the division as seen through binoculars from the bridge of the Torrin.

Flags   (*off*) They're all there, sir, don't show any signs of damage at all.

Scene 156

STUDIO EXT. BRIDGE. NIGHT.

MEDIUM SHOT, **Captain 'D'**, **Guns** *and* **Flags**.

Captain   Good.

Flags   (*down voice pipe*) Is that through yet? (*pause*) Very good – make the executive signal. (*to* **Pilot**) Executive signal for thirty-two knots. Pilot.

Pilot   (*down voice pipe*) Revolutions three-three-0.

Scene 157

INT. WHEELHOUSE. NIGHT

The **Cox'n** *is at the wheel and the* **Quartermaster** *at the starboard telegraph.*

Cox'n   (*up voice pipe*) Revolutions three-three-0, sir.

The **Quartermaster** *turns the revolution indicator and after a few seconds we hear the bell from the engine room. It rings three times and the* **Cox'n** *confirms up the voice pipe*

Cox'n   (*up voice pipe*) Three-three-0 revolutions on, sir.

(*Scenes 158–60 out*)

Scene 161

STUDIO EXT. SEA. (TANK). NIGHT.

MEDIUM SHOT, TRACKING. In the foreground of the picture is the ship's guardrail, beyond are the **survivors** *in the water.*

Scene 162

STUDIO EXT. NUMBER ONE GUN MOUNTING. NIGHT.

CLOSE SHOT, **Shorty** *and* **Joey***. They are both very hot and dirty and drinking mugs of cocoa.*

Joey   It seems wrong somehow leaving those poor bastards struggling about in the water.

Shorty   If you ask me it serves them bloody well right for being so saucy!

Scene 163

STUDIO EXT. NUMBER THREE GUN MOUNTING. NIGHT.

MEDIUM SHOT, **Walter**, *his tin hat on the back of his head. He is drinking cocoa and eating ship's biscuits.* **Brodie**, *the Torpedo Gunner's mate, enters picture.* **Walter** *stops him.*

Walter   I'll lay you ten to one they was all Germans – you'd never get the Macaronis to tackle a dangerous job like that not for love nor money.

Brodie   Go on – the Ityos will do anything for money!

Walter   Anything but fight – that's why they was so lousy in the last war – it's on account of their warm, languorous, southern temperament …

Brodie   Warm languorous southern temperament my – (*the rattlers sound cutting off his sentence*)

Scene 164

STUDIO EXT. NUMBER ONE GUN MOUNTING. NIGHT.

CLOSE SHOT, **Joey** *and* **Shorty** *as the rattlers are ringing. They finish their cocoa in one gulp and rush to their positions.*

Joey   'Ere we go again!

(R1)

Scene 165

STUDIO EXT. NUMBER THREE GUN MOUNTING. NIGHT

CLOSE SHOT, **Walter** *and* **Brodie***.*

Brodie   'Ere they come again. (*Runs out of picture towards the torpedo tubes*)

Walter   (*taking up his position at the gun*) Not a moment's peace in this bloody war.

DISSOLVE TO

Scene 166

EXT. STERN OF 'TORRIN'. DAWN. (LOCATION)

The sea is piling up and coming over the deck. The ship is doing 32 knots.

DISSOLVE TO

Scene 167

STUDIO EXT. CRETE COAST LINE. DAWN. (MODEL).

LONG SHOT, the Division. They are steaming in line ahead. The first streaks of dawn appear.

Scene 168

STUDIO EXT. BRIDGE. DAWN.

MEDIUM SHOT. Everyone is standing around smoking and drinking cocoa.

Captain   (*drinking cocoa*) Here comes the dawn of a new day, Flags. I wouldn't be surprised if it were a fairly uncomfortable one!

Flags   Yes, sir – very pretty sky, sir. Somebody sent me a calendar rather like that last Christmas.

Captain   Did it have a few squadrons of Dorniers in the upper right hand corner?

Flags   (*grinning*) No, sir.

Captain That's where Art parts company with reality.

Flags I'm afraid you're right – cigarette, sir?

Captain (*taking one*) Thanks.

Scene 169

STUDIO EXT. BRIDGE. DAWN.

CLOSE UP, the **Port Lookout***, his eyes are scanning the sky.*

(R2)

Scene 170

STUDIO EXT. NUMBER ONE GUN MOUNTING. DAWN.

Shorty, **Joey**, **Coombe** *and the rest of the gun's* **crew** *are smoking and drinking cocoa.*

Joey Pretty sky, ain't it? Looks like somebody'd painted it.

Shorty Yes – it's pretty all right, but there's a bloody sight too much of it!

DISSOLVE TO

Scene 171

EXT. SEA. DAY. (LOCATION).

LONG SHOT, sea and sky. The sun has now risen.

(*Scenes 172–219 out*)

Scene 220

STUDIO EXT. BRIDGE. DAY.

CLOSE UP, the **Starboard Lookout***. He is searching the sky. He looks towards the stern of the ship, sees something and yells.*

Lookout   Aircraft in sight astern. Angle of sight two-0.

Scene 221

STUDIO EXT. BRIDGE. DAY.

MEDIUM SHOT, **Captain 'D'***,* **Guns** *and* **Pilot***.* **Captain 'D'** *is standing near the voice pipe down to the Wheelhouse.*

Guns   That looks like a couple of squadrons of Junkers 87.

Captain   (*to* **Pilot**) Starboard twenty.

Pilot   Aye, Aye, sir. (*to* **Chief Yeoman**) One blast on the siren.

Scene 222

STUDIO EXT. BRIDGE. DAY.

CLOSE SHOT, the **Chief Yeoman***. He depresses the siren level once.*

Scene 223

STUDIO EXT. THE FUNNEL. DAY.

CLOSE UP, the siren gives one blast.

Scene 224

STUDIO EXT. BRIDGE. DAY.

CLOSE THREE SHOT, **Captain 'D'**, **Flags** *and* **Pilot**.

PILOT (*down voice pipe*) Starboard twenty.

The ship heels over to port.

Captain   (*to* **Flags**) Watch the Division.

Flags   They're all turning now, sir.

Scene 225

STUDIO EXT. CRETE COAST LINE. DAY. (MODEL).

LONG SHOT, the Division. All ships alter course to starboard.

Scene 226

STUDIO EXT. BRIDGE. DAY.

MEDIUM SHOT, **Captain 'D'**, **Guns**, **Pilot** *and* **Midshipman**.
The **Midshipman** *has a microphone in his hand on a wandering
lead. He passes the following order by loud speaker. The ship has
a list to port.*

Midshipman   Short range weapons – aircraft in sight. Starboard
– stand by for dive bombers.

Guns   Aircraft in sight, bearing green one-seven-o. Angle of
sight two-o. Open fire!

Scene 227

EXT. POM-POM PLATFORM. DAY.

*MEDIUM SHOT, the POM-POM gun as it trains on the target.
The other guns are heard as they open fire.*

Scene 228

EXT. SEARCHLIGHT PLATFORM. DAY.

MEDIUM SHOT of the two Hurlicane guns. Each gun has a **crew** *of two. They are preparing the guns for action. Another salvo is heard from the other guns.*

Scene 229

STUDIO EXT. SKY. DAY. (MODEL).

LONG SHOT, two squadrons of Junkers 87 as they break formation in preparation for diving.

Scene 230

STUDIO EXT. BRIDGE. DAY.

MEDIUM SHOT, **Captain 'D'**, **Flags** *and* **Guns**.

Flags   (*shouting*) They're breaking up for the attack.

Guns   (*to* **D.C.T.**) All guns – sector independent.

Captain   (*down voice pipe to wheelhouse*) The first wave are diving now. Hard a-port.

The ship keels over to starboard as two blasts on the siren are heard.

The **Captain** *looks up at the sky.*

Scene 231

STUDIO EXT. SKY. DAY. (MODEL).

A dive bomber is dropping like a stone towards camera.

Scene 232

STUDIO EXT. BRIDGE. DAY.

CLOSE UP, **Captain 'D'**. *He is looking up at the dive bomber which is coming from the port beam. He looks around to the next dive bomber which is coming from the stern.*

Scene 233

STUDIO EXT. SKY. DAY. (MODEL).

The second dive bomber is dropping towards the camera.

Scene 234

STUDIO EXT. BRIDGE. DAY.

CLOSE UP, **Captain 'D'**. *He looks at the third dive bomber, which is coming from the starboard quarter.*

Scene 235

EXT. SEARCHLIGHT PLATFORM. DAY.

MEDIUM SHOT, the two Hurlicane guns as they open fire.

Scene 237

EXT. POM-POM PLATFORM. DAY.

CLOSE SHOT, the Pom-Pom gun as it opens fire on the bomber which is diving to stern.

(Note: Now that the guns are firing independently the impression of noise is much greater. Throughout the following sequence the noise of the siren as it gives one blast for every time the ship turns

to starboard and two blasts every time the ship turns to port is also heard).

Scene 238

STUDIO EXT. SKY. DAY. (MODEL).

One of the two dive bombers, dropping towards the camera, receives a direct hit.

Scene 239

EXT. POM-POM PLATFORM. DAY.

MEDIUM SHOT. The Pom-Pom immediately trains to the other dive bomber, which is diving from the port beam.

Scene 240

STUDIO EXT. SEA. DAY. (MODEL).

The dive bomber crashes into the sea.

Scene 241

STUDIO EXT. BRIDGE. DAY.

TWO SHOT, **Captain** *and* **Guns**. *The roar of the remaining two bombers reaches a crescendo. The whistling of the bombs is heard, followed by six bomb explosions which send a shower of spray over the bridge.*

A cheer goes up all over the ship.

Captain   Hard a-starboard.

The ship returns to an even keel.

Captain   One bird out of that convoy. Try and get two out of the next one.

Guns   (*shouts*) All guns shift to the next wave.

Scene 242

STUDIO EXT. BRIDGE. DAY.

CLOSE UP, the **Midshipman** *with his microphone on a wandering lead.*

Midshipman   All close range weapons shift to the next wave.

Scene 243

STUDIO EXT. PORT SIDE SIGNAL DECK PLATFORM. DAY.

CLOSE SHOT, the point-five machine gun. The **crew** *of two train the gun to the next wave.*

Scene 244

EXT. POM-POM PLATFORM. DAY.

CLOSE SHOT, the Pom-Pom. The **crew** *train the gun to the next wave.*

Scene 245

EXT. SEARCHLIGHT PLATFORM. DAY.

CLOSE SHOT, the Hurlicane gun. It trains to the next wave.

Scene 246

STUDIO EXT. SKY. DAY. (MODEL).

Three more dive bombers go into a dive.

Scene 247

STUDIO EXT. BRIDGE. DAY.

CLOSE SHOT, **Captain** *and* **Flags**. *The Pom-Poms and point-fives open fire.*

Flags   The second wave are diving now, sir.

Captain   (*down voice pipe to* **Cox'n**) Hard a-starboard.

There is one blast on the siren.

Cox'n's voice   Hard a-starboard.

The ship heels over to port.

Scene 248

STUDIO EXT. PORT SIDE SIGNAL DECK PLATFORM.
DAY. B.P.

CLOSE SHOT from behind the point-five machine gun. The gun is firing at a dive bomber which is diving at the camera.

Scene 249

EXT. POM-POM PLATFORM. DAY

CLOSE SHOT, the Pom-Pom firing.

Scene 250

STUDIO EXT. SKY. DAY. (MODEL).

One of the aircraft diving at camera.

Scene 251

STUDIO EXT. PORT SIDE SEARCHLIGHT PLATFORM. DAY.

BIG CLOSE UP of **Number One** *of the gun's crew at the Hurlicane gun. The gun is firing and shaking as it recoils again and again.*

Scene 252

STUDIO EXT. SKY. DAY. (MODEL)

A dive bomber as seen through the Hurlicane gun sights. As it reaches the bottom of its dive a train of smoke appears.

Scene 253

STUDIO EXT. BRIDGE. DAY.

CLOSE SHOT, **Captain 'D'** *and* **Guns**.

Captain   Good shooting, Guns. We've winged that one.

There is the screaming of bombs. The whine of 'planes as they pull out of the dive.

Scene 254

STUDIO EXT. SEA. DAY. (MODEL).

Three bombs hit the surface and explode. Two small columns of

*water and one very large one shoot up into the air. The small
columns are caused by 250lb. bombs and would be about 5–7 feet
high the large column is caused by a 1000 pounder and would be
about 20'.*

Scene 255

STUDIO EXT. BRIDGE. DAY.

CLOSE SHOT, **Captain 'D'**, **Guns** *and* **Flags**. *The guns cease fire.*

Captain   (*down voice pipe to* **Cox'n**) Midships.

Cox'n's voice   (*up voice pipe*) Midships, sir.

The ship returns to an even keel.

Flags   (*to* **Captain**) Another wave on the port side, sir.

Scene 256

STUDIO EXT. SKY. DAY. (MODEL).

*Another formation of three dive bombers breaks formation and
begins to dive.*

Scene 257

STUDIO EXT. BRIDGE. DAY.

CLOSE SHOT, **Captain 'D'**, **Flags** *and* **Guns**.

Flags   They're breaking up for the attack.

The guns open fire.

Captain   (*down voice pipe to* **Cox'n**) Hard a-starboard.

One blast on the siren is heard.

Cox'ns voice   Hard a-starboard, sir.

The ship lists seven or eight degrees to port.

Scene 258

STUDIO EXT. SKY. DAY. (MODEL).

A dive bomber diving towards the camera.

Scene 259

STUDIO EXT. BRIDGE. DAY.

CLOSE SHOT, **Captain** *and* **Guns**. *They are on the port side, facing aft.*

Guns   The leader of this wave is coming much lower, sir.

Scene 269

STUDIO EXT. SKY. DAY. (MODEL).

The leading bomber diving lower and lower through a barrage of fire.

Scene 261

STUDIO EXT. BRIDGE. DAY.

CLOSE UP, **Captain 'D'**.

Captain   He'll probably hit our mast.

Scene 262

STUDIO EXT. SKY. DAY. (MODEL).

The mast of the ship is in the foreground of the picture. The bomber is diving from the port quarter. It just misses the wireless aerial. There is the whistle of a bomb.

Scene 263

STUDIO EXT. BRIDGE. DAY.

BIG CLOSE UP, **Captain 'D'**. *A FLASH of his face as the shadow of the bomber flashes over him.*

Scene 264

STUDIO EXT. SEA. DAY. (MODEL).

The bomber crashes into the sea off the port bow.

Scene 265

STUDIO EXT. BRIDGE. DAY.

CLOSE TWO SHOT, **Captain 'D'** *and* **Guns**. *There is a blinding flash.* **Captain 'D'** *and* **Guns** *are flung out of the picture.*

Scene 266

STUDIO EXT. BRIDGE. DAY.

CLOSE UP, **Torps**. *He is flung against the depth charge levers.*

Scene 267

STUDIO EXT. BRIDGE. DAY.

CLOSE UP, **Flags**. *He is flung on to the deck beside the compass.*

Scene 268

STUDIO EXT. BRIDGE. DAY.

CLOSE UP, **Number One**. *He is flung on to the deck.*

Scene 269

EXT. SKY. DAY. (LOT).

*CLOSE SHOT, the top of the mast with the 'Aircraft' flag flying.
The top of the mast topples over and falls out of picture.*

Scene 270

STUDIO EXT. DIRECTOR CONTROL TOWER. DAY.

CLOSE SHOT. The mast crashes on to the top of the D.C.T.

(R1)

Scene 271

STUDIO EXT. BRIDGE. DAY.

MEDIUM SHOT, **Captain 'D'** *and* **Flags** *at the foot of the
compass. Their noses are bleeding. The* **Captain** *drags himself to
his feet, clutching on to the compass.* **Guns** *staggers into picture.
His mouth is bleeding ...*

Captain   (*to* **Guns**) Well done, we've got him – but I'm afraid
he's got us too.

Scene 271a

STUDIO EXT. SEARCHLIGHT PLATFORM. CRATER IN
DECK. DAY. (B.P.)

*The screen is filled with smoke which gradually clears and
discloses a large crater in the deck by the searchlight platform.*

Scene 272

STUDIO EXT. BRIDGE. DAY.

CLOSE UP, **Captain 'D'**, *he pulls himself to the voice pipe.*

Captain   (*to* **Cox'n**) Midships.

Scene 273

INT. WHEELHOUSE. DAY.

The two **Quartermasters** *are lying unconscious on the deck. The* **Cox'n** *drags himself to his feet by clutching the wheel. His nose and mouth are bleeding.*

Cox'n   (*dazed*) Midships, sir.

He turns the wheel to port until the wheel is amidships. The ship does not respond but stays at an angle of seven or eight degrees to port.

Cox'n   (*dazed*) She won't answer her wheel, sir.

Scene 274

STUDIO EXT. BRIDGE. DAY.

CLOSE SHOT, **Captain 'D'** *and* **Number One** *at the compass. The camera PANS with* **Number One** *as he staggers over to the port side and looks over.*

Scene 275

EXT. 'TORRIN'. DAY. (LOCATION).

LONG SHOT, shooting down over the port side onto the upper deck. The ship is still travelling at 32 knots and heeling over to port.

Scene 276

STUDIO EXT. BRIDGE. DAY

MEDIUM SHOT, **Captain 'D'**, **Number One** *and* **Guns**.

Number One   (*crossing to* **Captain**) *The steering gear has gone west, sir, but the propellers seem all right.*

The roar of aircraft is heard.

Captain   Carry on firing – here comes the next wave.

Guns   All guns are still firing, sir.

Scene 278

STUDIO EXT. SEARCHLIGHT PLATFORM. CRATER IN DECK. DAY. B.P.

There is a large crater in the dock by the searchlight platform. The oil fuel tank in the engine room explodes with a roar – there is a vivid flash and volumes of dense smoke rush up through the crater.

Scene 279

STUDIO EXT. BRIDGE. DAY.

MEDIUM SHOT, **Captain 'D'**, **Number One**, **Guns** *and* **Flags**.

The list increases to 10–11–12 degrees to port. Everyone on the bridge grabs hold of the object nearest to them.

Captain   (*down voice pipe to* **Cox'n**) Stop both.

Scene 280

INT. WHEELHOUSE. DAY.

CLOSE SHOT, the **Cox'n**.

Cox'n   (*up voice pipe*) Stop both, sir.

He reaches over to the port and starboard telegraphs. There is no answering bell from the engine room.

Cox'n   (*up voice pipe*) No answer from the engine room, sir – the telegraphs must be shot away.

Scene 281

STUDIO EXT. BRIDGE. DAY.

MEDIUM SHOT, **Captain 'D'** *and all the* **Officers**.

Captain   (*to* **all**) I'm afraid we're going over. (*to* **Midshipman**) Pass the word for the hands not at the guns to cast loose the Carley floats.

Midshipman   (*on the microphone*) Hands not at the guns – case loose Carley floats.

The ship lurches over violently to port.

Scene 282

EXT. POM-POM PLATFORM. (BIG TANK). DAY.

CLOSE SHOT, a Carley float. The deck is awash. The men cast the float loose by cutting the lashings. The float slides into the water and is swept away.

Scene 283

STUDIO EXT. BRIDGE. DAY.

MEDIUM SHOT, **Captain 'D'**. *The ship is lurching over rapidly. The* **Captain** *grabs hold of the compass.*

Scene 284

EXT. NUMBER ONE GUN MOUNTING. (BIG TANK). DAY.

MEDIUM SHOT. The water rushes up over the forecastle and sweeps a few of the gun's **crew** *away.*

Scene 285

EXT. NUMBER TWO GUN MOUNTING. (BIG TANK). DAY.

The water sweeps the **crew** *away. MEDIUM SHOT.*

Scene 286

EXT. POM-POM PLATFORM. (BIG TANK). DAY.

MEDIUM SHOT. Half the platform is submerged by this rushing water. The ship lurches still more. Half the **crew** *are carried away.*

Scene 287

STUDIO EXT. BRIDGE. (BIG TANK). DAY.

MEDIUM SHOT, **Captain 'D'**. *He is still clinging on to the compass. The water rushes in like a maelstrom, tearing all away, except the* **Captain**, *who goes under with the bridge.*

Scene 288

STUDIO EXT. SEA. DAY. (MODEL).

LONG SHOT of the 'Torrin' as her masts hit the water. The ship is still travelling at 32 knots. There is a gigantic splash.

Scene 289

STUDIO EXT. UNDER WATER. (GLASS TANK). DAY.

MEDIUM SHOT. The upturned bridge comes into the top of the picture. The **Captain** *is still holding on to the compass. Bubbles rush up past the camera.*

Scene 290

STUDIO EXT. UNDER WATER. (GLASS TANK). DAY.

MEDIUM SHOT. Bubbles rush up past the camera. A heavy drumming noise is heard. The **Captain** *turns in the water and his face floats towards the camera into a BIG CLOSE UP. The drumming noise increases. The* **Captain***'s voice is heard, but his lips do not move*

Captain   I'll sign for her now … I'll sign for her now … I'll sign for her now … .

RIPPLE DISSOLVE TO

Scene 291

THE WHITE ENSIGN.

Fills the screen. It is SUPERIMPOSED over the Captain's day cabin, aft.

Scene 292

INT. CAPTAIN'S DAY CABIN. DAY.

LONG SHOT. The White Ensign fades away. The morning sun is pouring through the scuttles. It is a reasonably spacious cabin, at the moment in process of being tidied by **Edgecombe**, *the Captain's cabin hand.* **Edgecombe** *is a stocky, cheerful man in* *the early forties. He is hammering open a large packing case. The sofa is piled with odds and ends – cigarette boxes, watercolours in thin frames, books, etc. The only piece of furniture that is not cluttered up is the writing desk at which* **Captain 'D'** *is sitting reading through some papers. Standing by him is his Secretary,* **Paymaster-Lieutenant-Commander Charles Borrell – Secco.** *He is a pleasant-looking man in the early thirties.*

Captain   Satterthwaite hasn't been sighted yet, has he?

Secco   No, sir, but it's just on ten o'clock.

Captain   Stop that hammering for a minute, Edgecombe. I can't hear myself think.

Edgecombe   Aye, Aye, sir.

Captain   You'd better tell Number One to fall the hands in on the quarter deck.

Secco   Aye, Aye, sir.

Secco *goes out. The* **Captain** *turns to another pile of papers, as he does so he presses a bell.*

Scene 293

INT. CAPTAIN'S DAY CABIN. DAY.

CLOSE SHOT, **Edgecombe.** *He takes a silver framed photograph out of the packing case. It is of Alix and the children. He takes it over to* **Captain 'D'**, *camera PANNING with him to CLOSE TWO SHOT.*

Edgecombe   Shall we 'ave it on the desk or the shelf, sir?

Captain   Shelf for the moment. We'll have the usual one on the desk when you find it.

Edgecombe   Wedding dress, sir?

Captain   Yes.

Camera PANS with **Edgecombe** *as he goes over to the sofa.*

Edgecombe   It's here, sir.

Captain   (*off*) Good. Give it to me.

Camera PANS with **Edgecombe** *as he hands* **Captain 'D'** *the photograph. The* **Captain** *looks at it for a moment then stands it up on the desk and goes on reading. Above, on the quarter deck, there is the sound of orders being shouted and the tramp of men's feet.*

Scene 295

INT. CAPTAIN'S DAY CABIN. DAY.

CLOSE SHOT at the doorway. A **Messenger** *comes in, stands to attention cap in hand.*

Scene 296

INT. CAPTAIN'S DAY CABIN. DAY.

CLOSE SHOT, the **Captain**. *The* **Messenger** *comes into picture.*

Captain   Take these to the Gunnery Officer if he's not in his cabin leave them on his desk. (*hands* **Messenger** *a sheaf of papers.*)

Messenger   Aye, Aye, sir.

He takes the papers, stands to attention for a second then goes out. **Edgecombe** *comes into the picture.*

Edgecombe   (*conversationally*) We're in for a spot of trouble with the 'ot tap in the bathroom, sir.

Captain   What sort of trouble?

Edgecombe   Well, it kind of explodes every time you turn it on, sir – makes a very nasty noise, sir.

Captain   You've had to deal with worse snags than that in your time, Edgecombe.

Edgecomb   (*grinning*) Yes, sir.

Scene 296

INT. CAPTAIN'S DAY CABIN. DAY.

CLOSE SHOT at the doorway. **Flags (Signal Officer, Lieutenant E. G. Leggatt)** *comes in.*

Flags   Mr. Satterthwaite coming on board, sir.

Scene 297

INT. CAPTAINS DAY CABIN. DAY.

MEDIUM SHOT, **Captain**.

Captain   Is Number One bringing him down?

Flags   (*off*) Yes, sir.

Captain   Hands all aft?

Flags   (*off*) Yes, sir.

Captain   (*rising and putting on his hat*) Good.

Scene 298

INT. CAPTAIN'S DAY CABIN. DAY

MEDIUM SHOT at the doorway. **Number One** *ushers in* **Mr. Satterthwaite**. *He is a burly, genial looking man. He is the Manager of the Shipyard. Camera PANS with him as he crosses to* **Captain 'D'** *into a TWO SHOT.*

Captain   (*shaking hands with* **Satterthwaite**) Good morning, Satterthwaite.

Mr. Satterthwaite   Good morning, Captain Kinross.

Captain   Everything in order?

Mr. Satterthwaite   (*smiling and producing some papers from his brief case*) Certainly.

Captain   Well, we'd better get the little ceremony over then, hadn't we? Then we'll go on deck.

Mr. Satterthwaite   Were you satisfied with the full power trial?

Captain   (*smiling*) Yes – she's a well found ship. (*to* **Edgecombe**) We'll be hoisting the Ensign in a couple of minutes Edgecombe – you'd better get your cap and go on deck.

Edgecombe   (*off*) Aye, Aye, sir. (*He goes out*)

Captain   Now then.

Mr. Satterthwaite   Are you prepared to take over the ship, sir?

Scene 299

INT. CAPTAIN'S DAY CABIN. DAY.

CLOSE SHOT, the **Captain**.

Captain   Yes, I'll sign for her now.

Scene 300

INT. CAPTAIN'S DAY CABIN. DAY.

CLOSE SHOT, **Edgecombe** *to cover previous scenes.*

RIPPLE DISSOLVE TO

Scene 301

STUDIO EXT. UNDER WATER. (SMALL TANK). DAY.

The bridge is upside down in the water. **Captain 'D'** *swims towards the camera and, once clear of the bridge structure, he straightens up and begins to shoot to the surface.* **Edgecombe**'s *voice is heard*

Edgecombe's voice   Watch your head, sir.

RIPPLE DISSOLVE TO

Scene 302

STUDIO EXT. PLYMOUTH QUAYSIDE. DAY.

MEDIUM SHOT. The camera is on the deck of the 'Torrin' shooting down the gangway. At the bottom of the gangway is **Edgecombe**, *standing beside a drop-head Hillman Minx Coupe. He stands to attention as he sees* **Captain 'D'** *approaching.*

Captain 'D' *comes into the picture and walks down the gangway to the car.*

Scene 303

STUDIO EXT. PLYMOUTH QUAYSIDE. DAY.

CLOSE SHOT, **Captain 'D'** *and* **Edgecombe**.

Edgecombe   Will you drive, sir, or shall I?

Captain   I will.

Edgecombe   Watch your head, sir.

The **Captain** *gets into the driver's seat of the car.* **Edgecombe** *gets in after him and sits beside him.*

Scene 304

STUDIO EXT. PLYMOUTH QUAYSIDE. DAY. (SCHUFFTAN).

LONG SHOT, the car drives out of the picture.

DISSOLVE TO

Scene 305

STUDIO EXT. COUNTRY LANE. DAY. (B.P.)

CLOSE TWO SHOT, **Captain 'D'**, *driving, and* **Edgecombe** *sitting beside him.*

Captain   You can smoke if you like, Edgecombe.

Edgecombe   Thank you, sir. (*he takes a packet of cigarettes from his pocket*) Will you have one, sir?

Captain   Not at the moment thanks.

There is a pause while **Edgecombe** *lights his cigarette.*

Captain   Heard from your missus lately?

Edgecombe   Yes, sir – I 'ad a letter last week. One of the usuals – full of complaints.

Captain   What's wrong?

Edgecombe   Everything, sir, as far as I can see – she's got her married sister staying with 'er for one thing, that always makes her a bit fretful, then young Norman went and rammed a milk van on his new bike and buckled up the front wheel and cut 'is 'ead open and 'ad to 'ave three stitches in it, then 'er mother was took bad again and 'ad to go to 'ospital – that old woman's always in trouble – if you ask me I think she enjoys it!

Captain   What's the matter with her?

Edgecombe   Well, last time it was 'er back, sir. This time it's 'er stomach – it seems she can't keep anything down and if I know 'er it's not for want of trying.

Captain (*laughing*) I should think you're glad to be going to sea again aren't you?

Edgecombe That's putting it mildly, sir.

Captain By the way, did you talk to the steward about getting that stuff on board?

Edgecombe Yes, sir – I made out a list for 'im.

Captain How does he strike you – efficient?

Edgecombe Oh, he's a bit of a fusspot, sir, if you know what I mean, 'as to 'ave everything cut and dried before 'e'll move an inch, but 'e'll be all right when 'e's settled down a bit. I wish we could 'ave old Aquilina again, sir – Maltese or no Maltese 'e knew 'is job.

Captain Yes, Aquilina was a treasure all right – here's the turning – is there anything behind?

Edgecombe (*looking back*) No, sir – all clear, sir.

Scene 306

STUDIO EXT. COUNTRY LANE. DAY. (B.P.)

and

Scene 307

CLOSE UP, **Captain 'D'** to cover above scene. *CLOSE UP*, **Edgecombe** *to cover above scene.*

Scene 308

STUDIO EXT. CAPTAIN 'D'S HOUSE. DAY

LONG SHOT. The car turns into the drive and stops by the front door of the house.

Scene 309

STUDIO EXT. CAPTAIN 'D'S HOUSE. DAY

*MEDIUM SHOT at the front door. As the car comes to a
standstill the door opens and* **Alix Kinross** *comes out followed
tempestuously by* **Bobby,** *aged 10, and* **Lavinia,** *aged 8. Camera
TRACKS BACK to include* **Captain 'D',** *who is now getting out of
the car.*

The **children** *fling themselves at him,* **Alix** *stands back a little,
smiling. She is an attractive woman in the middle thirties.*

Bobby   (*excitedly*) We thought you were never coming, Daddy.
We've been waiting for hours and hours.

Lavinia   Mummy wanted us to go to bed but we wouldn't.

Captain   (*disentangling himself from the children and kissing*
Alix) Everything under control, darling?

Alix   Far from it – we've been in an uproar all day, ever since
your telegram came.

Bobby   We saw the ship, Daddy – we saw the ship … .

Lavinia   We took our tea on to the cliffs and saw it go by – quite
close … .

Bobby   Not 'it', Lavvy – 'her'.

Captain   That's right, son.

Alix   She looked beautiful, Teddy – it was thrilling.

Bobby   How fast was she going, Daddy – was she going forty
knots?

Captain   (*laughing*) Good Heavens no – only about twenty.

Bobby   But she *can* do more than that can't she?

Captain   You bet she can. Edgecombe, you'd better take the car
round and give Ellen a hand with the dinner.

Edgecombe   Aye, Aye, sir.

Camera PANS with the group as they go into the front door.

Captain   I hope it's a good dinner – I'm starving.

Scene 310

STUDIO EXT. CAPTAIN 'D'S HOUSE. DAY

to

Scene 313

CLOSE UP, the **Captain** *to cover previous scene. CLOSE UP,* **Alix** *to cover previous scene. CLOSE UP,* **Bobby** *to cover previous scene. CLOSE UP,* **Lavinia** *to cover previous scene.*

Scene 314

INT. CAPTAIN 'D'S HALL. DAY.

MEDIUM SHOT, PANNING as **Captain 'D'**, **Alix**, **Bobby** *and* **Lavinia** *come in through the front door.*

Lavinia   Can I tell him what it is, Mummy?

Bobby   Of course you can't – it's a surprise. She mustn't spoil it, must she, Mummy?

Alix   Do keep still, Bobby, there's a dear … (*to* **Captain**) How long have you got?

Captain   Only until the morning.

Bobby   Can we come to the dockyard tomorrow and see her?

Captain   I'm afraid not, old man. I shall be too busy. We're commissioning – making a rush job of it.

Bobby   But Mummy promised that if –

Alix   That's quite enough, darling. You heard what Daddy said.

Scene 315

INT. CAPTAIN 'D'S DRAWING ROOM. DAY.

The room is typical. Comfortable and unpretentious. There are chintz covers, lots of flowers, several silver framed photographs of the Captain at various stages of his career. There is a tray of cocktail things on the table.

LONG SHOT of the group entering from the hall.

Lavinia   But we shall be able to come on board before you go away shan't we?

Captain   Yes – we'll make time somehow.

Bobby   When, Daddy?

Alix   Don't be so persistent, Bobby. Let Daddy relax for a minute – give him a cigarette, there's a good boy …

Lavinia   Let me – let me …

They both make a dive for the cigarette box.

Alix   Sit down, darling, you must be exhausted. I'll mix you a drink – cocktail or whisky and soda?

Scene 316

INT. CAPTAIN 'D'S DRAWING ROOM. DAY.

MEDIUM SHOT, the **Captain** *and* **Alix**.

Captain   Seeing that it's a gala evening we'll have a Kinross Special – and I'll bet you've forgotten to lay in any Cointreau …

Alix   (*holding up a bottle*) Wrong again – here it is.

Bobby *and* **Lavinia** *enter the picture and* **Bobby** *offers the cigarette box.*

Bobby   Here, Daddy.

Captain   (*taking cigarette*) Thanks, old mate.

Lavinia   Let me light it.

Lavinia *lights the* **Captain***'s cigarette with great care.*

Captain   I knew something was missing – where's Trafalgar?

Alix   (*horrified*) Oh Bobby – we left him shut up in the nursery – fly like the wind.

Lavinia   Oh, poor Trafalgar.

Camera PANS with **Bobby** *and* **Lavinia** *as they rush out of the room.*

Scene 317

INT. CAPTAIN 'D'S DRAWING ROOM. DAY.

CLOSE SHOT, **Captain 'D'** *and* **Alix***.*

Alix   (*mixing cocktail*) Were the trials satisfactory, darling – were you pleased?

Captain   More than pleased – she's a lovely ship. Beautiful manners. Does what she's told without a murmur …

Alix   Why are you making such a rush job of the commissioning?

Captain   Oh, I don't know – I like getting things done quickly.

Alix   Is that the only reason?

Captain   We live in strange times, darling – it's as well to be prepared for anything.

Alix   (*looking at him gravely for a moment*) Yes – I suppose it is. (*She brings him the cocktail*) Here try this – it may be a little too sweet.

Captain   (*taking it*) Nothing to worry about.

Alix   (*with a quick smile*) Of course not.

Captain   (*raising his glass*) My love!

Alix   (*raising her glass*) My love!

Captain   (*after drinking a little*) Just right – not a bit too sweet.

There is the noise of feet scampering down the stairs.

Scene 318

INT. CAPTAIN 'D'S DRAWING ROOM. DAY.

LONG SHOT of the door. The door bursts open and **Trafalgar**,
a small Cocker Spaniel, rushes into the room followed by **Bobby**
and **Lavinia**. *Camera PANS with Trafalgar into a TWO SHOT as
he jumps up at* **Captain 'D'** *nearly knocking the glass out of his
hand.*

Alix   (*off*) Oh Traf, you are naughty.

Captain   Here, steady on. (*puts his glass down and squats on his
haunches to talk to the dog*) Poor old boy – so they locked you up
in the nursery, did they – what a damned shame.

Scene 319

INT. CAPTAIN 'D'S DRAWING ROOM. DAY.

TWO SHOT, **Bobby** *and* **Lavinia**.

Bobby   He got a rabbit yesterday and another one last week.
Lavvy cried.

Lavinia   I didn't –

Bobby   You did.

Scene 320

INT. CAPTAIN 'D'S DRAWING ROOM. DAY.

MEDIUM LONG SHOT, the **Captain**, **Alix**, **Bobby** *and* **Lavinia**.

Alix   Children, you really must go to bed now – it's dreadfully late.

Bobby   Oh Mummy.

Alix   Daddy will come up and say good night to you before dinner if you're quick.

Bobby   I want to hear about the ship, Mummy.

Captain   I'll tell you about her in the morning, Bobby. We'll have an early breakfast and you can fire as many questions at me as you like if you'll be good. Do as your mother tells you and go to bed now.

Lavinia   Can I ask questions too?

Captain   You never do anything else – go on, off with you both. I'll come up in ten minutes.

Bobby   Promise?

Captain   Promise.

Bobby   Are you coming too, Mummy?

Alix   Yes, darling.

Bobby   All right, come on Lavvy – I'll race you.

Camera PANS with them as they run out of the room.

Scene 321

INT. CAPTAIN 'D'S DRAWING ROOM. DAY.

and

Scene 322

CLOSE TWO SHOT, **Captain** *and* **Alix** *to cover above scene.*

CLOSE TWO SHOT, **Bobby** *and* **Lavinia** *to cover above scene.*

Scene 323

INT. CAPTAIN 'D'S DRAWING ROOM. DAY.

CLOSE TWO SHOT, **Alix** *and* **Captain**.

Alix   (*sitting down*) They've been wild with excitement all day.

Captain   (*sitting down beside her and putting his hand on hers*) Missed me?

Alix   Of course not. I've been far too busy – I never gave you a thought.

Captain   That's right … What's the surprise for dinner?

Alix   Grouse – Maureen sent us a brace from Scotland.

Captain   Good for Maureen – there's a girl of really fine perception.

Alix   They're a bit high – but I expect you'll like that, won't you?

Captain   Is that a new dress?

Alix   No dear – I've had it for ages.

Captain   I'll swear I've never clapped eyes on it before.

Alix   (*resting her head on his shoulder*) Only about twenty times, my darling.

Captain   (*putting his arm round her*) Perhaps it's you that looks new. As good as new anyway.

Alix   Is there going to be a war, do you think?

Captain   (*after a slight pause*) yes – I think there is.

Alix   Oh!

Captain   No use worrying about it till it comes – not much use really.

Alix   No.

Captain   (*giving her a gentle little shake*) Don't be sad.

Alix   I'm not sad really … I'm just gathering myself together.

Captain   Any more of that Kinross Special left in the shaker?

Scene 324

INT. CAPTAIN 'D'S DRAWING ROOM. DAY.

and

Scene 325

CLOSE UP, **Captain 'D'** *to cover above scene. CLOSE UP,* **Alix** *to cover above scene.*

Scene 326

INT. CAPATIN 'D'S DRAWING ROOM. DAY.

ANOTHER ANGLE, TWO SHOT, **Alix** *and* **Captain**.

Alix   (*rising*) Of course – where's your glass?

Captain   Mantlepiece.

Camera PANS with **Alix** *as she takes his glass and moves over to the table.*

Alix   However busy you are and however quickly you get your commissioning done, I should like to come on board once before you go to sea – just to give the ship my love.

Scene 327

INT. CAPTAIN 'D'S DRAWING ROOM. DAY.

CLOSE SHOT, **Captain 'D'** *watching* **Alix**.

Captain   You'll have to whether you like it or not – my cabin's got to be made presentable.

Scene 328

INT. CAPTAIN 'D'S DRAWING ROOM. DAY.

CLOSE SHOT, **Alix**. *Camera PANS with her to a TWO SHOT as she comes carefully over to* **Captain 'D'** *carrying the two glasses.*

Alix   Does the chintz look all right?

Captain   (*taking drink*) Very shiny – very smooth – gay as be dammed!

Alix   Good. We must drink this quickly and go up to the children. Dinner will be ready in a minute.

Scene 329

INT. CAPTAIN'S DRAWING ROOM. DAY

CLOSE UP, **Captain 'D'** *drinking.*

Captain   Here we go!

Scene 330

INT. CAPTAIN 'D'S DRAWING ROOM. DAY

CLOSE UP, **Alix** *drinking.*

Alix   Here we go!

RIPPLE DISSOLVE TO

Scene 331

STUDIO EXT. SEA. (SMALL TANK). DAY.

CLOSE SHOT, **Captain 'D'** *as he shoots to the surface of the water. He is choking and spluttering. Great piles of oil fuel are beginning to form. There is a terrific noise of machinery. He looks up out of picture.*

Scene 332

EXT. KEEL OF 'TORRIN'. (BIG TANK). DAY.

CLOSE SHOT, the upturned keel of the 'Torrin'. The propellors, which are now out of the water, are racing at full speed.

Scene 333

EXT. SEA. (BIG TANK). DAY.

In the foreground of the picture is **Captain 'D'** *and a few* **survivors**. *In the background is the upturned keel of the 'Torrin', which is still moving. There is a slight swell and as the water reaches the propellers great columns of spray shoot towards camera.*

Captain   Swim to the float … swim to the float.

Scene 334

STUDIO EXT. SEA. (SMALL TANK). DAY. (B.P. SPLIT MATTE).

LONG SHOT, heads and various bits of wreckage etc. The Carley float is in the foreground, the upturned keel of the ship in the background.

76   Noël Coward Screenplays

Scene 336

STUDIO EXT. SEA. (SMALL TANK). DAY.

CLOSE MEDIUM SHOT, **Shorty** *in the water dragging* **Walter**'s *unconscious body towards the float. There is the splutter of machine guns and the roar of aircraft.*

(R2)

Scene 336

STUDIO EXT. SEA. (SMALL TANK). DAY.

MEDIUM SHOT, the **Captain** *swimming towards the Float. Camera PANS with him to include the float on which are* **Flags, Number One, Torps, Guns, Parkinson, Joey Mackridge, Edgecombe, Young Stoker, Hollett** *and 3 other* **Ratings**.

The **Captain** *hangs on to one side of the float.* **Shorty** *drags* **Walter** *into the picture. The* **Captain** *helps them on to the float.*

Scene 337

STUDIO EXT. CARLEY FLOAT. (SMALL TANK). DAY.

CLOSE SHOT, **Number One** *and the unconscious* **Walter**.

Number One   I've got some brandy in my Gieve's.

He unscrews his brandy flask and pours some between **Walter**'s *lips.*

Camera TRACKS in to a CLOSE SHOT of **Walter**. *His eyelids flutter as he mutters*

Walter   Kath!

RIPPLE DISSOLVE TO

Scene 338

INT. HARDY'S HALL and FRONT ROOM. DAY.

CLOSE SHOT, shooting through the bannisters, of **Kath***'s legs as she descends the stairs. Camera PANS with her legs revealing a MEDIUM LONG SHOT of the front door.*

Kath *pulls the morning paper out of the letter box, turns, and walks towards the camera. When she arrives in waist figure camera TRACKS BACK with her into*

THE HARDY'S FRONT ROOM. *The room is cheerful and rather overcrowded with furniture. There are several ornaments and photographs on the mantelpiece, among them a wedding group of* **Kath** *and* **Walter**. *Camera PANS her across room to include* **Walter**, *who is seated at the table finishing his breakfast.*

Kath   Here's the paper, dear.

Walter   Thanks. (*he glances at the clock*) It's nearly half past – shan't have time to read more than the headlines.

Kath   (*opening paper*) Here you are then –

Walter   (*reading*) Umm – doesn't look too good, does it?

Kath   Oh, you can't believe anything they say. Look at all the fuss and fume we had last year – everybody flying about in aeroplanes and making speeches and after all that nothing happened.

Walter   Nothing happened to us, but a hell of a lot happened to other people.

Kath   Do you really think we're going to have another war?

Walter   It looks like it.

Kath   (*putting some used crockery on a tray*) Well, I'll believe it when I see it.

Walter   Well, if you ask me you'll see it quicker than you bargained for.

Kath I don't believe that Hitler'd be so silly – what would he expect to gain by having a war?

Walter World domination – that's what that little rat's after – you mark my words.

Kath Well, they haven't got enough to eat in Germany, as it is. Mrs. Blackett's nephew – you know, the one that travels in underwear – came back from Berlin two months ago – he said they was all half-starved.

Walter Well, I can't help what Mrs. Blackett's nephew says, I think we're for it.

Kath Well, if we have another war, I give up, see! After all we went through last time.

Walter All you went through! You was too young and innocent to know anything about it.

Kath (*bridling*) Don't talk so silly. You know perfectly well how old I am, and it's no use pretending you don't.

Walter (*grinning*) You'll always be young and innocent to me!

Kath Will I indeed, now? If you ask me, you've got a hangover from all that beer you put away last night.

Walter (*rising*) I must be going – is Mother coming down?

Kath I promised I'd call her. Wait a minute. (*she exits to the door and we hear her call off-screen*) Mother – Walter's just going – you'd better come down as you are.

Walter That'll be nice.

Scene 339

INT. HARDYS' FRONT ROOM. DAY.

and

Scene 340

CLOSE UP, Walter to cover above scene. CLOSE UP, **Kath** *to cover above scene.*

Scene 341

INT. HARDYS' FRONT ROOM. DAY.

MEDIUM SHOT, **Kath** *in the doorway. Camera PANS her back to a TWO SHOT with* **Walter**, *who comes in to meet her.*

Kath   (*as she moves away from door*) Will you get ashore again after commissioning – before you go to sea, I mean?

Walter   That all depends … (*he puts his arm round her*) Don't forget to put them bulbs in when the right time comes …   .

Kath   You and your bulbs …

Walter   (*kissing her*) Goodbye, old girl.

Kath   Why, Walter Hardy, whatever is the matter with you this morning? Anyone'd think you was going away for ever.

Walter   Well, you never know …

Kath   You ought to be ashamed of yourself saying such things.

Walter   (*listening to footsteps on the stairs*) Here comes Mother.

Scene 342

INT. HARDYS' FRONT ROOM. DAY

MEDIUM SHOT at the door. The door opens and **Mrs. Lemmon** *comes in. She is a fat, elderly woman and wears a wrapper, slippers, and a sort of bed cap over her curlers.*

Camera TRACKS and PANS her back to **Kath** *and* **Walter**.

Mrs. Lemmon   That spirit lamp of mine will be the death of me yet.

Kath   What's the matter with it?

Mrs. Lemmon   It blew up again – frightened the wits out of me.

Kath   You will put in too much methylated – anyway I don't see what you want to go fussing about with spirit lamps in your bedroom for – you could easily pop down into the kitchen – nobody'd see you.

Mrs. Lemmon   I've made my own tea in my own bedroom all my life, and I don't see any reason to stop now.

Kath   Yes, but that doesn't happen to be your own bedroom, it's my spare, and if you go on blowing things up in it every five minutes, it won't be fit to sleep in.

Walter   Stop it, you two – I've got to go now. Goodbye, Mother. (*he kisses her*)

Mrs. Lemmon   A nice thing when my own daughter starts criticizing me …

Kath   Oh shut up, Mother – say goodbye to Walter – that's what you came down for isn't it?

Mrs. Lemmon   (*to* **Walter**) Will you get ashore again?

Walter   That all depends on Hitler.

Mrs. Lemmon   Who does he think he is, anyway?

Walter   That's the spirit, Mother. Look after Kath for me – and don't go nagging at each other from morning till night –

Mrs. Lemmon   Nagging! I like that I must say.

Walter   Come on, Kath –

Camera PANS with them as they move away towards the door.
Mrs. Lemmon *remains standing at the front room door as* **Walter** *and* **Kath** *go on to the front door, away from camera.* **Walter** *puts on his hat, gives* **Kath** *a smacking kiss and opens the front door.*

Scene 343

INT. HARDYS' FRONT ROOM. DAY.

and

Scene 344

CLOSE TWO SHOT, **Walter** *and* **Kath** *to cover above scene.*
CLOSE TWO, **Mrs. Lemmon** *to cover above scene.*

Scene 345

STUDIO EXT. HARDYS' FRONT DOOR. DAY.

CLOSE SHOT. The door opens and **Walter** *and* **Kath** *come out.*

Walter   Goodbye, old girl.

Kath   Goodbye.

Scene 346

STUDIO EXT. HARDYS' FRONT DOOR. DAY.

LONG SHOT as **Walter** *runs down the street towards Camera.*
Kath *waves after him.*

RIPPLE DISSOLVE TO

Scene 347

STUDIO EXT. PLYMOUTH QUAYSIDE. DAY.

*The camera is TRACKING BACK between rows of men lined up
on the quayside and ends on a MEDIUM SHOT of* **Walter**. *The
Rippling comes to an end and we hear* **Number One**'s *voice
shouting*

Number One's voice   (*off*) Ship's Company – 'shun'.

Scene 348

STUDIO EXT. PLYMOUTH QUAYSIDE. DAY.

LONG SHOT. The 'Torrin' is lying alongside the jetty. There is a gangway on to the quarter deck. On the jetty are twelve **Officers** *in good monkey jackets, and white cap covers, and about two hundred and twenty* **men** *in good blue uniforms and white caps. They are fallen in in carefully dressed lines. The* **Captain** *is 'piped' as he comes down the gangway.*

Scene 349

STUDIO EXT. PLYMOUTH QUAYSIDE. DAY.

CLOSE SHOT, **Captain** *and* **Number One**.

Number One   Ship's Company present, sir.

Captain   (*acknowledging salute*) Thank you – stand them at ease, please.

Number One   Aye, Aye, sir. (*to* **Ship's Company**) Ship's Company – stand at – ease.

The **Captain** *advances and climbs on to a bollard. He stands for a moment looking over the troops.*

Captain   Break ranks and gather round me.

Scene 350

STUDIO EXT. PLYMOUTH QUAYSIDE. DAY.

LONG SHOT with **Captain 'D'** *in the foreground and the* **men** *breaking ranks. The* **Captain** *beckons them nearer.*

Captain   Come a bit nearer – I don't want to have to shout. Can you hear me all right in the back row?

Sailor   (*in back row*) Yes, sir – we can hear you fine.

Scene 351

STUDIO EXT. PLYMOUTH QUAYSIDE. DAY.

*LONG SHOT, different angle, with the **men** in foreground, and **Captain** in the background.*

Captain   Good. You all know that it is the custom of the Service for the Captain to address the Ship's Company on Commissioning Day to give them his policy and tell them the ship's programme. Now my policy is easy and if there are any here who have served with me before, they will know what it is. Are there any old shipmates of mine here?

About half-a-dozen hands go up eagerly in different parts of the crowd.

Scene 352

STUDIO EXT. PLYMOUTH QUAYSIDE. DAY.

CLOSE SHOT, **Captain 'D'** *as he recognises them one by one.*

Captain   Glad to see you again, Johnson.

Scene 353

STUDIO EXT. PLYMOUTH QUAYSIDE. DAY.

MEDIUM SHOT, **Johnson** *is in the crowd. The camera ZIP PANS to a group which includes* **Coombe**.

Captain   (*off*) ... and Coombe ...

ZIP PANS TO ADAMS.

Captain   (*off*) … and Adams …

ZIP PANS TO REYNOLDS.

Captain   (*off*) … and Reynolds …

The camera ZIP PANS to another group. We see a hand sticking up behind the heftily built **Chief Stoker***.*

Scene 354

STUDIO EXT. PLYMOUTH QUAYSIDE. DAY.

CLOSE SHOT, the **Captain***.*

Captain   Who's that small fellow hiding his face behind the Chief Stoker?

Scene 355

STUDIO EXT. PLYMOUTH QUAYSIDE. DAY.

MEDIUM SHOT, the crowd. *There is a general murmur of laughter as* **Parkinson** *steps clear.*

Parkinson   Parkinson, sir.

Scene 356

STUDIO EXT. PLYMOUTH QUAYSIDE. DAY.

CLOSE UP, the **Captain***.*

Captain   You were Cox'n of the 'All Comers' whaler in the Valletta weren't you?

Scene 357

STUDIO EXT. PLYMOUTH QUAYSIDE. DAY

CLOSE UP, **Parkinson**.

Parkinson   I was that, sir, when we won the 'All Comers' cup in the 1936 regatta.

Scene 358

STUDIO EXT. PLYMOUTH QUAYSIDE. DAY.

CLOSE UP, the **Captain**.

Captain   Yes, and fell into the ditch when you got back to the ship.

Scene 359

STUDIO EXT. PLYMOUTH QUAYSIDE. DAY.

LONG SHOT, over the **Captain***'s shoulder. There is loud laughter. The tension of the new Ship's Company is lightened, and a friendly, more free and easy air comes over them.*

Captain   Well, there are certainly old shipmates to tell the others what my policy has always been. Johnson, Combe, Adams, Reynolds, Parkinson – what sort of a ship do I want the *Torrin* to be? (*there is a slight pause*) Come on, Reynolds?

Scene 360

STUDIO EXT. PLYMOUTH QUAYSIDE. DAY.

CLOSE UP, **Reynolds**.

Reynolds   A happy ship, sir.

Scene 361

STUDIO EXT. PLYMOUTH QUAYSIDE. DAY.

CLOSE UP, **Captain**.

Captain   That's right.

Scene 362

STUDIO EXT. PLYMOUTH QUAYSIDE. DAY.

CLOSE UP, **Coombe**.

Coombe   An efficient ship, sir.

Scene 363

STUDIO EXT. PLYMOUTH QUAYSIDE. DAY.

MEDIUM SHOT, the **Captain**.

Captain   Correct. A happy and efficient ship. A very happy
and a very efficient ship. Some of you might think I am a bit
ambitious wanting both but, in my experience, you can't have
one without the other. A ship can't be happy unless she's efficient,
and she certainly won't be efficient unless she's happy. Now for
our programme. You've most of you seen the commissioning
programme of the *Torrin* published in Plymouth General Orders,
and you will have noted that this allows the customary three
weeks. In peace-time it takes all of three weeks to get a new
Ship's Company together, to let them sling their hammocks and
teach them their stations and various duties, to get all the cordite
and shells and oil fuel and stores on board and so on and so forth.
Well, you've read your papers and you know that Ribbentrop
signed a non-aggression pact with Stalin yesterday. As I see it,
that means war next week, so I will give you not three *weeks* but
exactly three *days* to get this ship ready to sail. None of us will
take off our clothes or sling our hammocks or turn in for the next

three days and nights until the job is finished, then we'll send
Hitler a telegram saying 'The *Torrin* is ready – you can start your
war!'

Scene 364

EXT. PLYMOUTH QUAYSIDE. DAY.

CLOSE UP, the **Captain** *to cover above speech.*

Scene 365

and

Scene 366

MEDIUM SHOTS of the crowd to cover the above speech.

Scene 367

STUDIO EXT. PLYMOUTH QUAYSIDE. DAY.

MEDIUM LONG SHOT, **Captain** *and* **crew.** *The* **Captain**
*gets off the bollard amid a great deal of friendly laughter and
chattering.*

Number One   Ship's Company … 'shun. Pick up your
hammocks, about turn, double march.

The **Ship's Company** *run off smartly to where their hammocks
are piled against a shod.*

MIX TO

Scene 368

STUDIO EXT. PLYMOUTH QUAYSIDE. DAY.

Shot of an endless stream of hammocks being carried on board at a brisk walk.

MIX TO

Scene 369

STUDIO EXT. UPPER DECK. PORT SIDE. DAY.

BIG CLOSE UP, **Walter**.

Walter   You four – bring in the sugar. You six – bring in the gas masks. You four – bring in the nutty and canteen stores – and I'll join you two to bring in the rum.

(R2)

Scene 370

STUDIO EXT. PLYMOUTH QUAYSIDE. DAY

to

Scene 375

Six shots of **men** *picking up boxes containing stores from the Quayside.*

Scene 376

STUDIO EXT. PLYMOUTH QUAYSIDE. DAY.

to

Scene 381

Six shots of **men** *crossing the Brow with boxes.*

Scene 382

STUDIO EXT. UPPER DECK. DAY.

to

Scene 387

Six shots of boxes and crates being put down and unpacked. They contain tin hats, gas masks, webbing equipment, buckets and books.

(Scenes 388–94 out)

Scene 395

STUDIO EXT. PLYMOUTH QUAYSIDE. DAY.

MEDIUM SHOT, the brow. A stream of **sailors** *carrying shells on their shoulders, walk over the brow.*

Scene 396

STUDIO EXT. PLYMOUTH QUAYSIDE. DAY.

CLOSE SHOT. A stream of **sailors** *carrying shells on their shoulders proceeding along the port side of the upper deck.*

Scene 397

INT. MESS DECKS. DAY.

LONG SHOT. A stream of **sailors** *with shells on their shoulders.*
They pass out of picture.

Scene 399

INT. SHELL ROOM. DAY.

MEDIUM SHOT, shooting down through the hatch from the
Stokers' mess deck, of the magazine. The shells are packed in
racks, which are now partially filled.

DISSOLVE TO

(*Scenes 398 and 400–6 out*)

Scene 407

INT. CAPTAIN'S DAY CABIN. DAY.

CLOSE UP, **Captain 'D'** *seated at his desk, writing.*

Scene 408

STUDIO EXT. PLYMOUTH QUAYSIDE. NIGHT.

MEDIUM SHOT, the brow. A stream of **sailors** *are carrying shells*
on their shoulders, walk over the brow. They are now working
under bright lights. (Yard Arm Groups).

Scene 409

STUDIO EXT. PLYMOUTH QUAYSIDE. NIGHT.

CLOSE SHOT. Working under the bright lights the stream of
sailors *with the shells on their shoulders, proceed along the port*
side of the upper deck.

Scene 410

INT. MESS DECKS. NIGHT.

LONG SHOT. Working under bright lights, the stream of **sailors** *carrying the shells on their shoulders.*

Scene 411

INT. SHELL ROOM. NIGHT.

MEDIUM SHOT from the Stokers' mess deck shooting down through the Hatch, into the magazine. The shells are packed in racks which are now nearly filled. The work is carried on under bright lights.

MIX TO

Scene 412

STUDIO EXT. UPPER DECK. NIGHT.

MEDIUM SHOT. There is great activity and the deck is lit by arc lamps. Two or three **sailors** *are stretched out, asleep.* **Joey**, *who is one of them, is lying against the guard rail.* **Shorty** *comes up to him and gives him a light kick on the behind.*

Shorty   Wake up, England – you've 'ad your hour – it's my turn now.

(R2)

FADE IN

Scene 413

STUDIO EXT. PLYMOUTH QUAYSIDE. DAY. (MODEL).

LONG SHOT. The 'Torrin' is lying alongside the quay. Various groups of **men** *are standing around listening to the wireless loud-speakers from which are heard the chimes of Big Ben.*

Scene 414

INT. CAPATIN'S DAY CABIN. DAY.

The **Captain** *is at his desk,* **Secco** *by his side with a lot of papers in his hand.* **Captain 'D'** *silently hands* **Secco** *a cigarette and has one himself. On the desk is a calendar showing the date 'September 3rd, 1939'.*

A B.B.C. Announcer*'s voice introduces* **Mr. Chamberlain**. *Then:*

Chamberlain   I am speaking to you from the Cabinet Room at No. 10 Downing Street. This morning the British Ambassador in Berlin handed the German Government a final note …

(*Scene 415 out*)

Scene 416

INT. WARDROOM. DAY.

Number One, **Torps**, **Pilot** and **Doc** *are listening to the loud speaker.*

Chamberlain   … stating that, unless we heard from them by 11 o'clock that they were prepared at once to withdraw their troops from Poland, a state of war would exist between us.

(*Scene 417 out*)

(R2)

Scene 418

INT. MESS DECK. DAY.

MEDIUM SHOT, a group of **sailors**, *among them* **Shorty**, **Joey**, **Parkinson** *and* **Hollett**, *sitting at the table listening to* **Mr. Chamberlain**'s *speech.*

Chamberlain   I have to tell you now that no such undertaking has been received and that consequently this country is at war with Germany. You can imagine what a bitter blow it is to me … .

Shorty   (*interrupting*) It isn't exactly a Bank Holiday for us!!

As **Mr. Chamberlain**'s *voice continues 'that all my long struggle to win peace has failed' the scene*

RIPPLE DISSOLVES TO

Scene 419

STUDIO EXT. CARLEY FLOAT. DAY. (B.P.)

MEDIUM SHOT. **Captain 'D'** *is clambering on to the Float, helped by* **Shorty**. *The upturned keel of the 'Torrin' is seen in the distance.*

Shorty   Are you all right, sir?

Captain   Yes thanks.

When, with the help of **Shorty**, *he has hauled himself on to the float he looks towards the keel of the ship.*

Scene 420

STUDIO EXT. KEEL OF 'TORRIN'. (MODEL).

LONG SHOT, the upturned keel.

Scene 421

STUDIO EXT. CARLEY FLOAT. DAY. (B.P.)

MEDIUM CLOSE SHOT, the **Captain**.

Captain   She's still afloat.

Shorty   (*off*) Yes, sir.

CAMERA TRACKS to a BIG CLOSE UP of **Captain**'s *face staring towards the keel of the ship.* **Alix**'s *voice is heard saying*

Alix's voice   God bless this ship and all who sail in her … God bless this ship and all who sail in her …

RIPPLE DISSOLVE TO

Scene 422

STUDIO EXT. PLYMOUTH QUAYSIDE. DAY.

LONG SHOT, the 'Torrin' lying alongside the quay. There is snow falling and the sound of men's voices singing. The camera TRACKS in to the ship as the singing becomes louder.

MIX TO

Scene 423

INT. MESS DECK. DAY.

LONG SHOT. About half the **Ship's Company** *are crowded into a confined space. There are paper Christmas decorations festooned from the hammock hooks.* **Captain 'D'** *is taking the Service …*
The **men** *are singing 'For Those in Peril on the Sea.*

The camera TRACKS FORWARD through the singing men and finishes on a CLOSE UP of the **Captain** *as he starts reading from a Prayer book.*

Captain   (*reading*) 'Oh Eternal Lord God, Who alone spreadest out the heavens, and rulest the raging of the sea Who has compassed the waters with bounds until day and night come to an end Be pleased to receive into Thy Almighy and most gracious

protection the persons of us thy servants and the Fleet in which
we serve. Preserve us from the dangers of the sea and from the
violence of the enemy that we may be a safeguard unto our most
gracious Sovereign Lord King George and his Dominions, and a
security for such as pass on the seas upon their lawful occasions
that the inhabitants of our island may in peace and quietness
serve Thee our God and that we may return in safety to enjoy the
blessings of the land with the fruits of our labours, and with a
thankful remembrance of Thy mercies to praise and glorify Thy
Holy Name, Through Jesus Christ our Lord, Amen.

The **Captain** *then announces the number of the next hymn.*

Scene 424

INT. MESS DECK. DAY.

MEDIUM LONG SHOT, the **men** *start to sing the Christmas
Carol 'Good King Wenceslas'. The scene then DISSOLVES.*

Scene 425

INT. MESS DECK. DAY.

to

Scene 429

FIVE CLOSE MEDIUM SHOTS *of* **men** *to intercut with Hymn.*

DISSOLVE TO

(R2)

Scene 430

STUDIO EXT. BLAKE HOUSE. DAY.

LONG SHOT. In the foreground of the picture is a group of **children** *standing in the slushy snow. They are singing, rather breathily, 'Good King Wenceslas', and anxiously scanning the windows. After a few bars a window opens and* **Shorty** *appears and throws them out some coppers. He waves his hand to them and goes in again, closing the windows.*

Scene 431

INT. BLAKES' LIVING ROOM. DAY.

MEDIUM SHOT, Shorty *at the window. Camera PANS with him as he walks over to the oval table around which are seated* **Mr.** *and* **Mrs. Blake**, **May**, **Uncle Fred**, **Nell Fosdick** (**Shorty**'s *sister*), *her husband,* **Albert**, *a Corporal in the Royal Marines. They are seated as follows* **Mr. Blake** *at the head of the table with his back to the window, opposite him at the other end,* **Mrs. Blake**. *On her right are* **Albert** *and* **May** *on her left,* **Shorty**, **Nell** *and* **Uncle Fred**, *who sits next to* **Mr. Blake**. *The atmosphere is very festive. The table is wildly untidy with crackers, bits of paper, sweets and fruit. Everybody is wearing paper caps. As* **Shorty** *sits down* **Mrs. Blake** *says*

Mrs. Blake   Them kids have been at it all day – it beats me why their mothers let 'em do it.

Nell   It's the Christmas spirit, Mum.

Mrs. Blake   I'd give 'em Christmas spirit – coming 'ome with their feet sopping and getting colds and giving them to everybody else …

Shorty   Now then Mother, this is the time for goodwill towards all men – can't 'ave you grumbling just as if it was an ordinary day!

Mrs. Blake   Me grumble … I like that, I must say.

Scene 432

INT. BLAKES' LIVING ROOM. DAY.

TWO SHOT, **Uncle Fred** *and* **Mr. Blake**.

Uncle Fred   I remember in the last war spending Christmas in the Red Sea – we was coming 'ome from Aden – Hot! You could have fried an egg on the deck and that's no lie.

Scene 433

INT. BLAKES' LIVING ROOM. DAY.

CLOSE SHOT, **Albert**.

Albert   You've said it – the Red Sea can be 'ot all right. So can the Persian Gulf. I was there two years ago in the *'Worcestershire'*. The Frig went wonky, everything went bad, including the language – oh dear! You certainly see life in the big ships …

Scene 434

INT. BLAKES' LIVING ROOM. DAY.

CLOSE UP, **Shorty**.

Shorty   We don't do so badly in the small ones, you know.

Scene 435

INT. BLAKES' LIVING ROOM. DAY.

CLOSE UP, **Nell**.

Nell   Oh, they're off again – stop them, somebody.

Scene 436

INT. BLAKES' LIVING ROOM. DAY.

CLOSE UP, **Albert**.

Albert   I'm not starting anything – but it's a damn sight more lively in a big Cruiser than a Destroyer – it stands to reason, don't it?

Scene 437

INT. BLAKES' LIVING ROOM. DAY.

CLOSE UP, **Shorty**.

Shorty   It don't do no such thing – you're a Marine you are – you don't know nothing about Destroyers … .

Scene 438

INT. BLAKES' LIVING ROOM. DAY.

CLOSE UP, **Albert**.

Albert   What's the matter with the Marines?

Scene 439

INT. BLAKES' LIVING ROOM. DAY.

CLOSE UP, **Shorty**.

Shorty   Well, Bert – I'm afraid I'll have to tell you.

Scene 440

INT. BLAKES' LIVING ROOM. DAY.

CLOSE UP, **Albert**.

Albert   Now look 'ere. Shorty, my lad – just answer me one question – where would the Navy be if it wasn't for the Marines?

Scene 441

INT. BLAKES' LIVING ROOM. DAY.

CLOSE UP, **Shorty**.

Shorty   If there wasn't a Navy, there wouldn't <u>be</u> no Marines.

Scene 442

INT. BLAKES' LIVING ROOM. DAY.

THREE SHOT, **Mrs. Blake**, **Shorty** *and* **Albert**.

Mrs. Blake   Oh, shut up, you two – who cares, anyway?

Shorty   (*shocked*) That's a nice way to talk and no mistake – you, the mother of a sailor.

Albert   And the mother-in-law of a Marine!

Mrs. Blake   Pass the port wine and don't talk so silly – I'm as dry as a bone.

Nell *leans into shot to pass the port.*

Nell   Mum's quite right – what's the sense in arguing …?

Albert   We wasn't arguing – that was a friendly discussion.

Mrs. Blake   You'll be telling me next that was a friendly discussion last night in 'The Green Man' – why you 'ad the whole place in an uproar …

Scene 443

INT. BLAKES' LIVING ROOM. DAY.

CLOSE UP, **Shorty**.

Shorty   (*springing to his feet*) Bert – I give you a Toast – 'The Royal Marines – God Bless 'em – and a Happy Christmas to every man jack of 'em …'

Scene 444

INT. BLAKES' LIVING ROOM. DAY.

CLOSE UP, **Albert**.

Albert   (*rising*) Thanks, Shorty old man. I will respond to that Toast in a fitting manner, and on behalf of my Corps, of which I am justly proud …

Shorty   (*off*) Hear – Hear –

Albert   Here's to Destroyers and the '*Torrin*' in particular – May her shadow never grow less!

He drinks.

Scene 445

INT. BLAKES' LIVING ROOM. DAY.

CLOSE UP, **Shorty**.

Shorty   (*simply*) It never will!

DISSOLVE TO

Scene 446

INT. HARDYS' FRONT ROOM. DAY.

CLOSE SHOT, **Walter**. *He is in the middle of his speech and the camera is TRACKING BACK to reveal this room. Round the table are seated* **Kath**, **Mrs. Lemmon**, **Frank Gordon**, *a young Aircraftman, and* **Freda Lewis**, **Kath**'s *niece. She is a very pretty girl of about twenty.* **Walter** *is standing at the head of the table making a speech. The same festive atmosphere prevails. Everyone is in paper hats, etc.*

Walter   I would like to take the opportunity of this festive occasion to drink the healths of one and all present and to thank a kindly Fate for so arranging that my ship should have to come home for boiler cleaning exactly two days before Christmas, a bit of luck which any sailor will tell you is nothing short of a bloody miracle!

(R1)

Kath   How can you, Walter – you know I don't like you using that word.

Walter   Be that as it may, Kath, it is a highly expressive word and, what is more, it has been bound up with Naval tradition since time immemorial …

Frank   I have heard it whispered in the R.A.F.

Walter   Be that as it may, I would like to add that I consider that we are bl- very happy to be all together on this happy day, taking into account the fact that there's a war on, and the whole of civilization happens to be trembling on the edge of an abyss …

Kath   There now!

Walter   What did you say, Kath?

Kath   I only said 'There now'.

Walter   Well don't say it again, dear, because it puts me off.

Freda   (*giggling*) Oh dear.

Walter   And what are you giggling about, Freda, if I may make so bold?

Freda   Nothing really – it's just the way you talk.

Walter   What you young flipperty gibbets don't seem to realise is that this is a very important war indeed.

Kath   War or no war you certainly like listening to the sound of your own voice all right.

Mrs. Lemmon   Let him get on with his speech, Kath.

Kath   Try and stop him!

(R1)

Walter   I will treat those paltry interruptions with the contempt they deserve and go on to propose the health of one who is very dear to me. She is a creature of many moods and fads and fancies – she is, to coin a phrase, very often uncertain, coy and hard to please – but I am devoted to her with every fibre of my being and hereby swear to be true to her in word and deed Ladies and Gentlemen – '*H.M.S. Torrin*'!

Scene 447

INT. HARDYS' FRONT ROOM. DAY.

to

Scene 448

CLOSE UP, **Walter** *to cover above scene. CLOSE UP,* **Kath** *to cover above scene. CLOSE UP,* **Frank** *to cover above scene.*

MIX TO

Scene 450

INT. WARDROOM. NIGHT.
CLOSE UP, a hammer tapping on the table three times.

Scene 451

INT. WARDROOM. NIGHT.

LONG SHOT, high angle. It is Christmas evening. The Wardroom is gaily decorated and on the table is a small Christmas tree. **Number One** *sits in the President's chair with* **Alix** *on his right and* **Mrs. Macaddo** (**Torp**'s *wife*) *on his left. Seated round the table are* **Flags** *with Maureen on his right,* **Torps, Lavinia, Secco, Bobby, Trafalgar** (*on a chair*), **Captain 'D'** *and* **Mrs. Farrell** (**Number One**'s *wife*) *and SUB. Mrs. Macadoo is nicely dressed and rather pretty.* **Mrs. Farrell** *is a little older than* **Mrs. Macadoo.** **Maureen Fenwick** *is a very pretty girl who is staying with* **Alix**. (*correct seating of guests to be checked up*)*

The port is being passed round and there is a subdued murmur of general conversation. A **Wardroom Steward** *pours water into the glasses of* **Bobby, Lavinia** *and* **Maureen**. *The port arrives back in front of* **Number One**.

Number One   The King.

The toast to the King is drunk sitting. (Actually when there are women present it is custom to stand, but I think in a small party such as the above it would be more effective for them to sit.)

The moment the King has been drunk to the **Steward** *places bowls of fruit on the table and proceeds to serve the coffee. Everyone begins to pull crackers.*

Alix   We can smoke now can't we, darling?

Captain   Of course

Cigarettes are lit.

Bobby   (*with a cracker in his hand*) You promised to pull the first one with me, Mummy.

Alix   All right.

Captain   (*with a cracker in his hand*) Come on, Lavvy – take a tight grip and pull …

Torps   (*across the table to his wife*) Come on, old girl. (*they pull a cracker*)

There is a general babel of conversation interspersed with the sound of crackers going off. Most of the actual dialogue overlaps.

Mrs. Farrell   (*across the table to* **Number One**) I wish the children were here.

Number One   They're probably having a whale of a time with Aunt Laura.

Captain   I must say it's lucky for us living so near.

Lavinia   Mummy – can I give Trafalgar some raisins?

Alix   Yes dear, if you think he'd care for them.

Lavinia   raf – Traf – come here …

Throughout the above scene the camera has been slowly dropping in height until **Flags** *and Maureen are now in a CLOSE TWO SHOT.*

Flags   (*quietly*) Enjoying yourself?

Maureen   Very, very much.

Flags   That cap's absolutely wizard – you ought to have a hat made like it.

Maureen   Doesn't the tree look sweet? Alix and I spent hours dressing it.

Flags   This is the best Christmas I've ever had.

Maureen   (*as he squeezes her hand under the table*) Is it?

Scene 452

INT. WARDROOM. NIGHT

CLOSE UP, **Alix**.

Alix   Stop whispering you two – Number One, you ought never to have put them next to each other.

Scene 453

INT. WARDROOM. NIGHT

CLOSE UP, **Captain 'D'**.

Captain   We ought to drink to them, come on everybody – to the 'Newly Betrothed'.

Scene 454

INT. WARDROOM. NIGHT.

LONG SHOT, the table as seen between **Flags** *and* **Maureen**.

Everybody   To the 'Newly Betrothed'.

They all drink.

Bobby   What's 'betrothed', Daddy?

Captain   The beginning of the end, my boy.

Flags   On behalf of my fiancée and myself – thank you very kindly.

Scene 455

INT. WARDROOM. NIGHT

CLOSE UP, **Captain 'D'**.

Captain   Alix, as Flags and Maureen are so bashful I think it only right and proper that you should make a speech.

Scene 456

INT. WARDROOM. NIGHT.

MEDIUM SHOT, the GROUP around **Alix**.

Alix No – no – I can't – honestly I can't …

Number One   Come on, Mrs. Kinross – I'll support you.

Mrs. Macadoo   Hear – hear – speech.

Everybody *calls for speech. Finally, still protesting,* **Alix** *rises to her feet.*

Alix   Teddy, I swear I'll never forgive you for this. Oh dear – what am I to say?

Captain   (*laughing*) Happy Christmas!

Alix   Just you wait.

Captain   Come on now – silence everybody – her Worship the Lady Mayoress is about to declare the bazaar open …

Number One   Don't let him get you down, Mrs. Kinross.

Alix   Ladies and Gentlemen – I'll begin by taking my husband's advice …

Captain   Hurray!

Alix   … and wish you all a very, very happy Christmas. I'm sure that Mrs. Farrell and Mrs. Macadoo will back me up when I say I am going to deliver a word of warning – on behalf of all wretched Naval wives – to Maureen, who has been unwise enough to decide on joining our ranks …

General laughter and murmurs of 'Hear-Hear!' from **Mrs. Farrell** *and* **Mrs. Macadoo**.

Scene 457

INT. WARDROOM. NIGHT

CLOSE TWO shot, **Maureen** *and* **Flags**.

Alix   (*off*) Dear Maureen – we all wish you every possible happiness but it's only fair to tell you in advance what you're in for …

Torps   (*off*) Shame – shame!

Scene 458

INT. WARDROOM. NIGHT.

CLOSE UP. **Alix**.

Alix   Speaking from bitter experience I can only say that the wife of a sailor is most profoundly to be pitied. To begin with her home life – what there is of it – has no stability whatever. She can never really settle down – she moves through a succession of other people's houses, flats and furnished rooms. She finds herself grappling with domestic problems in Hong Kong, Bermuda, Malta, or Weymouth – we will not deal with the question of pay! That is altogether too painful, but what we will deal with is the most important disillusionment of all and that is …

Scene 459

INT. WARDROOM. NIGHT

CLOSE UP, **Captain 'D'**.

Captain   Stop her, somebody – this is rank mutiny.

Scene 460

INT. WARDROOM. NIGHT.

CLOSE UP, **Alix**.

Alix   (*firmly*) That is, that wherever she goes, there is always in her life a permanent and undefeated rival – her husband's ship! Whether it be a sloop or a battleship, or a submarine or a destroyer … It holds first place in his heart – it comes before home, wife, children, everything. Some of us fight this and get badly mauled in the process – others, like myself, resign themselves to the inevitable. That is what you will have to do, my poor Maureen – that is what we all have to do if we want any peace of mind at all. Ladies and Gentlemen, I give you my rival – it is extraordinary

that anyone could be so fond and proud of their most implacable
enemy – This Ship – God Bless this Ship and all who sail in her.

She drinks as the scene dissolves.

Scene 461

INT. WARDROOM. NIGHT

to

Scene 464

CLOSE UP, **Captain 'D'** *to cover above speech.*

CLOSE UP, **Maureen** *to cover above speech.*

CLOSE UP, **Mrs. Macadoo** *to cover above speech.*

CLOSE UP, **Mrs. Farrell** *to cover above speech.*

RIPPLE DISSOLVE TO

Scene 465

STUDIO EXT. CARLEY FLOAT. DAY

CLOSE UP, **Captain**'s *face. The float drifts slowly away from
camera and discloses the group of men. Each of them is now
silent, thinking of the ship.*

Scene 466

STUDIO EXT. KEEL OF 'TORRIN'. DAY. (MODEL)

LONG SHOT, the upturned keel.

Scene 467

STUDIO EXT. CARLEY FLOAT. DAY.

MEDIUM SHOT. **Shorty** *breaks the silence, giving a quick look at the* **Captain** *as he says*

Shorty   Well, she did her stuff, sir.

Hollett   Best ship I ever served in, sir.

Parkinson   That goes for me too, sir.

Number One   A very happy and a very efficient ship, sir.

Captain   (*almost brusquely*) Thank you … You'd better wipe your face, Edgecombe, you don't want to get that oil fuel in your eyes.

Edgecombe   Aye, Aye, sir. (*He wipes his face with his sleeve*)

Shorty   Well, do you know what I'd like now? A nice hot cup of tea.

The rather dismal tension relaxes and the **men** *laugh.*

Parkinson   I'd rather have a beer myself.

Torps   Look out … Here come the bastards back again.

Scene 466

EXT. SKY, DAY.

LONG SHOT, two German aircraft dive towards the float.

Scene 469

STUDIO EXT. CARLEY FLOAT. DAY.

MEDIUM SHOT, **Captain**, **Shorty** *and* **Number One**.

Shorty   Only a couple! … Getting quite brave aren't they?

Captain   Keep your heads down – get as low as you can.

There is the noise of an aeroplane as it roars overhead, and the sound of machine gun bullets splashing into the water.

Shorty   Missed – butter fingers!

Scene 470

EXT. SKY. DAY.

MEDIUM SHOT, a single German aeroplane dives towards the float. It opens fire.

Scene 477

STUDIO EXT. CARLEY FLOAT. DAY.

MEDIUM SHOT, **Number One**, **Shorty** *and* **Parkinson**. *Machine gun bullets race towards them in the water.* **Shorty** *gives a sharp cry.*

Shorty Blimey! I spoke too soon. (*he's clutching his arm*).

Number One   (*leans forward*) Did it get you badly?

Shorty   Don't rightly know, sir.

Number One   Knife somebody.

Hollett (*off*) Here, sir.

His hand comes into picture offering the knife.

Number One   Cut his sleeve carefully.

Hollett *starts to slit* **Shorty**'s *sleeve.* **Parkinson** *looks up at the sky.*

Parkinson Dirty rats.

Shorty   (*weakly, trying to be cheerful*) Hit a mother with a baby in her arms, you would. Look boys, shot through the heart. I always did hate the sight of blood (*he faints*).

Number One   Got a piece of rag anybody?

*As **Number One** starts to wipe the blood away camera TRACKS in to a CLOSE UP of **Shorty**'s forearm showing the tattoo of a heart and the name 'Freda' written underneath it. Over this we hear the sound of **Freda**'s voice saying 'What's your name?'*

RIPPLE DISSOLVE TO

Scene 472

INT. RAILWAY CARRIAGE. NIGHT.

*LONG SHOT. The carriage is very crowded and dimly lit. In the foreground on the left are, **Heathcote** and **Burton** (two private soldiers), **Mona Duke**, a rather flashy-looking girl, **Freda Lewis** and **Shorty Blake**, in the far corner. Opposite **Shorty** sits **Joey** playing a mouth organ, then **Parkinson**, **Mrs. Naylor**, a youngish woman with a small baby, **Mrs. Banks** and **Mr. Banks** who is in foreground, camera right. **Burton** is passing a bottle of beer round.*

Mona   (*taking a swig*) Quite a loving cup isn't it?

Burton   You never know your luck – I always say travel broadens the mind.

He winks at her and gives her a playful little pinch.

Mona   (*giggling*) Now then, Saucy – you keep your hands to yourself. (*she passes the bottle to **Freda***) Want a drop, dear?

Freda   No, thank you.

Mona   (*with slight irritation*) Come on, it won't hurt you.

Freda   I'd rather not, thanks all the same. I don't like it.

Mona   (*rudely – in a mock grand voice*) Oh, fancy that now – very sorry I'm sure.

Shorty   If she doesn't want it, she doesn't have to have it, does she?

Mona (*leaning across to* **Joey**) Play a hymn, there's a dear – I didn't know we was in Sunday School.

Shorty   Some people don't know when they've had enough.

Mona   What was that you said?

Shorty   You heard … you ain't got cloth ears. (*to* **Freda**) Here, miss – you change places **with me**.

Freda   No – it's perfectly all right, really.

Shorty   Come on, now – you'll be more comfortable in the corner.

Freda, *without further argument changes places with him.*

Scene 473

INT. RAILWAY CARRIAGE. NIGHT.

MEDIUM SHOT, **Mona**, **Burton**, **Freda** *and* **Shorty**.

Mona   (*grandly to* **Burton**) I'd be very much obliged, I'm sure, if you'd change places with me too – my mother always warned me never to sit next to sailors.

There is a general laugh.

Shorty   Pity she didn't warn you about a few other things while she was at it.

Amid further laughter **Mona** *changes places with* **Burton**.

Mona   Who d'you think you are anyway – Father Flanagan?

Burton   Here – have a fag and shut up arguing – life's too short.

Scene 474

INT. RAILWAY CARRIAGE. NIGHT.

CLOSE UP, **Joey** *as he starts to play 'If you were the only girl in the world'. Everybody sings it.*

Scene 475

INT. RAILWAY CARRIAGE. NIGHT.

CLOSE TWO SHOT, **Shorty** *and* **Freda**.

Shorty   (*under cover of the singing*) Comfy?

Freda   (*smiling*) Yes thanks.

Shorty   What's your name?

Freda   Freda – Freda Lewis.

Shorty   Freda … it's a pretty name, isn't it?

Freda   Is it?

Shorty   D'you mind if I smoke?

Freda   Of course not.

Shorty   (*producing a packet of 'Players'*) Have one?

Freda   (*taking one*) I don't mind.

Shorty   (*lighting them*) These are special – H.M.'s ships only – we get 'em in the canteen.

Freda   My uncle by marriage is in the Navy. He's on a destroyer.

Shorty   Isn't that a coincidence now, so am I!

Freda   He's a Petty Officer. They all call him by a funny name.

Shorty   Yes, we often call Petty Officers funny names.

Freda   It begins with B.

Shorty   (*laughing*) It generally does.

Freda   (*laughing too*) You are awful.

Shorty   What's his ship?

Freda   I'm not supposed to tell you that, am I? It's careless talk.

Shorty   You can tell me – I'm in the same firm, as you might say.

Freda   Chief Buffer – that's what he is called – he's on the *Torrin*.

Shorty   Well, if it isn't a small world and no mistake – Joey – our Chief Buffer's her uncle by marriage!

Joey   That makes you sort of Siamese twins, doesn't it?

Shorty   This is my friend Joe Mackridge – Miss Lewis.

Freda   How do you do?

Joey   Pleased to meet you, I'm sure.

Freda   (*turning to* **Shorty**) What's your name?

Scene 476

INT. RAILWAY CARRIAGE. NIGHT.

to

Scene 478

CLOSE UP, **Shorty** *to cover above scene. CLOSE UP,* **Freda** *to cover above scene. CLOSE UP,* **Joey** *to cover above scene.*

DISSOLVE TO

Scene 479

STUDIO EXT. TRAIN. NIGHT. (MODEL).

LONG SHOT of the train roaring along through the night. It is very dark and all that can be seen is the slight glow from the engine and the tail light of the train as it goes away from camera.

DISSOLVE TO

(R2)

Scene 480

INT. RAILWAY CARRIAGE. NIGHT.

MEDIUM LONG SHOT, Everybody *in the carriage asleep.*
Camera TRACKS in to a CLOSE UP of **Shorty** *and* **Freda**. *Her*
head droops on to his shoulder. With a momentary look of surprise
he puts his arm gently round her. There is a little smile on his face.

RIPPLE DISSOLVE TO

Scene 481

STUDIO EXT. CARLEY FLOAT. DAY.

Shorty*'s face is dimly seen through the ripple.* **Joey***'s voice is*
heard saying

Joey's voice   He's not badly hurt, is he?

Number One's voice   No – he's only fainted.

Edgecombe's voice   It's the blood … some people are like that –
he'll be round in a minute.

Shorty*'s face disappears.*

RIPPLE DISSOLVE TO

Scene 482

INT. TOP OF BUS. DAY. (B.P.)

CLOSE TWO SHOT, **Shorty** *and* **Freda**. *There is a moment's*
pause.

Shorty   I could see you home first, honest I could – it wouldn't
take a minute.

Freda   I can manage – I can really – your family will all be
waiting for you.

Shorty   (*after a little silence*) Funny us meeting like that, wasn't it.

Freda   Yes

Shorty   Sort of unexpected.

(R2)

Freda   Yes.

Shorty   That long train, all them people in it, and I picked on that one carriage.

Freda   It's Fate, I shouldn't wonder.

Shorty   (*eagerly*) I feel that way too.

Freda   We're nearly there, aren't we? Nearly at where you live, I mean …

Shorty   Yes – worse luck.

Freda   How can you?

Shorty   Does your Aunt let you go out much?

Freda   Of course – she doesn't mind – so long as I don't get back too late.

Shorty   What's the matter with tomorrow night then? We might go to the old Palais-de-Danse – do you like dancing?

Freda   Yes.

Shorty   That's a date, then. Six o'clock at the bus stop, Victoria Station.

Freda   You don't waste much time, do you?

Shorty   Can't afford to – I've only got short weekend leave.

Freda   It's not very long, is it?

DISSOLVE TO

Scene 483

STUDIO EXT. BLAKE HOUSE. DAY.

LONG SHOT, **Shorty** *and* **Freda** *walk down the street towards the camera. They stop at the bottom of the steps leading up to the front door.*

(R2)

Scene 484

STUDIO EXT. BLAKE HOUSE. DAY.

CLOSE SHOT, **Freda** *and* **Shorty**.

Shorty   Here we are. Come in and meet my Mum and Dad.

Freda   Oh no, not now, I'd really rather not – I've got to be getting along – they wouldn't want a stranger butting in …

Shorty   You're not a stranger – not any more.

Freda   To them I would be – give me that bag – there's a dear …

Shorty   Not until you say it's okay about tomorrow night.

Freda   Oh, you are awful.

Shorty   Six o'clock Victoria Station bus stop?

Freda   All right.

Shorty   Cross your heart and hope to die?

Freda   (*grabbing the case out of his hand*) Cross my heart and hope to die …

Shorty   So long, Freda.

Freda   So long.

Freda *walks out of the picture.* **Shorty** *goes up the steps of his house, then turns and looks after her.*

(R2)

Scene 485

STUDIO EXT. BLAKE HOUSE. DAY.

CLOSE SHOT, **Freda** *walking away. She turns and waves. She is smiling.*

(*Scene 486 out*)

Scene 487

STUDIO EXT. BLAKE HOUSE. DAY.

CLOSE TWO SHOT, **Mrs. Blake** *and* **Shorty** *at the front door.*

Mrs. Blake   (*clasping* **Shorty** *in her arms*) Why, Shorty Blake – you ought to be ashamed of yourself and that's a fact – your telegraph only arrived a half-an-hour ago. You never said what time you was coming or nothing …

Shorty   Well I'm here okay, aren't I? – sound in wind and limb – you can't grumble.

Mrs. Blake   You bad boy, you …

RIPPLE DISSOLVE TO

Scene 488

STUDIO EXT. CARLEY FLOAT. DAY.

CLOSE UP, **Shorty**. *His face appears for a brief moment. The scene starts to ripple.*

Scene 489

INT. BLAKES' LIVING ROOM. DAY.

MEDIUM SHOT, **Shorty** *is sitting at the table drinking a cup of* *tea. The family are grouped admiringly round him.* **Mrs. Blake**, *a large cheerful woman,* **Mr. Blake**, *rather a gentle type – bald with glasses,* **Uncle Fred**, *big and genial, and* **May**, *aged 14, with a bridge on her teeth.*

Mrs. Blake   Doesn't he look well!

Mr. Blake   How's the war going, son? See any submarines?

Shorty   Hundreds – sunk fourteen last week and a couple of Cruisers thrown in …

May   Oh Mum – he's fibbing, isn't he?

Uncle Fred   In the last war I was in a convoy once and –

Mrs. Blake   Oh, put a sock in it, Fred – we've 'ad quite enough about all what you did in the last war.

Shorty   Dad …

Mr. Blake   Yes, old man?

Shorty   Where did you first meet Mum?

Mrs. Blake   (*laughing*) Why, whatever made you think of asking that?

Mr. Blake   We was in a train – coming back from Herne Bay …

Shorty   It's a small world and no error …

May   Mum, can't I leave my bridge out while Shorty's home?

Shorty   It was Fate, wasn't it?

Mrs. Blake   You drink up your tea, my lad, and don't talk so soft …

Scene 490

INT. BLAKES' LIVING ROOM. DAY

to

Scene 493

CLOSE UP, **Shorty** *to cover above scene. CLOSE UP,* **Mr. Blake** *to cover above scene. CLOSE UP,* **Mrs. Blake** *to cover above scene. CLOSE UP,* **May** *to cover above scene.*

RIPPLE DISSOLVE TO

(R2)

Scene 494

STUDIO EXT. CARLEY FLOAT. DAY.

The scene starts to ripple as the noise of 'planes is heard. We hear **Parkinson***'s voice.*

Parkinson's voice   They're coming over again.

Captain's voice   Keep your heads down. Get as low as you can.

There is the splutter of machine gun bullets and the **Blake** *living room suddenly disappears.*

Scene 495

STUDIO EXT. CARLEY FLOAT. DAY.

MEDIUM SHOT. Bullets are splashing in the water, and the men are crouching low. The noise of planes zooming past is heard. Camera TRACKS IN towards **Shorty***. As the noise of aircraft recedes the 'Wedding March' is heard faintly as the picture*

DISSOLVES TO

Scene 496

INT. AGAINST BLACK VELVET. DOUBLE EXPOSURE. DAY.

MEDIUM SHOT, **Freda** *walking towards the camera. She is wearing a neat little coat and skirt and hat, and carrying a bouquet. Rice is falling around her. The 'Wedding March' grows louder. The Carley float disappears.*

Scene 497

STUDIO EXT. BLAKE HOUSE. DAY.

BIG CLOSE UP, a still camera. From behind the camera the **Photographer**'s *head pops up into picture.*

Photographer   Now, nice and still everybody, please.

Scene 497a

STUDIO EXT. BLAKE HOUSE. DAY

MEDIUM SHOT, the **wedding group** *lined up outside the house. In the centre are* **Shorty** *and* **Freda** *and they are surrounded by the* **Blake family Kath**, **Walter**, **Joey**, **Freda**'s *Aunt*, **Mrs. Patchcock**, *and several others.*

Photographer   (*off*) Now steady – a nice smile – that's it – hold it …

Scene 498

STUDIO EXT. BLAKE HOUSE. DAY.

CLOSE UP, the **Photographer**. *He presses the bulb and the scene*

DISSOLVES TO

Scene 499

STUDIO EXT. BLAKE HOUSE. DAY

MEDIUM SHOT on door of a taxi. **Shorty** *and* **Freda** *are getting into the taxi while the surrounding group shower them with confetti and rice.*

DISSOLVE TO

Scene 500

STUDIO EXT. BLAKE HOUSE. DAY.

CLOSE SHOT, **May Blake** *at the back of the taxi. She is tying an old shoe on to the back.*

Scene 501

STUDIO EXT. BLAKE HOUSE. DAY.

CLOSE UP, **Shorty** *and* **Freda***. They are seated inside the taxi. More rice and confetti shower in on them.*

Scene 502

STUDIO EXT. BLAKE HOUSE. DAY.

CLOSE UP, the taxi window as seen by **Shorty** *and* **Freda***, who are out of the picture. Framed in the window are the* **Blake family***,* **Walter** *and* **Kath***. The taxi starts to move and the faces at the window are left behind, leaving only the railings of Blake House.*

DISSOLVE TO

Scene 506

INT. RAILWAY CARRIAGE. DAY. (B.P.)

LONG SHOT, the countryside sweeping past the camera as seen through a window of a train. The camera PULLS BACK and discloses the MEDIUM SHOT of **Shorty** *and* **Freda** *sitting in a Third Class compartment. There is a paper bag of sandwiches between them on the seat and* **Shorty** *is opening two bottles.*

Shorty   Here we go – ginger ale for you good old Worthington for me.

Freda   Be careful – it might go off pop.

Shorty   (*handing her the opened bottle of ginger ale*) Here's your little lot. (*opens his bottle*) Now then … cheerio, Mrs. Blake! (*he drinks*)

Freda   It does sound funny, doesn't it?

Shorty   You'll get used to it.

Freda   There's one thing I never shall get used to and that's you going away all the time.

Shorty   Well, it's your own fault for marrying a sailor – that's fairly asking for trouble, that is. Can't trust any of 'em an inch – wives in every port – always coming home unexpected and catching you 'aving tea with the lodger …

Freda   I'm the one that'll be the lodger if I'm going to live with Kath when you're at sea.

Shorty   That isn't for a whole week yet – think of it – seven whole days of glorious life! You'll like being with Kath, won't you?

Freda   Of course I shall – it's you being away and me wondering what's happening to you that I shan't like.

Shorty   Proceed with the following operations as ordered 1 – Give us a kiss. 2 – Chuck us another of Mum's sandwiches. 3 – Cheer up and remember this isn't a funeral it's a honeymoon and 4 – Give us another kiss. Now then – Ship's Company – 'shun!

Shorty *gives her a kiss.*

Freda   (*struggling slightly*) Shorty – leave off – be careful of my hat – somebody might see …

Shorty   (*kissing her again*) Who cares!

He suddenly stiffens and jumps to his feet.

Scene 504

INT. RAILWAY CARRIAGE. DAY. (B.P.)

and

Scene 505

CLOSE UP, **Freda** *to cover above scene. CLOSE UP,* **Shorty** *to cover above scene.*

Scene 506

INT. FAILWAY CARRIAGE. DAY. (B.P.)

MEDIUM SHOT, **Shorty** *and* **Freda**. *In the doorway we see* **Captain 'D'** *who has stepped backwards from the corridor to allow a woman to pass. He turns and sees* **Shorty**.

Captain   Hello, Blake – what are you doing here?

Shorty   I'm on my honeymoon, sir.

Captain   (*smiling*) Well that's splendid – congratulations.

Shorty   This is my wife, sir – Mrs. Blake.

Captain   (shaking hands) How do you do?

Freda   (*shyly*) Pleased to meet you, I'm sure.

Captain   Alix – come in and meet one of my shipmates and his wife – they've just been married.

Captain   (*introducing*) Ordinary Seaman Blake – Mrs. Blake ... my wife.

Alix   (*shaking hands with Freda*) I hope you'll be very happy.

Freda   (*with a shy smile*) Thanks ever so.

Alix   (*shaking hands with* **Shorty**) Why – we're old friends.
(*to* **Captain**) He practically saved my life when I came on board
the other day – my foot slipped on the gangway and I nearly as
anything fell into the ditch … (*to* **Shorty**) Do you remember?

Shorty   (*grinning*) Yes, Ma'am.

Alix   (*to* **Freda**) Are you going to live in Plymouth?

Freda   Yes … that is when he goes to sea again –

Shorty   (*breaking in*) Chief Petty Officer Hardy's her uncle by
marriage, sir – so she's going to live at their place for the duration,
as you might say. But we're spending the next few days in Torquay.

Captain   And very nice too. Just you begin as you intend to go
on, Mrs. Blake – keep him in order. My wife rules me with a rod of
iron and it's really been quite successful so far, hasn't it, darling?

Alix   Don't talk such nonsense. (*to* **Freda** *and* **Shorty**) I'm never
allowed to have my own way over anything.

Captain   Well – we won't interrupt you any longer. (*to* **Freda**)
You report him to me if he doesn't behave himself.

Alix   Goodbye – and the very best of luck.

Freda   Thanks very much.

Captain   Come along, Alix. (*to* **Freda** *and* **Shorty**) Have a good
time and enjoy your leave.

Shorty   Thank you, sir – goodbye for the present, sir.

Captain 'D' *and* **Alix** *go out.* **Shorty** *resumes his seat.*

Scene 506

INT RAILWAY CARRIAGE. DAY. (B.P.)

to

Scene 508

CLOSE UP, **Captain** *and* **Alix** *to cover above scene. CLOSE UP,* **Shorty** *to cover above scene. CLOSE UP,* **Freda** *to cover above scene.*

Scene 509

INT. RAILWAY CARRIAGE. DAY. (B.P.)

TWO SHOT, **Shorty** *and* **Freda**.

Shorty   That was my Captain.

Freda   He's ever so nice.

Shorty   Yes – he's all right – knows what he wants anyhow and doesn't waste time mucking about.

Freda   Have they been married long?

Shorty   Yes – got two kids.

Freda   She's pretty, isn't she?

Shorty   Not 'arf as pretty as you.

Freda   Don't talk so silly.

Scene 510

INT. RESTAURANT CAR. DAY. (B.P.)

MEDIUM SHOT, **Captain** *and* **Alix**. *They are sitting down at one of the tables. As they sit the camera TRACKS in to a CLOSE TWO SHOT.*

Alix   How pretty she was – wasn't she? And so very young.

Captain   Coincidence about them going to Torquay for their honeymoon, wasn't it.

Alix   (*smiling*) Yes – I thought of that at the time, but I didn't want to go on about it.

Captain   That first quarrel we had – do you remember? When you went stamping off to listen to the band all by yourself and came back in tears about half an hour later …

Alix   Only because they were playing 'The Blue Danube'. You know that always makes me sort of pent up and emotional …

Captain   That wasn't why you were in tears and it's no use pretending it was.

Alix   If I was in tears at all – which I hotly deny – it was probably because that was the very first time I discovered what a disagreeable, horrible character you had …

Captain   Still – it was a good honeymoon as honeymoons go.

Alix   It went awfully quickly.

Captain 'D' *starts to hum 'The Blue Danube' very softly.*

Alix   Stop it, Teddy … I refuse to be made sentimental in the middle of a Great Western lunch – eat up that delicious piece of railway fish and behave yourself.

Captain 'D', *noticing something beyond camera, looks up.*

Scene 511

INT. RESTAURANT CAR. DAY. (B.P.)

CLOSE UP, a newspaper held in the hands of a man at another table. The front page is towards the camera, it carries huge headlines of the 'Altmark' incident.

Scene 512

INT. RESTAURANT CAR. DAY. (B.P.)

TWO SHOT, **Captain** *and* **Alix**.

Captain   Damn!

Alix   What's the matter?

Captain   (*with a nod of his head towards the paper*) That thing positively haunts me.

Alix   I believe you're jealous.

Captain   Jealous – I should just say I was …

Alix   You promised at breakfast not to go on about it any more.

Captain   I always seem to be refitting or boiler cleaning or something when anything really exciting happens. I'd have given my eye teeth to have the chance of a show like that …

Alix   (*a trifle wistfully*) Never mind, dear, there'll be lots of other chances and lots of other shows before the war's over.

Scene 513

INT. RESTAURANT CAR. DAY. (B.P.)

and

Scene 514

CLOSE UP, **Captain** *to cover above scene. CLOSE UP,* **Alix** *to cover above scene.*

DISSOLVE TO

Scene 515

EXT. THE FLOTILLA. DUSK.

The Flotilla is steaming along the Channel under an overcast sky. It is drenched with rain.

Scene 516

STUDIO EXT. BRIDGE. DUSK.

MEDIUM SHOT. Rain is pouring down. Everyone on the bridge is in oilskins, sou'westers and sea boots. **Flags** *is Officer of the Watch. Next to him stands* **Number One** *and there are present also* **Chief Yeoman of Signals**, **Petty Officer Yeoman**, *two* **Signalmen** *and four* **Lookouts**.

Scene 517

STUDIO EXT. BRIDGE. DUSK.

CLOSE SHOT, **Number One** *and* **Flags**.

Flags   I believe some damned poet at some time or other wrote a very a appealing little piece about 'The tiny feet of the rain'. There's a man I'd like to meet! I'd teach him!

Number One   I'm going down to the Wardroom keep a stiff upper lip, old boy!

Scene 518

INT. WARDROOM. NIGHT.

MEDIUM SHOT, **Torps**, **Guns**, **Doc** *and* **Sub**. **Torps** *and* **Guns** *are playing Russion Bank.* **Sub** (**Peter Williams**) *is in an armchair with his legs over the side, reading 'Esquire'.*

Guns   … five on six – two on three – (*he turns another card*) and ten – just what the Doctor ordered.

Doc   The Doctor hasn't ordered a damn thing, apart from a few doses of Cascars and one splint since the ship commissioned. That, I may say, is what is getting the Doctor down! Years of expensive medical training resulting in complete atrophy! The Doctor wishes he was dead.

Guns   Somebody give the Doctor a drink. (*he turns up the queen of hearts*) There! Just the girl I wanted.

Torps   You do have the damndest luck.

Guns   Skill, old boy – sheer undiluted skill – the usual triumph of mind over matter.

(R1)

Scene 519

INT. WARDROOM. NIGHT.

CLOSE SHOT, at the door. **Number One** *enters. He takes his white scarf and hat off.*

Number One   It's a stinking awful night …

Camera PANS with him as he walks over to the hatch and yells for a pink gin.

Number One   Here's Peace, Peace, perfect Peace, with loved ones far away.

Torps   (*to* **Guns**) Stop – you ought to have put the nine on the ten.

Guns   I never saw the damned thing.

Scene 520

INT. WARDROOM. NIGHT.

CLOSE SHOT, the **Sub**. *He gets up from his chair and camera PANS with him as he goes to the door.*

Sub   The sea is getting up and I've got the middle watch.

DISSOLVE TO

Scene 521

STUDIO EXT. BRIDGE. NIGHT.

MEDIUM SHOT, the **Sub**. *He climbs up the ladder to the bridge and falls over a ring bolt and curses.*

Flags   Feeling all right, old man?

Sub   Yes – why?

Flags   Sure there's nothing wrong – not running a temperature or anything?

Sub   No – of course not.

Flags   (*looking at his watch*) I only wondered – this is the first time you haven't been late for a Watch since we commissioned. You're two minutes early.

Sub   Sorry, sir – it won't occur again, sir.

Flags *starts procedure of turning watch over to Sub.*

Flags   Now Sub course two-one-o revolutions 0-eight-0 …

Starboard   (*off*), (*and cutting in*) Vessel on fire –

Lookout   bearing green three-o.

Flags *immediately raises his binoculars.*

Scene 522

STUDIO EXT. SEA. NIGHT. (MODEL).

LONG SHOT. The horizon, as seen through binoculars. There is a dull glow of a fire.

Scene 523

STUDIO EXT. BRIDGE. NIGHT.

Flags *lowers his glasses and presses the bell which connects the bridge with the Captain's sea cabin.*

Scene 524

INT. CAPTAIN'S SEA CABIN. NIGHT.

CLOSE SHOT, the **Captain**. *He is lying down on his bunk resting but dressed in his sea clothes and is wearing his sea boots. The bell by his side rings and* **Flags**'s *voice comes down the voice pipe beside his head*

Flags's voice   Captain, sir, vessel on fire, bearing green three-0.

Captain 'D' *immediately jumps up and camera TRACKS back into MEDIUM SHOT.*

Captain   (*up voice pipe to* **Flags**) Sound off action stations?

He grabs his oilskin and sou'wester. The action Alarm is sounded and continues ringing as **Captain** *runs up the ladder leading to the bridge, camera PANNING with him.*

Scene 525

INT. MESS DECK. NIGHT.

LONG SHOT. The alarm rattlers are sounding. The **men** *are lying on lockers, on the deck, on the mess table, one or two of them are slung in their hammocks. They are all fully dressed. Everyone jumps to his feet and grabs his oilskins.*

Scene 526

INT. MESS DECK. NIGHT.

CLOSE SHOT, **Joey** *and* **Shorty** *who have been asleep on the deck. They jump to their feet as they hear the alarm rattlers sounding.*

Shorty   I was just dreaming I was in a Turkish hareem surrounded by gorgeous girls and some fat'ead 'as to go and sound off Action Stations!

Joey   I wondered why you were pinching me!

Camera PANS with them as they run towards and up the ladder leading to the Petty Officer's Mess. **Walter** *comes tearing down the ladder.*

Scene 527

INT. MESS DECK. NIGHT.

The alarm rattlers are sounding. CLOSE SHOT, **Walter**. *He reaches the deck as* **Shorty** *and* **Joey** *run into the picture. Camera PANS with* **Walter** *as he races across the Deck to the mess deck door.*

Scene 528

INT. PETTY OFFICERS' MESS. NIGHT.

CLOSE SHOT, **Shorty** *and* **Joey**. *The alarm rattlers are still sounding.* **Shorty** *and* **Joey** *climb up through the mess deck hatch, run across to the foc's'le bulkhead door, camera PANNING with them.*

(R2)

Scene 529

STUDIO EXT. NUMBER ONE GUN MOUNTING. NIGHT.

CLOSE SHOT, the foc's'le bulkhead door. **Shorty** *and* **Joey** *run out. Camera PANS with them as they take up their action stations at the gun. The alarm rattlers continue ringing in the distance.*

Scene 530

STUDIO EXT. BRIDGE. NIGHT.

CLOSE SHOT, **Captain 'D'** *and* **Flags**. **Captain 'D'** *is looking through binoculars.*

Captain   Looks like a line of Destroyers. (*turning to* **Flags**) Make to the Flotilla alarm starboard. Speed 30 knots, line of bearing two-five-o.

(*Scene 531 out*)

Scene 532

STUDIO EXT. NUMBER THREE GUN MOUNTING. NIGHT.

MEDIUM SHOT. The gun's **crew** *are busily preparing the gun for action.* **Walter** *hurries into picture.*

Walter   Report through to T.S. when closed up and cleared away.

Scene 533

INT. SHELL ROOM. NIGHT.

A **crew** *of three, consisting of the* **Young Stoker***, and two* **Ratings***, take up their position by the ammunition hoist. The foreground of the picture is filled with shells.*

Seaman   Start up the ammunition hoist up top!

In answer, the sound of a motor is heard and the hoist starts to move. The **crew** *commence to load shells on to the trays of the endless belt. Camera PANS up the ammunition hoist, as through with the shells, to the deck-head (ceiling).*

(Scene 534 out)

Scene 535

INT. MESS DECK. NIGHT.

CLOSE SHOT, the top of the ammunition hoist. Round the top of the hoist are gathered **Number One Supply Party**, *consisting of four* **Ratings** *and a* **Leading Seaman**. *One of the ratings is the* **Chef** *who is dressed in white.*

The shell arrives at the top of the hoist. One of the ratings takes it and carries it over to the shell hoist shoot, camera PANNING with him. He puts the shell on the shoot and the shell travels up towards the gun deck, camera PANNING with it.

Scene 536

STUDIO EXT. NUMBER ONE GUN MOUNTING. NIGHT.

CLOSE SHOT, the head of the shell hoist. The shell arrives on the deck. **Shorty** *picks it up and camera PANS with him as he places the shell on the loading tray.*

Scene 537

STUDIO EXT. NUMBER ONE GUN MOUNTING. NIGHT.

CLOSE SHOT, the **Communication Number** *reports by telephone to the transmitting station*

Seaman   Number One mounting closed up and cleared away. Bore clear.

Scene 538

STUDIO EXT. NUMBER TWO GUN MOUNTING. NIGHT.

(*TO BE SHOT ON* **Number One** *GUN MOUNTING*)

CLOSE SHOT, the **Communication Number** *reports by telephone to the transmitting station.*

Seaman   Number Two mounting closed up and cleared away. Bore clear.

(R2)

Scene 539

STUDIO EXT. BRIDGE. NIGHT.

CLOSE UP, the **Searchlight Manipulator** *on the port side.*

Searchlight Manipulator   (*reporting*) Searchlight crew closed up. Lamp has been tested behind shutter.

(*Scene 540 out*)

Scene 541

STUDIO EXT. UPPER DECK. NIGHT.

CLOSE SHOT, the **Telephone Operator** *standing by the torpedo tubes.*

T.O.   Tubes' Crew cleaned up tubes cleared away.

Scene 542

STUDIO EXT. NUMBER THREE GUN MOUNTING. NIGHT.

CLOSE SHOT, the **Communication Number** *reports by telephone to the transmitting station*

Seaman   Number Three mounting closed up and cleared away.
Bore clear.

Scene 543

STUDIO EXT. BRIDGE. NIGHT.

*LONG SHOT. The whole of the bridge personnel are now
in position for action stations, they all wear oilskins and
seaboots, some wear sou'westers, some ordinary caps. Those
present are* **Captain 'D'**, **Guns**, **Torps**, **Flags**, **Pilot**, **Number
One**, **Illumination Officer** *and the following Ratings* **Chief
Yeoman of Signals**, **Petty Officer Yeoman**, *three* **Signalmen**,
four **Searchlight Crew**, *four* **Lookouts**, *two* **Torpedo Control
Officers**.

Number One   (*to* **Captain**) All quarters closed up at action
stations, sir.

Captain   Very good. Open fire! I'm going on to thirty knots.

Guns   (*turning to* **I.O.**) Open shutter – star shell commence.
(*bends down to the telephone*) Open fire!

Scene 544

STUDIO EXT. SEARCHLIGHT PLATFORM. NIGHT.

BIG CLOSE UP as the searchlight shutter raises.

Scene 545

STUDIO EXT. SEA. NIGHT. (MODEL).

*LONG SHOT, four enemy destroyers caught in the beam of the
searchlight from the 'Torrin'. There is a roar as the guns fire their
first salvo.*

Scene 546

STUDIO EXT. BRIDGE. NIGHT.

MEDIUM SHOT, **Captain 'D'**, **Torps** *and* **Guns**.

Captain   Well done, Guns, we've beaten them to it.

Torps   (*to* **Captain**) May we train tubes to starboard, sir?

Captain   Yes. (*to* **Flags**) Make to the Flotilla 'train tubes starboard'.

Scene 547

STUDIO EXT. BRIDGE. NIGHT.

CLOSE SHOT, **Yeoman**. *He immediately picks up his Aldis signal lamp and flashes out 'T-T-S'.*

Torps   (*off*) Tubes ready starboard.

Tube Telephone Operator   (*off*) Tubes ready starboard.

Scene 548

STUDIO EXT. BRIDGE. NIGHT.

MEDIUM SHOT, **Captain 'D'** *and* **Illumination Officer**.

Captain   They've fired now!

A second salvo is fired from the 'Torrin', the flash illuminates the bridge

I.O.   (*to* **Searchlight Manipulator**) Train right a little – hold the leading destroyer. (*down voice pipe*) Right – four stars – go on!

The whine of shells passing overhead is heard.

Captain   They've gone over! (*he raises his binoculars*).

Scene 549

STUDIO EXT. SEA. NIGHT. (MODEL).

*The four enemy destroyers are illuminated as a star shell bursts.
The light slowly drops towards the sea like a parachute flare.
The searchlight goes out. A vivid flash comes from the leading
destroyer as a direct hit is scored from the 'Torrin'.*

Scene 550

STUDIO EXT. BRIDGE. NIGHT.

CLOSE TWO SHOT, **Captain** *and* **Guns**. *The searchlight is no
longer on but the bridge is illuminated as the 'Torrin' fires a third
salvo.*

Captain   We've hit. Keep it up! Stop star shell, we can see
without.

Guns   (*to* **Illumination Officer**) Stop star shell.

Scene 551

STUDIO EXT. SEA. NIGHT. (MODEL).

*LONG SHOT, the enemy destroyers. Another star shell has burst
over them. There is a second flash from the leading destroyer as it
is hit again.*

Scene 552

STUDIO EXT. BRIDGE. NIGHT.

CLOSE TWO SHOT, **Captain** *and* **Guns**.

Captain   We've hit again!

There is another whine of shells passing overhead.

Guns   The leading ship's on fire.

Scene 553

STUDIO EXT. SEA. NIGHT. (MODEL).

The line of enemy destroyers is turning to starboard. They are still illuminated by the star shells but are beginning to lay a smoke screen.

Captain's voice   Yes, she's finished. They're turning away under smoke.

Scene 554

STUDIO EXT. BRIDGE. NIGHT.

*CLOSE SHOT, the **Captain**.*

Captain   Look out for torpedoes. Pity we can't possibly fire ours while they're running away.

Scene 555

STUDIO EXT. NUMBER ONE GUN MOUNTING. NIGHT.

A salvo is fired. The whole deck shudders. MEDIUM SHOT, **Shorty** *and* **Joey** *and* **Coombe**. *As the gun is reloaded camera PANS down to the head of the ammunition hoist shoot.*

Scene 556

INT. MESS DECK. NIGHT.

A salvo is fired and the whole deck shudders. Camera starts on the ammunition hoist shoot and PANS across the deck to the ammunition hoist. The **Supply Parties** *are busily at work.*

Scene 557

INT. SHELL ROOM. NIGHT.

*MEDIUM SHOT. The **crew** of three are at work feeding the
ammunition hoist. The **Young Stoker** is placing a shell on the
tray as the ship fires another salvo. The Shell room shudders. The
camera starts to TRACK in towards the **Young Stoker**, who is
glancing nervously at the ship's side, perspiration pouring down
his face.*

(R2)

*Another salvo is heard. The room shudders and the **Young Stoker**
stops his work for a moment, then continues. Camera TRACKS
into a BIG CLOSE UP of the **Young Stoker**. Another salvo is
fired. He stops his work of placing shells on the trays and then
bolts for the ladder.*

Scene 558

INT. SHELL ROOM. NIGHT.

*MEDIUM SHOT, CAMERA PANS with the **Young Stoker** as he
runs up the hatch into the Stokers' mess deck.*

Scene 559

INT. WARDROOM. NIGHT.

*MEDIUM SHOT, CAMERA PANS with the **Young Stoker** as he
runs up the hatch into the Stokers' mess deck.*

Scene 559

INT. WARDROOM. NIGHT.

*MEDIUM SHOT. The wardroom is deserted except for the **Doc*** *and the* **sick berth attendant**. *The* **Doc** *is playing Patience. The* **attendant** *is arranging splints, steriliser, instruments, etc. A salvo is fired and the wardroom shakes violently.* **Doc** *continues playing Patience unperturbed.*

Scene 560

STUDIO EXT. BRIDGE. NIGHT.

MEDIUM SHOT, **Captain 'D'**, **Torps**, **Number One** *and* **Guns**.

Torps   (*shouting*) Torpedo tracks starboard, sir.

Captain   (*down voice pipe*) Hard a-starboard. Full ahead both.

Cox'n's voice   (*up voice pipe*) Hard a-starboard. Full ahead both, sir.

The ship heels over to port. There is a blinding flash. Everyone is thrown off their feet. Flames and smoke rise above the bridge blotting out everything.

Scene 561

STUDIO EXT. NUMBER ONE GUN MOUNTING. NIGHT.

LONG SHOT. The torpedo has hit the ship just below the gun. The smoke clears away. Everything is covered in oil fuel. Five **men** *are dead.* **Shorty** *is alive, his nose and mouth are bleeding. He staggers over the bodies to* **Coombe**.

Scene 562

STUDIO EXT. NUMBER ONE GUN MOUNTING. NIGHT.

CLOSE SHOT, **Shorty** *and* **Coombe**. **Coombe** *is dead.*

Scene 563

STUDIO EXT. BRIDGE. NIGHT.

CLOSE SHOT, **Captain**, **Number One**, **Guns**. *The bridge and the men on it are covered with oil fuel. Their faces are black and all are bleeding at the nose and mouth. They are all somewhat dazed. Gunfire is still coming from* **Number Three** *gun. The ship lists heavily to starboard and sinks appreciably.*

Captain   (*down voice pipe*) Stop both – midships. (*to* **Number One**) Close all water-tight doors. Jettison top weight. (*to* **Guns**) Keep those guns firing.

Guns *picks up a megaphone and shouts through it over the side.*

Guns   Number One and Number Two mountings, carry on firing.

Scene 564

STUDIO EXT. NUMBER ONE GUN MOUNTING. NIGHT.

CLOSE SHOT, **Shorty** *and* **Coombe**. **Shorty** *hears the order from the bridge, staggers to his feet, straddles* **Coombe***'s dead body and goes on firing the gun.*

(R1)

Scene 565

STUDIO EXT. BRIDGE. NIGHT

CLOSE SHOT, **Captain 'D'** *and* **Flags**.

Captain   Flags, use a hand lamp, make to *Tomahawk*. 'Take over, continue chase'.

DISSOLVE TO

Scene 566

INT. WARDROOM. NIGHT.

LONG SHOT. There are wounded **men** *all over the deck. The* **Doc***, assisted by the* **sick berth atendant***, is working hard.*

Scene 567

INT. WARDROOM. NIGHT.

MEDIUM SHOT, at the door. **Shorty** *comes in, assisted by two* **Ratings***. Camera PANS with them as he is put into a chair.*

Shorty   Me legs are still there, aren't they?

Rating   Yes – what there is of 'em.

Shorty   Well, in that case I can walk on 'em.

Rating   You sit down, son, and take it easy.

FADE OUT.

(R2)

FADE IN.

Scene 568

STUDIO EXT. SEA. DAWN. (MODEL).

LONG SHOT. Dawn is breaking. The rest of the Flotilla have returned from the chase. 'Tomahawk' has closed in to within ten yards of 'Torrin' which has a sharp list to starboard.

Scene 569

STUDIO EXT. BRIDGE. DAWN. (B.P.)

The bridge of the 'Torrin' is in the foreground. On it stands
Captain 'D'. *In the background (B.P. Plate) is the Bridge of the 'Tomahawk' on which stands* **Commander Spencer**.

Spencer   Is Captain 'D' alive?

Captain   Yes, old chap – you've not succeeded to the command of the Flotilla yet? What did you do to Jerry?

With **Commander Spencer** *on the 'Tomahawk' are two* **Lieutenants**, *a* **Sub-Lieutenant**, *a* **Warrant Officer**, *a* **Petty Officer Yeoman** *and four* **ratings**.

With **Captain 'D'** *on the 'Torrin' are* **Torps**, **Flags**, **Midshipman**, **Chief Yeoman**, **Petty Oficer Yeoman** *and thirteen* **Ratings**.

Scene 570

STUDIO EXT. BRIDGE OF 'TOMAHAWK', DAWN.

CLOSE SHOT, **Commander Spencer**.

Spencer   Sunk three. A fourth escaped in a smoke screen, but was badly hit.

Scene 571

STUDIO EXT. BRIDGE. DAWN.

CLOSE UP, **Captain 'D'**.

Captain   Not too bad. Tell 'Tancred' to take me in tow.

Scene 572

STUDIO EXT. BRIDGE. 'TOMAHAWK'. DAWN.

CLOSE SHOT, **Commander Spencer**.

Spencer   Aye, Aye, sir … (*down voice pipe*) Port thirty. Half ahead both.

Camera TRACKS back to give the impression of the 'Tomahawk' drawing away.

Scene 573

STUDIO EXT. BRIDGE. DAWN.

MEDIUM SHOT, **Captain 'D'** *and* **Midshipman**.

Captain   Snotty, ask the First Lieutenant if he is all ready to tow forward.

Midshipman   Aye, Aye, sir (*he dashes off*).

Guns *arrives on the bridge, enters picture and salutes.*

Guns   The power is off, as you know, sir, but we've got all the guns working in hand.

Scene 574

STUDIO EXT. BRIDGE. DAWN.

CLOSE UP, **Captain 'D'**.

Captain   Thank you. We'll need them, I expect.

DISSOLVE TO

Scene 575

STUDIO EXT. SEA. DAWN. (MODEL).

LONG SHOT. 'Tancred' is towing the 'Torrin' at 8 knots.

DISSOLVE TO

Scene 576

STUDIO EXT. BRIDGE. DAY.

*It is now broad daylight and has stopped raining. The ship still has a bad list to starboard. On the bridge are **Guns**, **Torps**, **Flags**, **Sub**, **Chief Yeoman**, two **signalmen** and two **Lookouts**. They are all still covered in oil fuel and looking very tired. The bridge **messenger** arrives and starts to hand round cocoa and ship's biscuits. The orders from the bridge are relayed from man to man along the whole length of the ship this is because all electrical equipment has been put out of action by the torpedo.*

Guns   (*to* **Torps**) We seem to be taking a bit of a strain on the wire for'ard – we'd better alter course to Port.

Torps   (*to* **Chief Yeoman**) Port five.

Scene 577

STUDIO EXT. BRIDGE. DAY.

*CLOSE UP, the **Yeoman of Signals**. He leans over the port wing of the bridge facing aft and shouts through a megaphone to a **Rating** on the port side of the upper deck.*

Chief Yeoman   Port five.

Scene 578

STUDIO EXT. UPPER DECK. FOC'S'LE BREAK. DAY.

*CLOSE UP, **Rating**. He passes the order to another **Rating** standing by the Pom-Pom platform.*

Rating   Port five.

Scene 579

STUDIO EXT. POM-POM PLATFORM. UPPER DECK. DAY.

CLOSE UP, **Rating**. *He passes the order to another* **Rating** *who is standing by the fore torpedo tubes.*

Rating   Port five.

Scene 580

STUDIO EXT. FORE TORPEDO TUBES. DAY.

CLOSE UP, **Rating**. *He passes the order to another* **Rating** *who is standing by the aft torpedo tubes.*

Rating   Port five.

Scene 581

STUDIO EXT. AFT TORPEDO TUBES. DAY.

CLOSE UP, **Rating**. *He passes the order to another* **Rating** *who is standing by the after Screen.*

Rating   Port five.

Scene 582

STUDIO EXT. AFTER SCREEN. DAY.

CLOSE UP, **Rating**. *He passes the order to another* **Rating** *who is standing at the top of the Tiller Flat.*

Rating   Port five.

Scene 583

STUDIO EXT. TILLER FLAT HATCH. QUARTER DECK. DAY.

CLOSE UP, **Rating**. *He kneels down and shouts the order down the hatch.*

Rating   Port five.

(*Note: The above shots have been split into Close Ups, but if possible it will best to combine as many as possible in a single shot. This depending on the set construction.*)

(R1)

Scene 584

STUDIO EXT. BRIDGE. DAY.

LONG SHOT, **Guns**, **Torps**, **Flags**, **Sub**, **Chief Yeoman**, *two* **Signalmen** *and two* **lookouts**. *The* **Starboard Lookout** *yells out*

Lookout   Aircraft in sight, bearing green one-two-0. Angle of sight one-five.

Guns   (*to* **Chief Yeoman**) Pass to Number Three mounting – 'Train on enemy aircraft, bearing green one-two-0. Angle of sight one-five – Rapid salvoes as soon as possible'.

The **Chief Yeoman** *raises his megaphone and shouts down to the* **Rating** *on the port side of the upper reck, by the foc's'le deck.*

Chief Yeoman   Number Three mounting – train on enemy aircraft bearing green one-two-o. Angle of sight one-five. Rapid salvoes as soon as possible.

This order is heard being passed down to **Number Three** *mounting via the* **Ratings** *stationed at the Foc's'le Break, Pom-Pom platform (upper deck), and ending at the fore torpedo tubes. As each man passes the order it gets fainter and fainter.*

Guns   The R.A.F. ought to be here soon.

Torps   A nice nippy little Fighter Squadron – neat but not gaudy – that's what we need.

Guns   I wish they'd get a move on.

Torps   Give 'em time, old boy.

Guns   I'm sick of wallowing about here like a sitting duck – it gives me the jitters.

(R1)

Scene 585

INT. WARDROOM. DAY.

LONG SHOT. The **wounded men** *have now been dressed. Their faces are still covered in oil fuel as there is no hot water obtainable. They are lying in rows on the deck covered by blankets, rugs, sheets, duffel coats or Officers' overcoats. Three or four men are groaning.*

The **Doc** *is bending over a* **badly wounded sailor** *who is lying on the deck by the fireplace. His head and face are covered in bandages leaving only the eyes and mouth uncovered.*

Captain 'D' *and* **Number One** *are talking to* **Shorty**, *who has a bandage wrapped round his temple as he is suffering from slight concussion.*

Captain   (*to* **Shorty**) Well, Blake – how are you feeling?

Shorty   Fine, sir – thank you, sir.

Captain   Got concussed a bit, didn't you?

Shorty   Yes, sir – I think so, sir.

Captain   The First Lieutenant tells me you stuck to the gun even when most of the crew were knocked out – is that true?

Shorty   Well sir, somebody 'ad to do it, sir.

Captain   You did damned well … I'm very proud of you.

Shorty   Thank you, sir.

The scene is interrupted by the delirious voice of the badly wounded sailor whom **Doc** *is attending.*

Badly Wounded Sailor   (*monotonously*) I want to see my Captain … I want to see my Captain … I want to see my Captain …

The guns start firing. The wardroom shakes. The **sailor**'s *voice continues as* **Captain 'D'** *leaves* **Shorty** *and move over to him.*

Scene 586

INT. WARDROOM. DAY.

MEDIUM SHOT, the **Captain**, **Doc** *and* **badly wounded sailor**. *The* **Captain** *kneels into picture beside the Sailor who is still repeating 'I want to see my Captain …' The* **Captain** *takes the* **sailor**'s *hand and holds it flat between his own hands and speaks to him very softly*

Captain   It's all right, old man – I'm here – don't try to talk – just rest … just rest

The **sailor** *is soothed and stops talking. The* **Captain** *glances at the* **Doctor**.

Scene 587

INT. WARDROOM. DAY.

CLOSE UP, the **Doc**. *He shakes his head.*

Scene 588

INT. WARDROOM. DAY.

CLOSE UP, **Captain 'D'**. *He looks back at the* **badly wounded sailor**. *We see in his face that the sailor is dead. He lowers his*

hand to the deck and takes off his cap. There is the whistle of a
bomb and an explosion shakes the wardroom again.

DISSOLVE TO

Scene 589

STUDIO EXT. EXTREME AFT. QUARTER DECK. DAY.

LONG SHOT, the whole of the remaining **Ship's Company**
(*excepting* **Guns, Torps, Chief Yeoman**, *two* **Lookouts, Stokers**,
Engine Room Ratings *and the* **Ratings** *forming the chain of*
communications between the bridge and the tiller flat) are lined up
on the quarter deck for the funeral service.

Captain 'D' *is standing in front of the two lines of Ship's Officers*
who are facing to starboard. The **Ship's Company** *are facing*
AFT. **Walter Hardy** (*the Chief Buffer*) *is in charge of a firing*
party of three **Ratings** *who are facing to starboard. In front of*
them is the dipping board with two **Ratings**, *one at each corner.*
The board is covered by the Union Jack. By the side of the dipping
Board are three bodies sewn up in canvas. A White Ensign covers
them. By their side are two **Ratings** *– The* **bearers** *– who are*
facing to starboard. The Ensign Staff is flying the White Ensign
at half mast. By it stands a **Signalman** *with the Ensign halyards*
in his hand. A **Rating** *stands by the tiller flat (the last in the line*
of Communications). The **Ship's Company** *are dressed in Action*
uniform (overalls, duffle coats, etc.) Nearly all are still black with
oil fuel and are tired and unkempt.

As the scene DISSOLVES, **Captain 'D'** *starts reading the*
following Prayer from a Prayer book. His cap is under his arm

Captain 'Forasmuch as it hath pleased Almighty God of His
great mercy to take unto Himself the soul of our dear brother here
departed, we therefore commit his body to the deep, to be turned
into corruption, looking for the resurrection of the body (when
the sea shall give up her dead) and the life of the world to come,
through our Lord Jesus Christ Who, at His coming shall change

our vile body, that it may be like His glorious body, according to the mighty working, whereby He is able to subdue all things to Himself.'

During the prayer the navigation orders are passed down the line of communications from the bridge to the **Rating** *at the tiller flat. There is a pause of two minutes and the order is passed back along the line to the bridge.*

Chief Yeoman   (*on bridge, in distance – off*) Starboard five.

Rating   (*at Foc's'le Break in distance – off*) Starboard five.

Rating   (*at Pom-Pom platform, nearer – off*) Starboard five.

Rating   (*at fore torpedo tubes, nearer still – off*) Starboard five.

Rating   (*at aft torpedo tubes, still nearer – off*) Starboard five.

Rating   (*at tiller flat, in picture, down hatch*) Starboard five.

PAUSE OF TWO MINUTES during Prayer. Then the orders start being passed back to the bridge.

Rating   (*down tiller flat, off*) Five of starboard helm on.

Rating   (*at tiller flat, in picture*) Five of starboard helm on.

Rating   (*at aft torpedo tubes, off – near*) Five of starboard helm on.

The **Captain** *finishes reading the Prayer. The first body is carried, with the White Ensign over it, to the dipping board. The* **Chief Buffer**, **Walter Hardy**, *gives the order.*

Walter   Volleys, load.

The **Firing Party** *load their rifles at the hip.*

Walter   Firing Party – High Port.

The **Firing Party** *hoist their rifles to their shoulders. The* **Ratings** *on the dipping board hold the corners of the White Ensign and Union Jack with their left hand and tip the board with their right. The body begins to slide into the water.*

Walter   Firing Party – Volleys, Fire.

The **Firing Party** *fire a salvo.*

The second body is carried, with the White Ensign over it, to the dipping board.

Walter   Volleys, load.

The **Firing Party** *load their rifles at the hip.*

Walter   Firing Party – High Port.

The **Firing Party** *hoist their rifles to their shoulders. The* **Ratings** *on the dipping board hold the corners of the White Ensign and Union Jack with their left hand and tip the board with their right. The second body begins to slide into the water.*

Walter   Firing Party – Volleys, Fire.

The **Firing Party** *fires a second salvo. The third body is carried with the White Ensign over it, to the dipping board.*

Walter   Volleys, load.

The **Firing Party** *hoist their rifles to their shoulders. The* **Ratings** *on the Dipping board hold the corners of the White Ensign and Union Jack with their left hand and tip the board with their right. The third body begins to slide into the water.*

Walter   Firing Party – Volleys, Fire.

The **Firing Party** *fire a third salvo.*

As the last salvo is fired the White Ensign is slowly hoisted by the **Signalman**.

FADE OUT.

Scene 590

STUDIO EXT. EXTREME AFT. QUARTER DECK. DAY.

to

Scene 596

LONG SHOT, the **Ship's Company** *to cover above scene. CLOSE PANNING SHOT, the* **Ship's Company** *to cover above scene. CLOSE SHOT,* **Walter Hardy** *and* **Firing Party** *to cover above scene. CLOSE UP,* **Walter Hardy** *to cover above scene. CLOSE UP,* **Firing Party** *to cover above scene. CLOSE UP, rifles firing salvoes to cover above scene. CLOSE UP,* **Captain 'D'** *to cover above scene. CLOSE SHOT, the dipping board* **Ratings** *to cover above scene. CLOSE UP, the White Ensign being hoisted for the above scene.*

FADE OUT.

(R2)

FADE IN

Scene 599

EXT. SEA. DAY. (NEWSREEL).

LONG SHOT, the 'Torrin' is towed into port by a tug.

Scene 600

NEWSREEL SHOTS.

to

Scene 609

… of the 'Torrin' arriving in port showing the damage done by the torpedo, including shots of Dockyard Mateys cheering.

Scene 609a

STUDIO EXT. QUAYSIDE. DAY.

CLOSE SHOT, **Mr. Satterthwaite** *for this sequence.*

Scene 610

STUDIO EXT. BRIDGE. DAY.

CLOSE UP, **Captain 'D'**. *He is utterly exhausted after ninety-six hours without sleep.*

FADE OUT.

FADE IN.

Scene 611

STUDIO EXT. PLYMOUTH QUAYSIDE. DAY.

LONG SHOT, the 'Torrin' lying alongside the quay. She still has a sharp list. Fifteen **Officers** *and 200* **men** *are grouped together in the waist of of the ship. The* **men** *are unshaven and exhausted.*

Number One   Ship's Company – 'shun. (*he salutes the* **Captain**) Lower deck cleared, sir.

Captain   (*acknowledging salute*) Thank you – Stand at ease.

Number One   Aye, Aye, sir – Ship's Company – Stand at – ease.

The **Captain** *starts to climb up on to the torpedo tubes.*

Scene 612

STUDIO EXT. PLYMOUTH QUAYSIDE. DAY.

MEDIUM SHOT, **Captain 'D'** *and group of* **sailors**. *The* **Captain** *takes up his position on the torpedo tubes.*

Captain   Make yourselves comfortable – we're all pretty tired. (*there is a slight pause and a little movement among the men*) There are one or two things I want to say to you.

Scene 613

STUDIO EXT. PLYMOUTH QUAYSIDE. DAY.

CLOSE UP, **Captain 'D'**.

Captain   First of all I want to tell you that I will hold a short memorial service next Sunday for our thirty-six shipmates who lost their lives, and to return thanks that the old ship herself has come through safely with many of her complement … I expect that Hitler is even now conferring the Iron Cross on the man who claims to have sunk us!

Scene 614

STUDIO EXT. PLYMOUTH QUAYSIDE. DAY.

LONG SHOT, the **men**, *shooting over the* **Captain***'s shoulder. There is a slight murmur of laughter.*

Captain   Secondly, I want to tell you that you all did pretty well in the trying time we've all been through. When a torpedo hits so small as ship as a destroyer the result is bound to be fairly devastating, if not fatal, and I can understand the tremendous temptation to think of your own skin first and of the ship and your shipmates second.

Scene 615

STUDIO EXT. PLYMOUTH QUAYSIDE. DAY.

CLOSE UP, the **Captain**.

Captain   In a way I suppose it is gratifying to think that of two hundred and forty-four survivors, two hundred and forty-three behaved as I hoped and expected they would. One man, however, did not. This man has been brought before me charged with leaving his post without permission.

Scene 616

STUDIO EXT. PLYMOUTH QUAYSIDE. DAY.

MEDIUM SHOT, the **men**'s *faces.*

Captain   (*off*) I need not tell you how serious an offence of this nature is in time of war, nor how drastic is the punishment that normally follows. You will, therefore, all of you be surprised to hear that I have let him off with a caution.

There is a pause and dead silence.

Scene 617

STUDIO EXT. PLYMOUTH QUAYSIDE. DAY.

CLOSE UP, **Captain 'D'**.

Captain   Or perhaps I should say with *two* cautions – one to him and one to me, for in a way I feel what happened was my fault.

Scene 618

STUDIO EXT. PLYMOUTH QUAYSIDE. DAY.

CLOSE UP, the **men**'s *faces. The camera PANS slowly from face to face as the* **Captain**'s *voice continues.*

Captain   (*off*) This man has only been in the Navy for six months, and he has only been in this ship for two months. Even so I feel that in that time I should have been able to make it clear to him that I did not expect and would not tolerate such behaviour …

The camera comes to rest on the face of the **Young Stoker**. *He is staring woodenly before him. The Captain's voice continues.*

Captain   (*off*) … I feel that I should have been able to get at least that much of my creed across, and I have failed. I will not punish a man for an action for which I must largely take the blame, but I should like you all to know that after this there will be no more cautions.

Scene 619

STUDIO EXT. PLYMOUTH QUAYSIDE. DAY.

MEDIUM SHOT, **Captain** *as seen over the heads of the men.*

Captain   Next time we run into trouble, and as Leader of a Striking Force this ship should be in plenty more scraps, I know that, come what may, no one will fail to do his duty to the very end. Thank you for making my task so easy and the *'Torrin'* a ship to be so very proud of (*he starts to move off the torpedo tubes*).

Number One   Ship's Company – 'shun … Dismiss!

(R2)

Scene 620

STUDIO EXT. PLYMOUTH QUAYSIDE. DAY.

MEDIUM SHOT, the **Young Stoker**. *The* **men** *around him break up. He turns his back to the camera and starts to move off.*

DISSOLVE TO

Scene 621

STUDIO EXT. PLYMOUTH QUAYSIDE. NIGHT.

Groups of **men** *are seen moving away from the ship and* *disappearing into the darkness. Then the* **Young Stoker***, all by himself, picking his way along the dockside.*

DISSOLVE TO

Scene 622

INT. SMALL PUBLIC HOUSE. NIGHT.

MEDIUM SHOT. The camera is behind the bar, shooting over the counter into the public bar. The room is filled with chattering people. Drinks are being served by a good-humoured, florid-looking **Barmaid***. The* **Young Stoker** *pushes his way to the bar.*

Stoker   Beer, please, miss.

Girl in the Crowd   Hold on to your hats, girls – the Fleet's in.

The chatter and noise fade away as the scene

DISSOLVES TO

Scene 623

INT. SMALL PUBLIC HOUSE. NIGHT.

LONG SHOT. The room is deserted except for the **Young Stoker** *and the* **Barmaid***.*

Barmaid   Look here, I've got to close up now – it's no use your staying on any longer, you can't 'ave any more to drink, it's after hours.

Stoker   What's the matter with having some music?

Barmaid   If you've got a penny, you 'ave it. If you 'aven't, you can't.

Stoker   (*laconically*) I 'ave.

Barmaid   Well, put it in the slot, then – that's what it's there for.

Stoker   I will.

He walks over to the automatic piano.

Barmaid   Will you be requiring anything more before we close?

Stoker   (*putting penny into electric piano*) Look 'ere miss –
judging by all I've 'ad tonight I ought to be drunk, see? … I
want to be drunk. I want to be drunk more than I've ever wanted
anything in my whole life. (*the piano bursts into the tune of 'Run
Rabbit Run'*) … Who says sailors don't bloody well care?

He stumbles out and the door slam starts a

RIPPLE DISSOLVE TO

Scene 624

STUDIO EXT. CARLEY FLOAT. DAY.

CLOSE UP, the **Young Stoker**. *The sound of the automatic piano
has changed to that of Joey's mouth organ. The float slowly drifts
away from camera and discloses* **Joey**.

Stoker   Play another tune, for God's sake.

Joey   Anything to oblige.

*He starts to play 'Roll out the Barrel'. Camera PANS down to
the CLOSE UP of* **Walter**. *He seems to notice the tune in his
sub-conscious mind and gives a slight smile. Camera TRACKS in
CLOSER and an orchestra takes up the tune.*

RIPPLE DISSOLVE TO

Scene 625

INT. PALACE THEATRE. PLYMOUTH. NIGHT. (LONDON
VARIETY THEATRE)

LONG SHOT of the stage as seen from the stalls. The atmosphere is thick. On the stage are a row of **Chorus Girls** *and a* **Revue Artiste***. They and the* **audience** *are singing 'Roll out the Barrel'.*

Scene 626

INT. PALACE THEATRE. PLYMOUTH. NIGHT.

CLOSE SHOT, **Walter***,* **Kath***,* **Shorty** *and* **Freda***. They are all singing lustily.*

Scene 627

INT. PALACE THEATRE. PLYMOUTH. NIGHT.

CLOSE SHOT, **Chorus Girls** *and* **Revue Artiste** *continuing the number.*

Scene 628

INT. PALACE THEATRE. PLYMOUTH. NIGHT.

LONG SHOT, the Auditorium as seen from the stage. The singing ends. There is wild applause as the scene

DISSOLVES TO

Scene 629

STUDIO EXT. DOCKYARD GATES. PLYMOUTH. DAWN.

It is a grey, early morning. A constant stream of **sailors** *pass the camera.* **Freda***,* **Shorty***,* **Walter** *and* **Kath** *enter picture and stop.*

Freda   Well – goodbye, Walter …

Walter   Goodbye, Freda – don't go over-exerting yourself, now …

Shorty   Goodbye, Kath.

Kath   Be good – go on, Freda – go on up to the gate with him – I'll wait here.

Camera TRACKS with **Freda** *and* **Shorty** *as they walk a few yards to the gate. They stop. The stream of* **sailors** *continues.*

Shorty   You shouldn't 'ave come really, you know – it's bad for you.

Freda   Don't be so silly – it would be much worse sitting at home – why we've had a whole half hour extra. It's better than last time somehow – perhaps I'm getting used to it.

Shorty   Come on – give us a kiss and 'op it – no sense in 'anging about …

Freda   All right.

She puts her arm round his neck, kisses him and turns away.

Shorty   Now then – none of that …

Freda   (*not looking at him*) Go on – be a good boy – and don't get your feet wet …

Scene 630

STUDIO EXT. DOCKYARD GATES. PLYMOUTH. DAWN.

CLOSE SHOT, **Walter** *and* **Kath** *exchanging a hurried farewell kiss.*

Walter   Goodbye, old girl.

Kath   Goodbye. I won't forget about having the mower mended.

Walter   That's right – and if things get bad you can always go to Dorothy's, can't you?

Kath   They'll have to be good and bad before I do that.

Walter   All right obstinate … Cheerio!

Kath   Cheerio!

Walter *goes.* **Freda** *joins* **Kath**. *They stand together for a moment then, as they turn their back to the camera and begin to walk away against the stream of* **sailors** *the camera CRANES UP.*

DISSOLVE TO

Scene 631

EXT. 'TORRIN'. DAY.

LONG SHOT, high angle from the mast on to the stern of the ship. The stream of sailors becomes the stream of water cut by the term of the 'Torrin'.

DISSOLVE TO

Scene 632

INT. MESS DECK. NIGHT.

Joey *is laboriously darning a sock.* **Shorty** *is at the table writing a letter. Two or three* **men** *are asleep, one of them stretched full length on a wooden bench.*

Shorty   How d'you spell 'porpoise'?

Joey   P-o-r-p-o-u-s, I suppose, why?

Shorty   I was trying to explain to my missus that we've been escorting a convoy of them!

DISSOLVE TO

Scene 633

EXT. 'TORRIN', DAY.

The 'Torrin' ploughing through a very heavy sea – decks awash.

DISSOLVE TO

Scene 634

INT. PETTY OFFICERS' MESS. NIGHT.

CLOSE TWO SHOT, **Walter** *and* **Brodie** *seated at the wooden table. There is a motoring magazine open in front of them.*

Walter (firmly) You can take all your 'Packards' and all your 'Cadillacs' and you know what you can do with them … give me a Rolls Royce every time!

Brodie You're old fashioned – that's what you are. Time marches on, you know.

Walter What does the King 'ave?

Brodie (*triumphantly*) A Daimler.

Walter I suppose you think that's old fashioned, too?

(R1)

Brodie So it is – compared to a snappy 1940 Packard.

Walter You couldn't 'ave the King whizzing along the streets in a flash roadster, could you?

Brodie Who said anything about roadsters?

Walter I said before, and I'll say it again – there isn't nothing on land or sea to beat a good old conservative British make – give me a Daimler every time.

Brodie You wanted a Rolls-Royce just now. You can't have both, you know, looks like profiteering …

Walter Now look here, old man …

Brodie Oh, give it a rest.

DISSOLVE TO

Scene 634a

EXT. 'TORRIN'. DAY. (LOCATION).

LONG SHOT, the flotilla. The sea is calm. It is a perfect day.

DISSOLVE TO

Scene 635

INT. WARDROOM. DAY.

Flags, **Torps**, **Guns**, *the* **Snotty** *and* **Secco** *are finishing lunch.*

Flags   Anybody seen the Chief after the royal raspberry he got this morning?

Torps   Poor old Chiefy.

Guns   He hasn't been in to lunch yet.

The CHIEF *comes in.*

(R2)

Flags   Hullo, Chief – we were just talking about you.

Chief   Damned nice of you, I'm sure.

Guns   Been making any more filthy vapours?

Chief   You shut up, Guns – I've had quite enough of all that.

Flags   I thought it looked very attractive – all those clouds of dense black smoke belching from the funnel!

Chief   (*pouring himself out some water*) I'll thank you all to lay off it.

Torps   Never mind, Chiefy!

Guns   I must say old *'Tomahawk'* went one better round about 10 o'clock. I thought she was on fire.

Chief   (*to* **Steward** *through hatch*) Bring me some food, Mitchell.

Mitchell   Yes, sir.

Flags   Has 'Sparks' picked up any titbits about the war?

Torps   Nothing since yesterday – pretty bad show.

Guns   My young brother's in the B.E.F. He wasn't far from G.H.Q. in Arras. God knows where he is now.

Chief   The whole thing's been a lash up.

DISSOLVE TO

(*Scenes 635c–37 out*)

Scene 638

STUDIO EXT. UPPER DECK. DAY.

LONG SHOT. **Captain 'D'** *is standing on the platform by the side of the torpedo tubes. Sixteen* **Officers** *in old monkey jackets and blue caps and 240* **men** *in all sorts of rigs, duffle coats, overalls, blue uniforms and blue caps are listening to him.* **Reynolds** *is at the very back of the crowd in foreground of picture.*

Captain   Come a bit nearer, I don't want to have to shout. Can you hear me all right, Reynolds?

Reynolds   (*answering from back*) Yes, sir.

Captain   Well, you probably all know what we've got to do, don't you? The whole of the British Expeditionary Force is falling back on Dunkirk. Now in peace time, as you know, there is a lot of leg-pulling between the Services, but the soldiers are our brothers in arms and it's up to us to get them off, so that they can live to fight again. No operation of war that the Navy can be called upon to perform is less pleasant than an evacuation. There is none of the glory or thrill of battle, or running troops into a landing. We have got to go in in greater heart than we have ever had before. Let 'em see how much we admire the way they've fought. Don't forget that the success of our evacuation is measured by the smallness of the military casualties, not the Naval ones. The soldiers are our guests and their lives will be in our hands.

(R2)

Scene 639

STUDIO EXT. UPPER DECK. DAY

to

Scene 641

CLOSE UP, **Captain 'D'** *to cover previous scene. LONG SHOT, group over* **Captain***'s shoulder to cover previous scene. PANNING SHOT,* **men***'s faces to cover previous scene.*

DISSOLVE TO

(Scenes 642–51 out)

Scene 652

INT. MESS DECKS. NIGHT.

The decks are packed tightly with **soldiers***.* **Shorty***,* **Parkinson** *and* **Coombe** *are serving out cocoa and ship's biscuits. As the ship rolls the tightly packed* **soldiers** *sway in unison from side to side. There is the roar of* **Number Three** *gun as it fires, followed immediately by the roar of an aircraft and whistle of a bomb. The deck shakes violently. Wherever they can find room, the* **soldiers** *proceed to tidy themselves, wiping their faces with bits of rag, polishing their boots, trying to straighten their uniforms, etc.*

Scene 653

INT. MESS DECKS. NIGHT.

CLOSE SHOT, **Shorty** *and group of* **soldiers***.*

Shorty   Here y'are, chums – try dipping the biscuit in the cocoa – it can't hurt the cocoa and it *can* save your teeth.

Joey Here, Mate – pass it along, will you?

Soldier Righto.

Shorty (*to a* **Soldier**) 'Ere – don't you want any?

Soldier Can't 'old it, son – me 'and's gone wonky.

Shorty 'Arf a mo' – Joey, take this a minute. (*gives* **Joey** *his tray and proceeds to feed the* **Soldier** *with cocoa*) Don't gulp it now – you'll burn yourself.

Soldier Thanks, son.

(R2)

Scene 654

STUDIO EXT. NUMBER THREE GUN MOUNTING. NIGHT– EARLY DAWN.

MEDIUM SHOT, **Walter** *and the gun's* **crew**. *At the rear of the gun are crowds of* **soldiers**. *The gun's* **crew** *are reloading as the sound of an aircraft is heard approaching. A* **Corporal** *staggers forward wearily to try to help.*

Walter Relax, Mate – you've done your whack. The Navy's in charge now. 'Ere we go again!

The **crew** *start to train the gun.*

Scene 655

STUDIO EXT. BRIDGE. EARLY DAWN.

MEDIUM SHOT. On the bridge are **Captain 'D'**, **Flags**, **Torps**, **Guns**, **Number One**, **Sub**, **Midshipman/Chief Yeoman**, **Petty Officer Yeoman**, *two* **Signalman**, *six* **Lookouts**, *an Army Colonel,* **Colonel Charles Lumsden**, *and an Army Captain,* **Captain Jasper Fry**. *They are all looking up at the approaching cliffs of*

Dover. The two soldiers are being regaled with a jug of hot Bovril and sherry.

Lumsden   Why did we never think of this for elevenses in the mess, Jasper? It's damned good.

Captain   It's only ordinary Bovril rather heavily laced with sherry.

Number Three *gun fires and the flash illuminates the bridge.*

Jasper   How's the old country looking, sir? I feel as if I've been away for years.

Captain   We've been away quite a while too – we put in up North every now and again to refuel. The country was looking much the same as usual the last time I saw it – gentle, you know. Not exactly smug but, well – not exactly warlike either …

Lumsden   There'll always be an England, eh? I suppose that's as good a conviction as any.

Jasper   A good deal better than most, if I may say so, sir (*his voice rises as the whistle of a bomb is heard*).

The whistle of the bomb becomes louder.

Lumsden What?

Jasper   (*shouting*) A good deal better than most, if I may say so, sir.

The bomb explodes nearby.

Lumsden   All right, all right, Jasper – don't start one of your damned arguments.

Number Three *gun fires again.* **Colonel Lumsden** *turns to* **Captain 'D'**.

Lumsden   Fry's one of these jingoistic fellows – brought up on G.A. Henty and Kipling and all that sort of thing – quite a bore sometimes in the mess.

Scene 655a

INT. MESS DECK. NIGHT.

MEDIUM SHOT, **Shorty***,* **Joey** *and* **Parkinson***, forcing their way through the crowd of* **Soldiers***, camera TRACKING with them. They stop as they reach a* **Soldier** *who is slumped over a table on which are lying two other* **men***.*

Shorty   Here, somebody – give me a hand with this one.

Helped by two **Soldiers***, they get the man up on to the table. His head rests beside the boots of another man, whose head is out of picture.*

Shorty   Here, Cock! Here's a nice cup of cocoa. (*he hands it to the* **Soldier**)

Joey   Want a biscuit?

The **Soldier** *shakes his head weakly.*

Shorty   Go on, leave it with him, he might fancy it later.

Soldier   I'd never have thought I'd be so glad to see a cup of cocoa.

During this dialogue **Parkinson** *has been unlacing the boots of the other* **Soldier***.*

Parkinson   (*as he begins to pull them off*) Come on, chum, it's better with your boots off.

Scene 655b

STUDIO EXT. BRIDGE.

MEDIUM SHOT, **Captain 'D'***,* **Lumsden** *and* **Fry***.*

Lumsden   I believe you know a great friend of my wife's, Kinross – Deidre Lorrimer?

Captain   Yes, rather, of course I do. I haven't heard from her for ages.

Lumsden   She married some chap in the Diplomatic Service, didn't she, and went away somewhere or other?

Captain   Yes – Freddy Blakely – I believe they're in South America.

Lumsden   That's the bloke. Looked a bit wet to me but she seemed to fancy him.

Jasper   We're getting quite close – good old white cliffs of Dover …

Lumsden   Look better with the sun on them – still, can't have everything, I suppose.

Jasper   Damned lucky to see them at all, sir.

Colonel   Quite right, Jasper. Haven't had a chance to say thank you for all you've done for us, Kinross. The Navy's put up a fine show – don't think we're not grateful – perhaps you'd care to dine one night when you get a spot of leave.

Captain   Thanks – I'd love to.

Colonel   We'd better get below, Jasper, and start getting the troops lined up. (*to* **Captain 'D'**) I expect you'll be wanting to shove off again as soon as possible?

Captain   Yes – you've struck rather a busy day.

Colonel   Goodbye then for the present.

Captain   (*shaking hands*) Goodbye, forgive my not coming down with you.

Jasper   Goodbye, sir – thanks very much.

Captain   Goodbye – good luck.

Colonel   Just ordinary Bovril and sherry?

Captain   Just ordinary Bovril and sherry.

Colonel   Good – thanks.

Scene 656

STUDIO EXT. BRIDGE. EARLY DAWN.

and

Scene 657

CLOSE SHOTS to cover the above scene.

Scene 658

EXT. DOVER CLIFFS. EARLY DAWN. (LOCATION).

LONG SHOT, the cliffs of Dover as seen from the Bridge of the 'Torrin'.

DISSOLVE TO

Scene 659

STUDIO EXT. DOVER QUAYSIDE. DAWN.

The 'Torrin' is alongside the quay. The **Guards** *are filing off the ship in perfect order and are fallen in on the quay by a* **Sergeant Major** *and a few* **Officers***. The* **Sergeant Major** *'dresses' them. The wounded and dying are carried off from another gangway.*

Scene 660

STUDIO EXT. DOVER QUAYSIDE. DAWN.

MEDIUM SHOT. The camera TRACKS down the line of **Guards** *as they 'dress' themselves in straight lines.*

Scene 661

STUDIO EXT. DOVER QUAYSIDE. BRIDGE. DAWN.

CLOSE UP, **Captain 'D'** *as he stands on the bridge watching the* **Guards**.

Scene 662

STUDIO EXT. UPPER DECK. DAWN.

CLOSE SHOT, **Shorty** *and* **Joey**. *They are sweaty, dirty and exhausted but are also watching the* **Guards**.

Scene 663

STUDIO EXT. DOVER QUAYSIDE. DAWN.

LONG SHOT, from the bridge shooting over **Captain 'D'** *on to the* **Guardsmen**. *They are given the order to march off towards the waiting trains at the head of the quayside. They turn and start to march past in perfect order.*

Scene 664

STUDIO EXT. BRIDGE. DAWN.

CLOSE UP, **Captain 'D'**. *The camera slowly TRACKS into a VERY BIG CLOSE UP. As it does so the strains of a Military March fade in an, SUPERIMPOSED over* **Captain 'D'**'s *face is a shot of*

Scene 665

EXT. BUCKINGHAM PALACE. DAY. (NEWSREEL).

It is a sunny morning outside Buckingham Palace in peace time. The **Guards** *are parading in bearskins and full regimental regalia. The martial music swells.*

After a moment the picture fades away and leaves only **Captain 'D'***'s face.*

Scene 666

STUDIO EXT. DOVER QUAYSIDE. DAWN.

MEDIUM SHOT, the **Guards** *march away.*

Scene 667

STUDIO EXT. UPPER DECK. DAWN.

CLOSE SHOT, **Shorty** *and* **Joey**.

Shorty   If I wasn't so tired, I'd give the bastards a cheer.

Scene 668

STUDIO EXT. DOVER QUAYSIDE. DAWN. (MATTE).

LONG SHOT, the Quayside with the masts and rigging of the 'Torrin' in the foreground of the picture. Beyond are the **Guards** *marching away from camera towards the waiting trains, in the distance. The MUSIC rises to a crescendo.*

FADE OUT.

Scene 669

STUDIO EXT. PLYMOUTH QUAYSIDE. DAY.

Half the **Ship's Company***,* **Liberty Men***, are lined up on the* *quay. The camera starts on a CLOSE SHOT of* **Shorty** *who is now spick and span in contrast with his appearance at Dover. The camera PULLS BACK and PANS over to* **Number One**.

Sub   Liberty Men – 'shun.

Number One   Thank you. Stand them at ease.

Sub   Liberty Men – stand at ease.

Number One   (*getting up on to a box*) Now then all of you … you've got four days leave, there are just a few things I want to remind you of before you go. First, I suggest it would be wiser not to take the very last train back, but the one before the last. Then, don't forget that you are not allowed to take more than 80 cigarettes out of the Dockyard. I would also like to suggest that you do not apply for extension of leave for any such trivial matter as pneumonia or marriage, but only for something really important and then in good time! Remember also not to discuss the ship or its whereabouts in any public places such as railway carriages, 'buses or Pubs. In fact – keep a weather eye on the King's Regulations – have a thundering good leave and enjoy yourselves.

He then climbs off the box.

Sub   Liberty Men – dismiss!

Scene 670

STUDIO EXT. PLYMOUTH QUAYSIDE. DAY.

and

Scene 671

CLOSE UP, **Number One** *to cover above scene. LONG SHOT, the* **Liberty Men** *to cover above scene.*

Scene 672

STUDIO EXT. DOCKYARD GATES, PLYMOUTH. DAY.

MEDIUM SHOT. A stream of **sailors** *is passing out through the gates*

DISSOLVE TO

Scene 673

STUDIO EXT. PLYMOUTH HOE. DAY.

LONG SHOT, **Freda** *and* **Shorty** *are sitting on a seat, backs to camera. In the background is the sea in the evening sunlight.*

Scene 673

STUDIO EXT. PLYMOUTH HOE. DAY.

CLOSE UP, **Shorty** *and* **Freda** *on the seat.*

Shorty   It's funny to think this is such a little island, isn't it?

DISSOLVE TO

Scene 675

INT. CINEMA. NIGHT.

The screen is filled with the title

'HITLER IN PARIS'

Scene 676

INT. CINEMA. NIGHT

NEWSREEL shot of Hitler in Paris.

Scene 677

INT. CINEMA. NIGHT. (B.P.)

CLOSE SHOT, **Walter** *and* **Kath** *sitting in the Cinema watching the Hitler Newsreel.*

Walter   Well, he's got France now, and France is only 20 miles from England – makes you think, doesn't it?

DISSOLVE TO

Scene 678

LIBRARY SHOT.

LONG SHOT of a dogfight in the sky. There is the distant noise of an aircraft and the white lines from exhausts, etc.

Scene 679

STUDIO EXT. SUSSEX DOWNS. DAY.

MEDIUM SHOT. **Captain 'D'**, **Alix**, **Bobby**, **Lavinia** *and* **Trafalgar** *are having a picnic.* **Captain 'D'** *is tremendously interested in the dogfight, but the others are more interested in the lunch. Bobby gives Trafalgar a bit of sausage roll which the dog disdains.*

Bobby   Mummy, Trafalgar won't eat sausage roll.

Alix   That's probably because you've thoroughly spoiled him.

There is the whine of a diving aircraft.

Captain   (*excitedly*) Look, Bobby – quickly – that one diving is a Hurricane.

Bobby   (*calmly*) No it isn't, Daddy – it's an M.E.109 like the one they brought down last Tuesday.

Lavinia   Don't talk with your mouth full.

DISSOLVE TO

Scene 680

STUDIO EXT. SUSSEX DOWNS. DAY.

MEDIUM SHOT. The whine of the aircraft fades away in the dissolve. Camera shows a LONG SHOT of the rolling Downs with the sea beyond. It is a perfect summer day. Camera PANS a little to disclose **Captain 'D'** *and* **Alix**. *The picnic is finished and the children are packing up the hamper.*

Alix   What a perfectly lovely day it's been – (*she looks up at the sky*) Lovely for us, I mean. I suppose that's selfish of me, isn't it?

Captain   Extremely.

Alix   I can't believe that it's so dreadfully wrong to forget the war every now and then – when one can – just for a little ...

Captain   I think it's very clever of you, with all hell breaking loose just over our defenceless heads!

Alix   I made a tremendous effort and pretended that it wasn't real at all – that they were toys – having a mock battle – just to keep us amused.

Captain   That's a most shameful confession – sheer escapism.

Scene 681

STUDIO EXT. SUSSEX DOWNS. DAY.

CLOSE UP, **Alix**.

Alix   I don't care – it has been a lovely day, the sun has been shining and the country does look so very green and sweet and peaceful and you are on leave even if it's only until the day after tomorrow ... oh, Teddy – (*she breaks off*) I wonder where we shall be this time next year?

Scene 682

STUDIO EXT. SUSSEX DOWNS. DAY.

CLOSE UP, the **Captain**.

Captain   (*laughing lightly*) A lot may happen between now and this time next year!

DISSOLVE TO

Scene 683

INT. PADDINGTON STATION. DAY

The big station clock fills most of the screen. The time is a few seconds before 10 o'clock. There is the noise of station whistles, loud speakers giving directions, etc. The big hand of the clock jerks to the hour.

Scene 684

INT. PADDINGTON STATION. DAY.

CLOSE SHOT, Flags and **Maureen**. **Flags** *is leaning out of the window of a First Class carriage.* **Maureen** *is on the platform.*

Maureen   Take care of yourself, darling.

The train whistle blows.

Flags   It was a good honeymoon while it lasted.

The train moves off taking **Flags** *out of picture.*

Scene 685

INT. PADDINGTON STATION. DAY

CLOSE UP, **Maureen** *looking after train as it moves away.*

DISSOLVE TO

Scene 686

EXT. SEA. DAY. (NEWSREEL).

LONG SHOT, the 'Torrin' escorting a large convoy.

DISSOLVE TO

Scene 687

INT. CORNER OF BEDROOM. NIGHT.

CLOSE UP, **Mrs. Macadoo** *on the telephone.*

Mrs. Macadoo   It's all right – I had a letter this morning – they must have been miles north of where we thought they were … no dear, I can't – it's my night shift at the Canteen.

DISSOLVE TO

Scene 688

STUDIO EXT. LONDON ROOF TOPS. NIGHT. (MODEL).

LONG SHOT. The noise of droning aircraft and of Ack-Ack fire. Cones of searchlights fill the sky.

DISSOLVE TO

Scene 689

INT. LONDON AIR RAID SHELTER. NIGHT.

MEDIUM SHOT, **Mr.** *and* **Mrs. Blake**, **Fred**, **Nell Fosdick**, **May** *and several* **other people** *including a* **Little Boy** *of about seven. There is the sound of gunfire from outside. The* **Little Boy**, *with his father's walking stick as a machine gun, monotonously shouts*

Little Boy   Bang … bang … bang

Mrs. Blake   Stop it, Albert – they're making enough noise outside without you giving us a 'eadache in 'ere …

DISSOLVE TO

(R2)

Scene 690

INT. BUTCHER'S SHOP. DAY. (INSERT).

BIG CLOSE UP. Meat sheet in ration book. A pair of scissors is cutting out a coupon.

DISSOLVE TO

Scene 691

STUDIO EXT. BUTCHER'S SHOP. DAY.

MEDIUM SHOT, **Freda** *and* **Kath** *in a queue outside this butcher's shop. They both have string bags and carriers.*

Kath   Any more of this queuing up and I'll turn vegetarian like Hitler.

DISSOLVE TO

Scene 692

INT. KINROSS DRAWING ROOM. DAY.

CLOSE UP of an illustrated cover of 'Alice in Wonderland'. Camera TRACKS BACK to show **Alix** *reading to* **Bobby** *and* **Lavinia**.

Alix   (*reading*)

'The sun was shining on the sea

Shining with all its might,

He did his very best to make

The Billows smooth and bright ...'

Scene 693

EXT. 'TORRIN'. DAY.

A depth charge explodes. The screen is filled with flying spray.

DISSOLVE TO

Scene 694

STUDIO EXT. BRIDGE. NIGHT.

MEDIUM SHOT, **Torps** (*who is* **Officer of the Watch**), *and the* **Yeoman of the Signals**. *Beyond them is a starlit sky.* **Torps** *is standing muffled up with a scarf round his neck and he has a cup of cocoa in his hand. He is looking out to sea.*

Torps   This cocoa gets thicker and thicker every night.

Chief Yeoman   It's warming anyhow, sir. Lines the stomach, as you might say.

Torps   It's practically porridge!

There is the roar of aircraft far away overhead. They both look skywards.

Chief Yeoman   There goes another lot, sir.

Torps   Looks as if poor old Plymouth is going to get it again.

Scene 695

INT. HARDY'S FRONT ROOM. NIGHT.

MEDIUM SHOT. In the foreground of the picture is **Freda**,

obviously soon to have a baby. She is sitting by the fire sewing.
Mrs. Lemmon *and* **Kath** *are clearing away the supper things from the table in the background.*

Kath   Well, I will say one thing for that bit of fish – there may not have been much of it, but what there was was tasty.

Mrs. Lemmon   It's that Mr. Morgan – he always favours us. It's Freda that gets round him. The moment we got into the shop this morning up he come with a chair as if we was Royalty.

Kath   Oh, he's all right, if only he wasn't quite so nosey.

She goes out of the room with the tray. **Mrs. Lemmon***, who is folding the table cloth, walks over to* **Freda***. Camera TRACKS up into a CLOSE TWO SHOT.*

Mrs. Lemmon   How are you feeling, dear?

Freda   Fine, thank you.

Mrs. Lemmon   That letter from Shorty must have cheered you up…

Freda   I wish he was home … I wish the ship could get just a little damaged – not so that anyone was hurt, I mean – just enough for him to get a bit of leave.

Mrs. Lemmon   Never mind, dear – 'Men must work and women must weep' – that's what I always say.

Scene 696

INT. HARDYS' FRONT ROOM. NIGHT.

MEDIUM SHOT, at door. Kath comes back into the room.

Kath   That sink's stopped up again – it never rains but it pours.

Camera PANS with **Kath** *into the room and including* **Freda** *and* **Mrs. Lemmon***.*

Mrs. Lemmon   Better get Mr. Luton in.

Kath   He was blitzed out last week – don't know where he's moved to.

She goes to the sideboard and gets some paper patterns out of the drawer and brings them to the table.

Kath   Anybody seen my scissors?

Freda   Yes, I've got them – here they are.

Kath   (*taking them*) Thanks, dear.

The Air Raid Warning begins to wail.

Mrs. Lemmon   Oh my God – they're here again!

Kath   (*glancing at the clock*) Bit later than they were last night (*She proceeds to spread the paper pattern on the table*).

Mrs. Lemmon   I wish you'd go down to the Shelter, Freda.

Freda   Oh please don't start all that again, Mrs. Lemmon – you know I hate being shut up down there – it makes me feel sick – I'd much rather stay here, really I would.

Mrs. Lemmon   But in your condition, dear, I honestly do think –

Kath   It's no use, Mother – why don't you leave her alone?

Mrs. Lemmon   It's all very fine you being so calm and collected but I'll tell you one thing here and now … my nerves won't stand much more of this night after night, and that's the truth.

Kath   You can go down to the shelter, if you want to – nobody's stopping you.

Mrs. Lemmon   Try as I may, I can't understand why you won't shut up the house and evacuate.

Kath   I've told you why till I'm blue in the face. (*she starts cutting out the pattern*)

From outside comes the sound of running feet as people hurry down the street to the Public Shelters.

Mrs. Lemmon   When you *could* go away somewhere quiet it seems just plan silly to sit here and ask for it …

Kath   Could go away? Where – I should like to know!

Mrs. Lemmon   Well, there's Dorothy for a start – she's got a spare room.

Kath   Thank you for nothing – I've slept in it.

Mrs. Lemmon   It may be a bit pokey but it's safe.

Scene 697

INT. HARDYS' FRONT ROOM. NIGHT.

CLOSE UP, **Kath**. *She stops cutting out and turns round.*

Kath   Now, once and for all, Mother, will you do me a favour and shut up about this. I've told you how I feel and that's that. This is Walter's home, see, and he expects to find me in it when he comes back on leave. What do you suppose he'd think if he turned up unexpected one day and found the house locked up and me hiding somewhere in the country. He might only have a few hours. That would be a nice thing, wouldn't it?

Scene 698

INT. HARDYS' FRONT ROOM. NIGHT.

CLOSE UP, **Mrs. Lemmon**.

Mrs. Lemmon   Well, you could let him know where we were, couldn't you?

Scene 699

INT. HARDYS' FRONT ROOM. NIGHT.

CLOSE UP, **Kath**.

Kath   Oh, it's 'we' now is it? I thought there was a catch in it …

Scene 700

INT. HARDYS' FRONT ROOM. NIGHT.

CLOSE UP, **Mrs. Lemmon**.

Mrs. Lemmon   Why, Kathleen Hardy, how can you say such a thing to your own Mother?

The noise of the Blitz begins to be heard.

Scene 701

INT. HARDYS' FRONT ROOM. NIGHT.

THREE SHOT, **Mrs. Lemmon** *and* **Freda** *in foreground,* **Kath** *in background at the table.*

Kath   I'm sorry but you make me tired sometimes – really you do …

Mrs. Lemmon   I'm sure I was only trying to be sensible.

Kath   What about the garden – and Walter's bulbs that he's so proud of? Who'd look after them?

Mrs. Lemmon   Bulbs don't need any looking after – they just come up.

A bomb is heard to fall nearby. There is a good deal of gunfire.

Kath   Come on, Freda – under the stairs you go – your chair's all ready for you.

Freda   I'm all right here, Kath – honest I am …

Kath   Never mind about that, just you do as you're told there's a good girl. We'll leave the door open like we did before so you won't feel lonely.

Freda   (*rising reluctantly*) Oh, Kath …

Kath   Come on, I'll bring your sewing – the light's quite good in the hall.

Camera PANS with **Freda** *and* **Kath** *as they go into the hall.*

Scene 702

INT. HARDYS' HALLWAY. NIGHT.

MEDIUM SHOT, placed under the stairs is a cane armchair with a cushion in it. As **Freda** *sits down there is a very near explosion.*

Mrs. Lemmon   (*off*) Oh dear – that sounded like a land mine.

Kath   (*as she returns to the front room*) No – just an ordinary H.E. … land-mines make more of a rumble.

The sound of the Blitz gets much worse.

Scene 703

INT. HARDYS' FRONT ROOM. NIGHT.

CLOSE SHOT, **Mrs. Lemmon** *and* **Kath**.

Mrs. Lemmon   (*shouting to make herself heard*) I don't like this, Kath, and it's no use pretending I do.

Kath   (*going over to her*) I know you don't, Mother – nobody does – but there's no use in making a fuss, is there? (*she suddenly puts her arms round her*) Cheer up, there's a dear. (*she raises her voice and calls*) Are you all right, Freda?

Scene 704

INT. HARDYS' HALLWAY. NIGHT

CLOSE UP, **Freda**.

Freda   Yes, thanks.

Kath   (*off*) If you're cold I can run up and get you an eiderdown.

Freda   I'm quite warm.

Kath   (*off*) We'll have some tea in a minute anyway – just to keep us going …

There is the sound of a high explosive whistling down. It is louder than any that have been before.

Scene 705

INT. HARDYS' FRONT ROOM. NIGHT.

MEDIUM SHOT, **Kath** *and* **Mrs. Lemmon.** **Kath** *puts her arm round* **Mrs. Lemmon** *again and they both look up at the ceiling. Then they both duck, shielding their heads with their arms. The roof collapses, there is a deafening explosion, pitch darkness, and then, for a few seconds, dead silence.*

Then comes, still in the darkness, the ominous sound of the house crumbling. A side of the wall caves in and the staircase is seen silhouetted against the flickering light.

DISSOLVE TO

Scene 706

INT. WRECKED HOUSE. NIGHT.

MEDIUM SHOT. A few figures working as though in a fog. A.R.P. **Wardens** *and* **Fire Watchers** *with spades. A stretcher looms up towards camera.*

DISSOLVE TO

Scene 707

STUDIO EXT. WRECKED HOUSE. NIGHT.

A stretcher, with Kath on it, is placed in an Ambulance. The scene is lit by flickering fires. The Ambulance drives off.

DISSOLVE TO

Scene 708

INT. AMBULANCE. NIGHT.

CLOSE UP, **Kath**. *Her face and clothes are black with soot. Her eyes are closed. An* **Ambulance Man** *is sitting by her.*

Kath   (*almost inaudibly – opening her eyes*) Tell Walter ... tell him I didn't want to leave the house. (*Her head drops back*)

DISSOLVE TO

Scene 708

INT. CORNER OF HOSPITAL WARD. NIGHT.

MEDIUM SHOT, **Freda**, *begrimed with soot, lying in bed. A* **nurse** *is bending over her.*

Freda   (*weakly*) *Is* it all over?

Nurse   Yes, don't worry, dear, it's all over ... Mother and child both doing well.

The 'All Clear' is heard in the distance.

FADE OUT.

FADE IN.

Scene 710

STUDIO EXT. SCAPA FLOW. DAY. (MODEL) (B.P.)

LONG SHOT. The 'Torrin' at anchor. The bleak coast line can be seen beyond the ship.

DISSOLVE TO

Scene 711

INT. MESS DECK. DAY. (B.P.)

MEDIUM SHOT, **Shorty**, **Joey**, **Hollett**, **Coombe**, **Parkinson**, **Edgecombe**, **Reynolds** *and a few others in various stages of relaxation. One, for instance, is stretched on table asleep; another two are playing draughts;* **Shorty**, *wearing a singlet and trousers, is seated at the table reading a magazine.* **Joey**, *as usual, is darning a sock.* **Hollett**, *stripped to the waist, is shaving before a small mirror propped up against a suitcase. Most of them are smoking and the air is pretty thick.*

Parkinson   (*looking dismally through the scuttle*) This is the fourth time in three months we've put in to this dead-and-alive 'ole …

Joey   Don't worry, cock – we'll be off again tonight, I shouldn't wonder.

Parkinson   I know – I know – no need to rub it in. I am two blocks with this place.

Joey   Well, where could you go if you *could* get ashore? (*he rises and joins* **Parkinson** *at the scuttle*) Look at it – nothing but sheep and seagulls – not even a tree.

Shorty   What do you expect in the North of Scotland – a bloody casino?

Parkinson   There must be one bottle of beer somewhere in Scotland – just one wonderful bottle of beer …

Joey   Here comes Posty, anyway.

Scene 712

INT. MESS DECK. DAY.

and

Scene 713

CLOSE UP, **Parkinson** *to cover above scene. CLOSE UP,* **Shorty** *to cover above scene.*

Scene 714

INT. MESS DECK. DAY.

MEDIUM SHOT, as **Adams** *comes in with a pile of letters. Great animation sets in. Camera PANS with* **Adams** *as he starts to dole out the letters.*

Adams   Edgecombe – Blake – 'ere you are, Shorty – Coombe – Hollett …

Hollett   Stick it on the table – my hands are wet. I suppose it's a bill from my tailor!

Adams – Jordan – Fisher – Mackridge …

Joey   Only one?

Adams   That's right.

Joey   (*gloomily*) It's from my young sister – after months of mucking about in the North bloody Sea, all I get is a letter from my young sister …

Shorty   Cheer up – it may be bad news!

Edgecombe   (*opening his letter and beginning to read it*) Oh dear – more trouble …

Hollett   What's up?

Edgecombe   Some fat'ead left the lid off the coalhole and my old woman fell down it.

Shorty, *who has been opening his letter in the background suddenly leaps to his feet and rushes wildly towards Joey.*

Scene 715

INT. MESS DECK. DAY.

CLOSE UP **Shorty** *and* **Joey**.

Shorty   (*wildly excited*) Joey – Joey – it's come – the baby's come – it weighs seven pounds and it's a boy … listen to what she says – it was born in the middle of a blitz and (*he stops dead*) … oh!

Joey   What's the matter?

Shorty   (*slowly*) Kath Hardy – Kath and her Mother – the whole house went and they got killed.

Hollett   Mrs. Hardy?

Shorty   yes – my missus was living with them, you know. I wonder if anyone's told him …

Joey   They hadn't got any kids, had they?

Shorty   No – they hadn't got any kids. (*he reaches for his cap*) I think I'd better go along and see if I can find him …

Still clutching his letter **Shorty** *goes slowly out.*

Scene 716

INT. PETTY OFFICERS' MESS. DAY.

In the foreground of the picture is **Walter**, *writing a letter. In the background are* **Brodie**, **Stevens**, **Hooper** *and* **Ridgeway**. **Brodie** *and* **Stevens** *are reading.* **Hooper** *is doing his accounts.* **Walter** *dips his pen in the ink and starts to write again.*

Scene 717

INT. PETTY OFFICERS' MESS. DAY

CLOSE UP, **Walter**'s *letter.*

'My dear wife – well here we are, old darling, in port again for a bit – so near and yet so far – as you might say'.

Scene 718

INT. PETTY OFFICERS' MESS. DAY.

MEDIUM SHOT, **Walter**. *In the background* **Shorty** *can be seen coming into the mess.*

Walter   (*looking up and seeing* **Shorty**) Hello, Shorty … come in.

Shorty *takes off his cap and comes up to* **Walter**.

Shorty   (*rather haltingly*) I – er – I just popped along to see if you'd had any news from home –

Walter   Not so much as P.C. … That's Kath all over – in all the years we've been married she never got a post right yet. Have you heard from Freda?

Shorty   Yes.

Walter   How's she doing?

Shorty   She's all right.

Walter   (*noticing something strained in* **Shorty**'s *manner*) What's the matter?

Shorty   It's Kath, Walter … she and Mrs. Lemmon … you see they was all in the house together and … and it got blitzed …

Walter   What do you mean?

Shorty   (*miserably*) Kath got killed … both of them did – Freda was all right – she was under the stairs.

Walter   (*after a pause*) Oh – oh, I see.

Shorty   I thought I'd better tell you, seeing that – well – I mean …

Walter   Thanks, son, I'm much obliged – thanks very much. (*he rises*) I think I'll go out on deck for a bit …

Shorty   Righto.

Walter   (*as he moves away, he stops*) I'm glad Freda's all right.

Shorty   (*with an attempt at a smile*) Yes – she's fine. (*almost apologetically*) We got a son.

Walter   (*coming back and giving* **Shorty** *a pat on the shoulder*) That's good … Congratulations.

Walter *walks away from camera into a LONG SHOT and goes out of the mess.*

Scene 719

INT. PETTY OFFICERS' MESS. DAY.

and

Scene 720

CLOSE UP, **Shorty** *to cover above scene. CLOSE UP,* **Walter** *to cover above scene.*

(R2)

(*Scene 721 out*)

DISSOLVE TO

Scene 722

STUDIO EXT. QUARTER DECK. DAY. (B.P.)

MEDIUM SHOT, **Walter**. *He reaches the extreme aft of the quarterdeck and looks towards the shore. He suddenly discovers that his unfinished letter to* **Kath** *is in his hand. He looks at it almost unseeing for a moment, then crumples it up and throws it over the side.*

Scene 723

STUDIO EXT. (SMALL TANK). DAY. (INSERT).

CLOSE SHOT, the water, from above. The crumpled letter falls into the water and drifts away out of picture.

RIPPLE DISSOLVE TO

(*Scenes 724–5 out*)

Scene 726

STUDIO EXT. CARLEY FLOAT. DAY.

CLOSE SHOT, **Walter**. *He is unconscious. The float drifts away a little and discloses the group of* **men**. ***Shorty***, *who is busy wiping oil fuel from his eyes, suddenly looks up past the camera.*

Shorty   She's going, sir.

Scene 727

STUDIO EXT. 'TORRIN'. DAY. (MODEL).

CLOSE SHOT, the keel of the 'Torrin' is sinking rapidly under the water.

Scene 728

STUDIO EXT. CARLEY FLOAT. DAY.

CLOSE UP, **Captain 'D'**.

Captain   Three cheers for the ship.

Scene 729

STUDIO EXT. CARLEY FLOAT. DAY. (MODEL). (B.P.)

MEDIUM SHOT, the group on the float. Beyond them the keel of the 'Torrin' is disappearing under the water. The **men** *cheer huskily. The cheering is suddenly cut by the roar of aircraft and the splashing of bullets. Everybody ducks.*

Scene 730

EXT. SKY. DAY.

LONG SHOT, a German aeroplane diving towards camera. It fires a burst.

Scene 731

STUDIO EXT. CARLEY FLOAT. DAY.

CLOSE SHOT, the **Young Stoker**. *A line of bullet splashes race towards him. He is hit and gives a cry.*

(R2)

Scene 732

STUDIO EXT. CARLEY FLOAT. DAY.

CLOSE UP, **Number One**. *He is hit and falls into the sea. The bullet splashes race away.*

Scene 732a

STUDIO EXT. CARLEY FLOAT. DAY.

CLOSE SHOT, **Flags**. *Camera PANS with* **Flags** *as he flings* *himself into the water and swims into a TWO SHOT with* **Number One**, *who is obviously unconscious.*

Scene 732b

STUDIO EXT. CARLEY FLOAT. DAY.

CLOSE SHOT, **Flags** *and* **Number One**. **Flags** *is grappling with* **Number One** *in the water. Finally he gets his head above the surface. He shouts to the* **Captain**.

Flags   It's all right, sir, I've got him.

As he begins to swim with **Number One** *towards the float there is the roar of another plane and the racing splash of machine-gun bullets.* **Flags** *gives a cry, writhes in the water and disappears with* **Number One** *below the surface.*

DISSOLVE TO

Scene 733

STUDIO EXT. 'TOMAHAWK' BRIDGE. DAY.

On the bridge are **Commander Spencer**, *two* **Lieutenants**, *a* **Sub-Lieutenant**, **Petty Officer Yeoman** *and six* **Lookouts**. *The funnel of the 'Tomahawk' has one white band instead of the black band of the 'Torrin'. Everyone is sweeping the sea with their binoculars in search of survivors. The* **Yeoman** *reports*

Yeoman   Dark object floating off starboard bow, sir. It looks like a raft.

Spencer   (*looking through binoculars*) You're right, Yeoman. (*to* **First Lieutenant**) Stand by to pick up survivors.

Lieutenant   Aye, Aye, sir.

(R2)

Scene 734

STUDIO EXT. CARLEY FLOAT. DAY.

MEDIUM SHOT. **Number One** *and* **Flags** *are missing. The* **survivors** *are searching the horizon for a rescue ship.* **Captain 'D'** *sees something.*

Captain   Keep your spirits up – I believe they've arrived at last.

Everyone pulls himself together and gazes off at the approaching Destroyer. **Joey** *starts again to play 'Roll out the Barrel'. Everyone makes an attempt to sing.*

DISSOLVE TO

Scene 735

STUDIO EXT. CARLEY FLOAT. DAY.

and

Scene 736

CLOSE UP, **Captain 'D'** *to cover above scene. CLOSE UP,* **Joey** *to cover above scene.*

Scene 737

STUDIO EXT. 'TOMAHAWK' UPPER DECK. DAY. (B.P.0)

CLOSE SHOT, **Commander Spencer** *and* **Captain 'D'**.

Spencer   I'm damned glad you're all right, sir.

Captain   (*smiling*) Thanks, old boy – I warned you, you won't get command of the Flotilla yet.

Spencer   It was the most extraordinary bit of luck finding you.

The Chief Yeoman spotted you just at the last minute when we were about to give up …

Captain   How many of my men have you picked up?

They start to move, camera TRACKING with them.

Spencer   Ninety, sir, all told. Some of them are rather badly knocked about, I'm afraid.

Captain   Where are they?

Spencer   Mostly between decks, sir – the dive bombing's pretty incessant …

Scene 738

INT. 'TOMAHAWK' BETWEEN DECKS. DAY.

LONG SHOT. The 'Torrin' **survivors** *are packed like sardines.* **Spencer** *and* **Captain 'D'** *enter and, as they pass along, those who are sitting or lying down make an attempt to rise.*

Scene 739

INT. 'TOMAHAWK' BETWEEN DECKS. DAY.

MEDIUM SHOT, TRACKING with **Captain 'D'** *and* **Spencer**.

Captain   (*to the* **men**) It's all right – don't move.

Fisher   Glad you're okay, sir.

Moran   He was getting a bit worried about you, sir.

Captain   Thanks, Moran – nothing like a good swim before breakfast.

Moran   (*grinning*) That's right, sir.

The scene is broken by the sound of the ship's guns and the roar of dive bombers.

Scene 740

INT. 'TOMAHAWK' BETWEEN DECKS. DAY.

MEDIUM SHOT, **Shorty** *and* **Walter** *are wedged between several other men. There is the sound of bombs dropping. The* **men** *are flinching a bit.*

Shorty 'Ere we go again – anybody got any Flit?

Walter Anyone know where we happen to be going?

Clark Alexandria, I expect. Join the Navy and see the world.

Scene 741

INT. 'TOMAHAWK' BETWEEN DECKS. DAY.

CLOSE SHOT, **Shorty** *and* **Walter**.

Shorty Looks to me as if it's going to be the next world.

There is the further roar of aircraft, and the guns renew their firing.

Walter Of all the persistent bastards – you'd think they'd get tired wouldn't you?

Shorty I'll tell you something strictly between you and I ... I'm scared pink and it's no good pretending I'm not – if I could be at a gun or something I shouldn't mind ... but this lying about asking for it's getting me down.

Walter Brace up – remember Nelson.

Shorty Yes – look what happened to him!

Scene 742

INT. 'TOMAHAWK' MESS DECK. DAY.

MEDIUM SHOT. The mess deck has been turned over to the very badly wounded. They are packed very close. The camera PANS across the **men** *and finishes on a CLOSE SHOT of* **Captain 'D'** *and* **Reynolds**. *The* **Captain** *is still in his wet clothes and covered in oil fuel. He is half-sitting and half-lying next to* **Reynolds**. *With his left hand he is gripping* **Reynolds'** *left hand, with his right he is scribbling in a notebook.*

Reynolds   (*almost inaudibly*) It's – It's number 17. Just as you turn out of the High Street.

Captain   (*gently*) All right, old man, I've got the address straight – I'll let her know.

Reynolds   Thank you, sir.

His head falls back. **Captain** *gently disengages his hand and looks at* **Reynolds** *carefully for a moment. Camera TRACKS with the* **Captain** *as he crawls across* **Reynolds** *to the* **Young Stoker**. *He props him up and slips his arm round his shoulders. The* **Young Stoker** *makes an effort to say something.*

Captain   (*whispering*) I can't quite hear – try again … (*he bends very close and listens, then writes something in his notebook*) Yes – I've got that – you'll be all right – don't worry. I'll write and tell them they can be proud of you.

The **Young Stoker** *gives a little smile of relief.* **Captain 'D'** *lowers him gently down on to the deck again and goes over to the next man as the scene*

FADES OUT.

(R2)

FADE IN.

Scene 743

STUDIO EXT. BLAKE HOUSE. DAY.

MEDIUM SHOT. A barrel-organ is in the foreground of the

picture, playing 'There'll always be an England'. A **Telegraph Boy** *rides into the picture. He gets off his bicycle and, leaning it against the steps, goes up to the front door.*

(*Scene 744 out*)

Scene 745

INT. BLAKES' LIVING ROOM. DAY.

Camera is on a CLOSE SHOT of the table on which lies the morning paper. The headlines tell of the Naval action off Crete. CAMERA PANS up to reveal **Freda** *stretched out on the sofa, sodden with tears. By her side is her baby.*

The front door bell rings there is the sound of footsteps and **Mrs. Blake** *comes from the kitchen. As she enters picture the camera PANS with her as she goes to the door.*

Scene 746

STUDIO EXT. BLAKE HOUSE. DAY.

CLOSE SHOT, the **Telegraph Boy**, *at the front door. The door opens and* **Mrs. Blake** *appears. She sees the telegram and looks horrified.*

Boy   Name of Blake?

Mrs. Blake   Yes, that's right.

Boy   Here you are, then.

Mrs. Blake   Thanks. (*she takes the telegram and opens it. As she reads her whole expression changes*) There's no answer.

Mrs. Blake *slams the door in the boy's face.*

(R2)

Scene 747

INT. BLAKES' LIVING ROOM. DAY.

MEDIUM SHOT. Camera PANS with **Mrs. Blake** *as she runs screaming across the room.*

Mrs. Blake   Fred ... May ... Dad ... Freda – He's safe ... he's all right ... he's safe.

Camera PANS with her into the TWO SHOT with **Freda**. **Freda** *raises her head.*

Freda   What is it? It's not –

Mrs. Blake   It's from him – he's sent a telegram – it's from 'imself – he's all right – my boy's all right.

Freda   But the ship went down, didn't it? It said so in the papers.

Mrs. Blake   (*handing her the telegram*) Look ...

Freda   Okay – love ...

She gives a little cry and **Mrs. Blake** *puts her arm round her.*

Mrs. Blake   There, there dear – there isn't nothing to cry about no more.

(*Scenes 748–9 out*)

(R2)

Scene 750

STUDIO EXT. KINROSS HOUSE. FRONT DOOR. DAY.

CLOSE SHOT, a **Telegraph Girl**. *She is wearing an ordinary blouse and skirt, with the uniform hat. The front door is opened by* **Emily**, *the housemaid. She takes the telegram offered her with a look of great apprehension.*

Girl   Shall I wait for an answer?

Emily   Just a minute, I'll see.

She goes into the hallway in the direction of the drawing room.

Scene 751

INT. DRAWING ROOM. DAY.

MEDIUM SHOT, **Alix**, **Bobby** *and* **Lavinia** *are having tea. The* **children** *are chattering at the top of their voices.* **Alix** *is spreading some jam on a sponge cake for Lavinia.* **Emily** *comes in with the telegram.* **Alix** *closes her eyes for a moment, puts the sponge cake down and takes the telegram. The* **children** *stop talking abruptly and look at her in silence.*

Emily   The girl is waiting for an answer, ma'am.

Alix   Thank you, Emily.

She reads the telegram and a look of indescribable relief passes over her face – she looks up.

Alix   There's no answer – tell Mrs. Bates and John that it's from the Captain and everything's all right.

Emily   (*breathlessly*) Yes'm – I'm so glad'm …

Alix   Thank you, Emily.

Emily *goes out.* **Alix**, *with an effort, picks up the sponge cake and goes on spreading jam on it. She is obviously trying to behave calmly. When she has her voice more or less under control she speaks.*

(R2)

Alix   It's from Daddy, darlings – he was picked up and taken to Alexandria – he's quite safe (*her voice trembles*).

Bobby *jumps up and puts an arm round her shoulders.* **Alix** *puts down the sponge cake again, hugs him to her and puts her other hand out to* **Lavinia**. *As the scene fades she is smiling but her eyes are filled with tears.*

Scene 752

INT. DRAWING ROOM. DAY

and

Scene 753

CLOSE UP, **Alix** *to cover above scene. CLOSE UP,* **Bobby** *and* **Lavinia** *to cover above scene.*

DISSOLVE TO

Scene 754

INT. LARGE SHED. ALEXANDRIA. DAY. (MATTE).

LONG SHOT. Five **Officers** *and ninety* **men** *are gathered. They are dressed in a variety of borrowed tropical clothing – vest, singlets, shirts, shorts or trousers, white or khaki. No hats or caps. Several men are bandaged. The* **R.N.V.R. Sub-Lieutenant** *calls out*

Sub-Lieutenant   Ship's Company – 'shun!

Scene 755

INT. LARGE SHED. ALEXANDRIA. DAY.

MEDIUM SHOT. **Captain 'D'** *and the* **Sub-Lieutenant.** *The latter comes to attention, but does not salute as he has no cap.*

Sub-Lieutenant   Ship's Company present, sir.

Captain   Thank you – stand easy, please.

Sub-Lieutenant   Ship's Company – stand – easy!

Captain   I have come to say goodbye to the few of you who are left. We have had so many talks but this is our last … I have always tried to crack a joke or two before and you have all been friendly and laughed at them. But today I am afraid I have run out of jokes, and I don't suppose any of us feel much like laughing. The *Torrin* has been in one scrap after another – but even when we have had men killed the majority survived and brought the old ship back. Now, she lies in fifteen hundred fathoms and with her more than half our shipmates. If they had to die, what a grand way to go, for now they lie all together with the ship we loved, and they are in very good company. We have lost her but they are still with her. There may be less than half the *Torrin* left but I feel that each of us will take up the battle with even stronger heart. Each of us knows twice as much about fighting and each of us has twice as good a reason to fight. You will all be sent to replace men who have been killed in other ships, and the next time you are in action, remember the *Torrin*. As you ram each shell home into the gun, shout *Torrin*, and so her spirit will go on inspiring us until Victory is won. I should like to add that there isn't one of you that I wouldn't be proud and honoured to serve with again. Goodbye, good luck and thank you all from the bottom of my heart.

DISSOLVE TO

Scene 756

INT. LARGE SHED. ALEXANDRIA. DAY.

to

Scene 762

CLOSE UP, **Captin 'D'** *to cover above scene. MEDIUM SHOT, group of* **men** *over Captain's shoulder to cover above scene. CLOSE UP,* **Shorty** *to cover above scene. CLOSE UP,* **Walter** *to cover above scene. CLOSE UP,* **Joey** *to cover above scene. CLOSE SHOT,* **Torps** *and* **Guns** *to cover above scene. CLOSE SHOT,* **Edgecombe** *and* **Hollett** *to cover above scene.*

Scene 763

INT. LARGE SHED. ALEXANDRIA. DAY.

CLOSE SHOT, **Captain 'D'**. *The* **men** *file past and he shakes hands with each one.*

Men   (*mumbling*) Good luck, sir … Thank you, sir … etc., etc.

Shorty   Goodbye, sir. (*he shakes hands with the* **Captain**)

Walter   (*shaking hands*) Goodbye, sir.

Camera TRACKS CLOSER and CLOSER to the **Captain**'s *face. The MUSIC swells and the scene*

FADES OUT.

FADE IN.

Scene 764

MONTAGE.

to

Scene 778

The MUSIC swells and the voice of the **Commander**, *who spoke the Prologue to the film, says*

Leslie Howard (voice over)   Here ends the story of a ship. But there will always be other ships, for we are an island race and through all our centuries the sea has ruled our destiny. There will always be other ships and men to sail in them. It is those men in peace or war to whom we owe so much.

Above all victories, beyond all loss, in spite of changing values in a changing world, they give to us, their countrymen, eternal and indomitable pride.

God bless our ships and all who sail in them …

There are a series of shots of minelayers, sloops, destroyers, trawlers, aircraft carriers, submarines, cruisers, tugs, converted liners, tankers, M.T.B.'s and battleships.

Scene 779

STUDIO EXT. CRUISER GUN TURRET. DAY.

CLOSE UP, **Walter** *standing by the gun. Round him is a group of* **sailors***. He is giving them instructions. He is just heard to say one line of technical gunnery instruction.*

Scene 780

STUDIO EXT. BATTLESHIP GUN TURRET. DAY.

CLOSE UP, **Shorty** *and several* other **Ratings***. Sweat is pouring down his face as he rams the shells into the breech. He is saying very softly, between clenched teeth*

Shorty   *Torrin …*

Scene 781

STUDIO EXT. SHIP'S BRIDGE. DAY

CLOSE UP, **Captain 'D'**. *Round him are a group of entirely different* **Officers** *from those we have seen before. There is the usual babble of technical directions going on.*

Captain 'D' *is looking through his binoculars. He lowers them, raises his right hand and says*

Captain   Open fire!

He lifts his binoculars again – there is a burst of gunfire and the MUSIC swells.

THE END

Twenty-ninth
DECEMBER,
1941.

British Lion PRESENTS

NOEL COWARD'S

"IN WHICH WE SERVE"

A TWO CITIES FILM

Directed by NOEL COWARD & DAVID LEAN
Photographed by RONALD NEAME

NOEL COWARD · JOHN MILLS
BERNARD MILES · CELIA JOHNSON
JOYCE CAREY · KAY WALSH

Noel Coward's
BRIEF ENCOUNTER
starring
CELIA JOHNSON · TREVOR HOWARD
with
STANLEY HOLLOWAY
JOYCE CAREY   CYRIL RAYMOND

In charge of production
ANTHONY HAVELOCK-ALLAN · RONALD NEAME

A Noel Coward-Cineguild Production

Directed by DAVID LEAN

J. ARTHUR RANK presents

NOEL COWARD'S

The ASTONISHED HEART

Another triumph from the star and the author of "Brief Encounter"

STARRING

CELIA JOHNSON

NOEL COWARD

MARGARET LEIGHTON

A DARING *Experiment* IN LOVE!

Leonora Vail (Margaret Leighton) and Barbara Faber (Celia Johnson) were old school friends. Years later they meet by accident, share a pot of tea … and their lives are never to be the same. (*The Astonished Heart*)

In spite of himself, Christian (Noël Coward) finds himself falling in love with Leonora (Margaret Leighton) – who is by no means averse to the idea. (*The Astonished Heart*)

'Good luck, sir …' The few survivors of the *Torrin* – played mostly by real sailors – say their goodbyes to Capt. 'D' in Alexandria. (*In Which We Serve*)

Capt. 'D' comforts the wounded. Richard Attenborough made his screen debut in the film as a young stoker. (*In Which We Serve*)

As the *Torrin* sinks, Capt. 'D', Shorty Blake (John Mills) and Walter Hardy (Bernard Miles) cling to the Carley raft. (*In Which We Serve*)

'I'll see you to your train'. The first realization that something out of the ordinary is happening. Laura Jesson (Celia Johnson) talks out of the train window to Dr Alec Harvey (Trevor Howard). (*Brief Encounter*)

As the relationship deepens, the night scenes take on a certain threat. Their shadows precede them, dwarfing them, anticipating what is going to happen. (*Brief Encounter*)

Love among the teacups. The parallel 'romance' between ticket inspector Albert Godby (Stanley Holloway) and Myrtle Bagot (Joyce Carey), manageress of the refreshment room at Milford Junction. (*Brief Encounter*)

Academy of Motion Picture Arts and Sciences

CERTIFICATE

FOR

DISTINCTIVE ACHIEVEMENT

Noel Coward

has been judged worthy of the Academy's

CERTIFICATE OF MERIT

for **his outstanding production achievement**

"In Which We Serve"

This judgment being rendered with reference to
Motion Pictures First Regularly Exhibited in
the Los Angeles district during the
year ending December 31, 1942

[signature]
PRESIDENT

Pete Smith
SECRETARY

Brief Encounter

Introduction to *Brief Encounter*

It began life in 1936 as *Still Life*, one of the nine one act plays in the *Tonight at 8.30* sequence.

In 1945 – following their second successful collaboration on *In Which We Serve* (1942), *This Happy Breed* (1943) and *Blithe Spirit* (1945) – Noël's 'little darlings' (David Lean, Ronald Neame and Anthony Havelock-Allan), joined forces one last time, as it turned out, to film Noël's screenplay of the piece.

What should it be called? Somehow 'still life' didn't seem appropriate for a moving picture. The title should be short for maximum impact. Noël's designer, Gladys Calthrop, came up with the answer. 'What about *Brief Encounter*?'

Brief Encounter it was.

Noël had already done some of the groundwork in writing the original play. As always, he needed to know who his characters were in the world they inhabited ...

> LAURA. She is an attractive woman in her thirties. Her clothes are not particularly smart but obviously chosen with taste. She looks exactly what she is – a pleasant, ordinary married woman, rather pale, for she is not very strong and with a definite charm of personality, which comes from natural kindliness, humour and reasonable conscience.
>
> Alec is about 35. He wears a moustache, a mackintosh and a squash hat, and carries a small bag. His manner is decisive and 'unflurried'.

(The moustache did not survive subsequent incarnations! It was presumably intended to help distinguish between the three different characters Noël would be performing on any given evening.)

Tonight at 8.30 had been sold to MGM, along with several other plays of Noël's. Later, British producer Sydney Box had managed to buy them and proceeded to sell them off piecemeal. *Still Life* went to Cineguild – the successor production company to Two Cities – for £60,000. The film came in at £270,000.

Anxious to continue their successful collaboration, Noël produced a draft film script. Lean showed interest. Not being by nature someone with a marked sense of humour, he had one fundamental question. Was the comedy counterplot with the station master and the lady who runs the station buffet absolutely necessary?

Havelock-Allan had the immediate answer to that. 'Noël was an extremely skilful theatre writer and he knew that the story would have been intolerably sad otherwise. They provided some relief from the central situation, which was building up to be increasingly painful, both for the audience and for the two principals, for whom the audience feels deep sympathy'.

He might have added that Shakespeare had also been known to offer parallel relationships for much the same reason.

Taking a lesson learned from *In Which We Serve*, Noël also played with the time sequence. On Lean's suggestion he begins the narrative with Laura and Alec parting in the station buffet. As Alec leaves to catch his train he touches her shoulder briefly. We sense something was left unsaid, because of the interruptive arrival of Laura's voluble acquaintance.

Then Laura's thought voice takes up the backstory of who they are and how their lives led them to this point. From then on it becomes Laura's story … until it reaches this same scene, when the touch on the shoulder has much more emotional significance.

Whereas the play told the story chronologically and the two characters were equally important, what Noël and Lean created in the film is a woman's story. The viewer is given an 'attitude' point of view the play necessarily lacks.

One of the reasons for the film's lasting appeal is that it allows middle-aged, middle class women to identify with a woman in whom they can credibly see themselves, as opposed to the traditional screen beauties who are enviable but irrelevant.

Here is a woman like them who can fantasize about the Great Love That Can Never Be in the library books she borrows from Boot's Lending Library by a writer like Kate O'Brien, who specialises in the conflict between chaste romance and everyday life. Having borrowed her latest, you settled down in the Kardomah Café for tea and cake. Then a movie – usually a romance – then the train home. Same routine very week. Dream safely packaged until one day – real life bursts in.

***

With the structure settled, Noël found the writing easy. Dialogue was never a problem. He had had that facility from the outset and it never failed to amaze his 'little darlings'.

Havelock-Allan recalled one instance when Noël was touring and entertaining the troops in India ... 'We managed to get cables through to him saying we needed thirty seconds of dialogue for the scene in the boat and we got a cable back giving us two lines of dialogue and saying: "This runs forty-eight seconds; if you want to shorten it, take out the following words ..."'

***

Before writing the original play he had gone into even greater detail about the characters.

> *Laura Fayne* – born 1900 in Cornwall – childhood school in Cornwall, holidays at home by the sea – married Frederick Jesson in 1922 – solicitor's clerk in London. They live there a few years, then move to Ketchworth, Fred's home town. Fred becomes, first of all, Junior Partner in his father's office then, on death of his father in 1930, Senior Partner at Jesson, Holford & Rhys. Laura's children, Freddie, aged 13, Betty, aged 11, and Robin, aged 9.

> FACTS:

> Laura's mother died of cancer 1918. Her father still alive and married again. One married sister, Mary, and one unmarried brother, rather a waster, tea planter in Ceylon.

> (Note: Noël's own late brother, Erik, had had the same occupation.)

> INTERESTS:

> Children, animals – books, average – mostly novels – Walpole, Phyllis Gibbs, Sheila Kaye-Smith, etc. Bored by Shaw – not particularly musical – loves movies, particularly gangster ones, 'Silly Symphonies' (on account of the children) and 'Travelogues'.

He does the same for Alec ...

> *Alec Harvey*. Born Aberdeen 1901 – educated Aberdeen High School – is in training at Aberdeen University O.T.C.

in 1918 aged 17. Decides to take up medicine like his
older brother, Gordon – is qualified – aged 23. Comes to
London – attached to Guy's – rooms in Bloomsbury – meets
Madeline Loring at a party in Hampstead – they marry 1925.
In 1929 they settle in Churley where, through an agency,
Alec has obtained a practice. They have two children, James
born in 1926 and John, born in 1928.

Alec's main interest outside his practice is 'Preventative
Medicine', particularly in reference to 'Pneumoconiosis' – a
slow process of fibrosis of the lung due to the inhalation of
particles of dust.

Alec's friend, Stephen Lynn, who was at the university
with him, is Physician to General Hospital at Milford and
invites Alec once a week as assistant physician to take over
for him, thereby giving him a chance for a certain amount of
research of his special subject, as there are coal mines near
Milford and lots of authentic cases.'

***

The brief encounter begins when Laura gets a piece of grit in her eye
from the passing express train. While the point is never laboured,
it's possible to see the power of the express as the excitement her
daily life lacks.

At the end of the film the express represents even greater danger
for her, when – now that Alec has gone out of her life forever – she's
tempted to throw herself under it.

I really meant to do it – I stood there trembling – right on
the edge – but then, just in time I stepped back – I couldn't
– I wasn't brave enough.

Nor was she brave enough to follow her heart and turn her brief
encounter into something more. She returns to the world she knows
where romance is safely contained and at a distance in a novel, a
film about someone else's life – or a piece of music.

Originally Noël had said Laura was not 'musical' but now he
changed his mind. At home with Fred he has her turn on the radio
and listen to Rachmaninoff's 2nd Piano Concerto with its sweeping
melodies.

During filming the piece became briefly contentious. Musical Director Muir Mathieson was in favour of having an original composition as background music, as many British films were doing at that time. Noël would have none of it. He might have quoted himself and said – 'Extraordinary how potent cheap music can be'. Instead he said – 'No, no, no. She listens to Rachmaninoff on the radio, she borrows her books from the Boot's library and she eats at the Kardomah'. End of conversation.

The images drawn from the romantic fictional world that Laura inhabits constantly recur. Riding home in the train she imagines – and we see her in the reflection in the carriage window – waltzing with Alec, sitting in a box at the theatre, reclining in a Venetian gondola ... literally in a world of her own.

Occasionally Noël throws in a private joke.

In the early 1920s, when he had written *Easy Virtue*, he had been abroad when the play was meant to be tried out in Manchester prior to the West End. One day he received an anguished cable from director Basil Dean. The local Watch Committee, which acted as censors for the city, had banned the use of the play's title. They claim they had thought it was EASY MONEY. Consequently, it appeared as 'A New Play in Three Acts by Noël Coward'. In London it resumed its real title.

When he got to see his 'new play in three acts' in Manchester, Noël observed that the cinema next door to the theatre was advertising its current feature – *Flames of Passion*. The Watch Committee apparently had no jurisdiction over films.

Twenty years later, when Laura and Alec leave a cinema, laughing at the absurdity of what they have been watching, we see the title – *Flames of Passion*!

The way Noël reslanted the material makes it 'Laura's film' but that wouldn't have worked anything like as well as it does without Celia Johnson.

After *In Which We Serve* and *This Happy Breed*, she had become a founder member of the Coward/Lean troupe.

Critic C. A. Lejeune summed up her unique appeal. 'To my mind, Miss Johnson's face and her walk and her eyes can tell a story or impart a mood or reveal a confidence without the help of any narrative ... Good acting needs no explanation'.

Celia Johnson seized on the reference to her eyes in her modest disclaimer, since she happened to be extremely short-sighted. 'It's my *eyes*. It's a great advantage when everything is a blur beyond a certain point'.

David Lean had learned by now that there was rather more to it than that. 'Movie acting is thinking, which a lot of people don't understand. If you're thinking right, it changes the way you walk or put your head or whatever it is in the correct way...'. In the scene where Laura decides to go back to Alec in the flat and hurries to the station exit, 'on her back you could read her thoughts, and all this thinking is transformed into the physical!'

When the shot ended, he asked Johnson how she had worked out what to do. 'I didn't work it out', she replied, 'She would just do that, wouldn't she?'

***

When the film was released, reactions were interestingly mixed. The French and Europeans generally couldn't understand why Laura and Alec hadn't gone to bed together. These English were strange creatures. To begin with the 'strange creatures' didn't know what to make of it and there would often be nervous laughter. These people on screen were just like them – and what would *they* have done in the conservatively-structured society of the day?

But as time went by, the emotional honesty of the piece and the performances got through and it was not long before the film settled on critics' top ten lists – where it has stayed.

On a regular basis potential filmmakers approach the Coward Estate with a proposal to make an updated (as they call it) version. Of course, in today's world, they argue, Laura and Alec would have been to bed together. The new film would be about their *guilt* ...

At which point the conversation ends. They clearly don't understand that the impossibility of their relationship is what makes it romantic. Their version would turn a brief encounter into a *longueur* ...

***

Seventy years on ... and *The Guardian* runs a poll on the most romantic films of all time.

Third is *Gone with the Wind* (1939)... second is *Casablanca* (1942).

And the winner is ... *Brief Encounter.*

Credits

In Charge of Production	Anthony Havelock-Alan
	Ronald Neame
Producer	Nöel Coward
Director	David Lean
Screenplay	Nöel Coward
Director of Photography	Robert Krasker
Art Director	L. P. Williams
Art Supervisor to Nöel Coward	G. E. Calthrop
Continuity	Margaret Sibley
Editor	Jack Harris
Sound Editor	Harry Miller
Sound Recordists	Stanley Lambourne
	Desmond Dew
Production Manager	E. Holding
Assistant Director	George Pollock
Camera Operator	B. Francke

Cast

Laura Jesson	Celia Johnson
Alec Harvey	Trevor Howard
Albert Godby	Stanley Holloway
Myrtle Bagot	Joyce Carey
Fred Jesson	Cyril Raymond
Dolly Messiter	Everley Gregg
Beryl Waters	Margaret Barton
Stanley	Dennis Harkin
Stephen Lynn	Valentine Dyall
Mary Norton	Marjorie Mars
Mrs. Rolandson	Nuna Davey
Woman Organist	Irene Handl
Bill	Edward Hodge
Johnnie	Sydney Bromley
Policeman	Wilfred Babbage
Waitress	Avis Scutt
Margaret	Henrietta Vincent
Bobbie	Richard Thomas
Clergyman	George V. Sheldon

Rachmaninoff Piano Concerto No. 2
Played by Eileen Joyce with the National Symphony Orchestra
Conducted by Muir Mathieson

The action of this film takes place during the Winter of 1938/39.

FADE IN.

Scene 1

EXT. MILFORD JUNCTION STATION. NIGHT. (LOCATION)

LONG SHOT, Number 1 Platform of Milford Junction Station. It is early evening. A local train is pulling into the station as a voice over the station loud speaker announces

'MILFORD JUNCTION' – 'MILFORD JUNCTION'

The engine of the train comes closer and closer to the camera until it fills the picture. A great cloud of steam hisses out from the engine, and the screen becomes white. The main titles appear.

DISSOLVE

Scene 2

EXT. MILFORD JUNCTION STATION. NIGHT. (LOCATION)

The screen is filled with steam. As the last Title fades out the steam disperses, revealing a shot of the Engine, which starts to pull away from camera out of the station.

CUT TO

Scene 3

EXT. MILFORD JUNCTION STATION. NIGHT. (STUDIO)

MEDIUM SHOT of **Albert Godby** *at the ticket barrier. He is somewhere between 30 and 40. His accent is North Country. He collects the last few tickets from the passengers of the departing train and moves off out of picture, towards the edge of the platform.*

CUT TO

Scene 4

EXT. MILFORD JUNCTION STATION. NIGHT. (LOCATION)

MEDIUM LONG SHOT. The camera is shooting from between the rails, which adjoin Number 2 platform. An express is approaching in the distance. **Albert** *jumps down from Number 1 platform on to the track. He walks up into MEDIUM SHOT and waits for the express to pass. It roars over the camera, practically blotting out the picture.*

CUT TO

Scene 5

EXT. MILFORD JUNCTION STATION. NIGHT. (STUDIO)

CLOSE SHOT of **Albert** *as he watches the train go by. The lights from the carriage windows flash across his face. From his waistcoat pocket he takes out a watch and chain and checks the time of the train. By the look of satisfaction on his face we know that it is punctual. He puts the watch back and the lights cease flashing on his face. The train has passed. He follows it with his eyes.*

Scene 6

INSERT of **Albert**'s *WATCH, reading 5.35 to cut into above scene.*

CUT TO

Scene 7

EXT. RAILWAY TUNNEL. NIGHT. (LOCATION)

LONG SHOT. The train roars into a tunnel.

CUT TO

Scene 8

EXT. MILFORD JUNCTION STATION. NIGHT. (STUDIO)

MEDIUM SHOT of **Albert Godby** *as he crosses the lines, over which the express has just passed. He jumps up on to Number 2 platform and crosses over to the Refreshment Room. The camera PANS with him.*

CUT TO

Scene 9

INT. MILFORD JUNCTION STATION. REFRESHMENT ROOM. NIGHT.

MEDIUM LONG SHOT. The camera PANS with **Albert** *as he crosses the Refreshment Room and goes over to the counter behind which stand* **Myrtle Bagot** *and her assistant* **Beryl Waters**. **Myrtle** *is a buxom and imposing widow. Her hair is piled high, and her expression reasonably jaunty except on those occasions when a strong sense of refinement gets the better of her.* **Beryl** *is pretty but dimmed, not only by* **Myrtle**'s *personal effulgence, but by her firm authority.*

Albert   Hullo! Hullo! Hullo!

Myrtle   Quite a stranger, aren't you?

Albert   I couldn't get in yesterday.

Myrtle   (*bridling*) I wondered what happened to you.

Albert   I 'ad a bit of a dust-up.

Myrtle   (*preparing his tea*) What about?

Albert   Saw a chap getting out of a first class compartment, and when he comes to give up 'is ticket it was third class, and I told 'im he'd 'ave to pay excess, and then he turned a bit nasty and I 'ad to send for Mr. Saunders.

Myrtle   Fat lot of good he'd be.

Albert   He ticked him off proper.

Myrtle   Seein's believing –

The camera PANS off **Albert** *and* **Myrtle** *on to a table at the far end of the refreshment room. Seated at the table are* **Alec Harvey** *and* **Laura Jesson**. *He is about 35 and wears a mackintosh and a squash hat. She is an attractive woman in the thirties. Her clothes are not smart, but obviously chosen with taste. They are in earnest conversation, but we do not hear what they are saying.*

Albert   (*off*) I tell you, he ticked 'im off proper – 'You pay the balance at once', he said, 'or I'll 'and you over to the Police'. You should 'ave seen the chap's face at the mention of the word 'Police'. Changed his tune then 'e did – paid up quick as lightning.

Myrtle   (*off*) That's just what I mean. He hadn't got the courage to handle it himself. He had to call in the Police.

Albert   (*off*) Who said he called in the Police?

Myrtle   (*off*) You did, of course.

Albert   (*off*) I didn't do any such thing. I merely said he mentioned the Police, which is quite a different thing from calling them in. He's not a bad lot, Mr. Saunders. After all, you can't expect much spirit from a man who's only got one lung and a wife with diabetes.

Myrtle   (*off*) I thought something must be wrong when you didn't come.

CUT TO

Scene 10

CLOSE SHOT of **Albert** *and* **Myrtle**. **Beryl** *is in the background.*

Albert   I'd have popped in to explain, but I had a date and 'ad to run for it the moment I went off.

Myrtle   (*frigidly*) Oh, indeed.

Albert   A chap I know's getting married.

Myrtle   Very interesting, I'm sure.

Albert   What's up with you, anyway?

Myrtle   I'm sure I don't know to what you're referring.

Albert   You're a bit unfriendly all of a sudden.

Myrtle   (*ignoring him*) Beryl, hurry up – put some coal in the stove while you're at it.

Beryl   Yes, Mrs. Bagot.

Myrtle   I'm afraid I really can't stand here wasting my time in idle gossip, Mr. Godby.

Albert   Aren't you going to offer me another cup?

Myrtle   You can 'ave another cup and welcome when you've finished that one. Beryl'll give it to you – I've got my accounts to do.

Albert   I'd rather you gave it to me.

Myrtle   Time and tide wait for no man, Mr. Godby.

Albert   I don't know what you're huffy about, but whatever it is I'm very sorry.

Scene 11

CLOSE UP of **Albert** *to cover above scene.*

Scene 12

CLOSE UP of **Myrtle** *to cover above scene.*

CUT TO

Scene 13

MEDIUM SHOT. The door from the platform opens and **Dolly**
Messiter *bustles into the refreshment room. She is a nicely dressed*
woman with a rather fussy manner. She is laden with parcels. The
camera PANS with her as she hurries over to the counter and
addresses **Myrtle**.

Dolly   A cup of tea, please.

Myrtle   Certainly. Cake or pastry?

Dolly   (*looking around the room*) No, thank you.

Her eyes light up suddenly as she sees:

CUT TO

Scene 14

MEDIUM SHOT of **Alec** *and* **Laura** *from* **Dolly***'s view-point. They*
have not seen **Dolly** *and are still in deep conversation.*

CUT TO

Scene 15

MEDIUM SHOT of **Dolly** *at the counter. Forgetting her tea, she*
hurries across the room and the camera PANS with her into a
THREE SHOT with **Laura** *and* **Alec**.

Dolly   Laura! What a lovely surprise!

Laura   (*dazed*) Oh, Dolly.

Dolly   My dear! I've been shopping 'till I'm dropping. My feet
are nearly falling off, and my throat's parched. I thought of having
tea in Spindle's, but I was terrified of losing the train. I'm always
missing trains and being late for meals, and Bob gets disagreeable
for days at a time – he's been getting those dreadful headaches

you know – I've been trying to make him see a doctor, but he won't. (*flopping down at their table*) Oh dear.

Laura   This is Doctor Harvey.

Alec   (*rising*) How do you do?

Dolly   (*shaking hands*) How do you do. Would you be a perfect dear and get me my cup of tea? I don't think I could drag my poor old bones back to the counter again. I must get some chocolates for Tony, too, but I can do that afterwards.

She offers him money.

Alec   (*waving it away*) No, please …

He goes drearily out of picture towards the counter.

CUT TO

Scene 16

CLOSE SHOT of Dolly and Laura.

Dolly   My dear – what a nice-looking man. Who on earth is he? Really, you're quite a dark horse. I shall telephone Fred in the morning and make mischief – that is a bit of luck. I haven't seen you for ages, and I've been meaning to pop in, but Tony's had measles, you know, and I had all that awful fuss about Phyllis – but of course you don't know – she left me.

Laura   (*with an effort*) Oh, how dreadful.

CUT TO

Scene 17

MEDIUM SHOT of Alec at the counter. He is standing next to Albert, who is finishing his cup of tea. Albert leaves and Myrtle hands Alec the change for Dolly's cup of tea.

Dolly   (*off*) Mind you, I never cared for her much, but still Tony did. Tony adored her, and – but never mind, I'll tell you all about that in the train.

The camera PANS with **Alec** *as he picks up* **Dolly**'*s tea and moves back to the table into a THREE SHOT with* **Laura** *and* **Dolly**. *He sits down again.*

Dolly   Thank you so very much. They've certainly put enough milk in it – but still, it'll be refreshing. (*she sips it*) Oh, dear – no sugar.

Alec   It's in the spoon.

Dolly   Oh, of course – what a fool I am – Laura, you look frightfully well. I do wish I'd known you were coming in today, we could have come together and lunched and had a good gossip. I loathe shopping by myself anyway.

There is the sound of a bell on the platform, and a loud speaker voice announces the arrival of the Churley train.

Laura   There's your train.

Alec   Yes, I know.

Dolly   Aren't you coming with us?

Alec   No, I go in the opposite direction. My practice is in Churley.

Dolly   Oh, I see.

Alec   I'm a general practitioner at the moment.

Laura   (*dully*) Doctor Harvey is going out to Africa next week.

Dolly   Oh, how thrilling.

There is the sound of **Alec**'*s train approaching.*

Alec   I must go.

Laura   Yes, you must.

Alec   Goodbye.

Dolly   Goodbye.

He shakes hands with **Dolly**, *looks at* **Laura** *swiftly once and gives her shoulder a little squeeze. The train is heard rumbling into the station. The camera PANS with* **Alec** *as he goes over to the door and out on to the platform.*

Scene 18

CLOSE UP of **Laura** *to cover above scene.*

Scene 19

CLOSE UP of **Alec** *to cover above scene.*

Scene 20

CLOSE UP of **Dolly** *to cover above scene.*

CUT TO

Scene 21

CLOSE UP of **Laura** *and* **Dolly**. **Laura** *is gazing at the door through which* **Alec** *has just passed. She seems almost unaware of the chattering* **Dolly** *at her side, who proceeds to fumble in her handbag for lipstick and a mirror. The camera starts to TRACK SLOWLY FORWARD to a CLOSE UP of* **Laura**.

Dolly   He'll have to run or he'll miss it – he's got to get right over to the other platform. Talking of missing trains reminds me of that awful bridge at Broadham Junction – you have to go traipsing all up one side, along the top and down the other. Well, last week I'd been over to see Bob's solicitor about renewing the lease of the house – and I arrived at the station with exactly half a minute to spare … .

CUT TO

Scene 22

CLOSE UP of **Dolly**, *who is applying lipstick to her chattering mouth and watching the operation in her little hand-mirror.*

Dolly   ... My dear, I flew – I had Tony with me, and like a fool, I'd bought a new shade for the lamp in the drawing room – I could just as easily have got it here in Milford.

CUT TO

Scene 23

CLOSE UP of **Laura**.

Dolly   (*off*) ... It was the most enormous thing and I could hardly see over it – I've never been in such a frizz in my life – I nearly knocked a woman down.

CUT TO

Scene 24

MEDIUM SHOT of the door on to the platform from **Laura**'s *eye line.*

Dolly   (*off*) ... Of course, by the time I got home it was battered to bits.

There is the sound of a bell on the platform.

CUT TO

Scene 25

CLOSE SHOT of **Laura** *and* **Dolly**.

Dolly   Is that the train?

She addresses **Myrtle**.

Dolly   Can you tell me, is that the Ketchworth train?

Myrtle   (*off*) No, that's the express.

Laura   The boat train.

Dolly   Oh yes – that doesn't stop, does it?

She gets up and the camera follows with her into a TWO SHOT with **Myrtle** *at the counter.*

Dolly   Express trains are Tony's passion in life – I want some chocolate, please.

Myrtle   Milk or plain?

Dolly   Plain, I think – or no, perhaps milk would be nicer. Have you any with nuts in it?

The express is heard in the distance.

Myrtle   Nestlé's nut-milk – shilling or sixpence?

Dolly   Give me one plain and one nut-milk.

The noise of the express sounds louder. The express roars through the station as **Dolly** *finishes buying and paying for her chocolate. She turns.*

CUT TO

Scene 26

MEDIUM SHOT of **Laura**'*s table from* **Dolly**'*s viewpoint.* **Laura** *is no longer there.*

CUT TO

Scene 27

CLOSE SHOT of **Dolly** *and* **Myrtle**.

Dolly   Where is she?

Myrtle   (*looking over the counter*) I never noticed her go.

There is the sound of a door opening and they both look up.

CUT TO

Scene 28

MEDIUM SHOT. **Laura** *comes in through the door from Number 2 platform, looking very white and shaky. She shuts the door and leans back against it.* **Dolly** *enters the picture.*

Dolly   My dear, I couldn't think where you'd disappeared to.

Laura   I just wanted to see the express go through.

Dolly   What on earth's the matter? Do you feel ill?

Laura   I feel a little sick.

The camera PANS with **Laura** *as she goes slowly over to her table, where* **Dolly** *helps her into a chair. The platform bell goes, and the loud speaker announces the arrival of the Ketchworth train.*

Laura   That's our train.

Dolly *goes out of picture towards the counter.*

Dolly   (*off*) Have you any brandy?

Myrtle   (*off*) I'm afraid it's out of hours.

Dolly   (*off*) Surely – if someone's feeling ill …

Laura   I'm all right, really.

CUT TO

Scene 29

CLOSE SHOT of **Dolly** *and* **Myrtle**.

Dolly   Just a sip of brandy will buck you up (*to* **Myrtle**).
Please …

Myrtle   Very well …

*She pours out some brandy as the train is heard approaching the
station.*

Dolly   How much?

Myrtle   Tenpence, please.

CUT TO

Scene 30

MEDIUM SHOT of **Laura** *at the table.*

Dolly   (*off*) There!

The train is heard rumbling into the station. **Dolly** *hurries into
picture with the brandy.*

Dolly   Here you are, dear.

Laura   (*taking it*) Thank you.

She gulps down the brandy as **Dolly** *proceeds to gather up
her parcels. The camera PANS with them as they hurry across
the refreshment room and out of the door leading to Number 3
platform.*

CUT TO

Scene 31

EXT. MILFORD JUNCTION STATION AND INT. RAILWAY
CARRIAGE. NIGHT. (STUDIO). B.P.

MEDIUM SHOT. The camera PANS and TRACKS with **Dolly** *and* **Laura** *as they cross the platform to the train. A* **Porter** *opens the door of a Third Class compartment. The camera TRACKS FORWARD with them into the compartment. There is the sound of the door slamming, off. Through the carriage window at the far end can be seen platform Number 4.* **Laura** *sits down out of picture.* **Dolly** *bustles over to the corner seat opposite her.*

Dolly   Well, this is a bit of luck, I must say ...

The carriage gives a jolt and the train starts to pull out of the station.

Dolly   ... This train is generally packed.

Dolly*, having placed her various packages on the seat beside her, leans forward to talk to* **Laura***.*

Dolly   I really am worried about you, dear – you look terribly peaky.

CUT TO

Scene 32

CLOSE SHOT of **Laura** *over* **Dolly***'s shoulder.*

Laura   I'm all right – really I am – I just felt faint for a minute, that's all. It often happens to me you know – I once did it in the middle of Bobbie's school concert! I don't think he's ever forgiven me.

She gives a little smile, it is obviously an effort, but she succeeds reasonably well.

CUT TO

Scene 34[1]

CLOSE SHOT of **Dolly** *over* **Laura**'s *shoulder.*

Dolly   (*after a slight pause*) He was certainly very nice-looking.

Laura   Who?

Dolly   Your friend – that Doctor whatever his name was.

CUT TO

Scene 35

CLOSE SHOT of **Laura** *over* **Dolly**'s *shoulder.*

Laura   Yes. He's a nice creature.

Dolly   Have you known him long?

Laura   No, not very long.

The camera starts to track SLOWLY FORWARD into a CLOSE UP of **Laura**, *who smiles again, quite casually, but her eyes remain miserable.*

Laura   I hardly know him at all, really …

Dolly   (*off*) Well, my dear, I've always had a passion for doctors. I can well understand how it is that women get neurotic. Of course some of them go too far. I'll never forget that time Mary Norton had jaundice. The way she behaved with that Doctor of hers was absolutely scandalous. Her husband was furious and said he would …

Dolly's words fade away. **Laura**'s *mouth remains closed, but we hear her thoughts.*

Laura's voice   I wish I could trust you. I wish you were a wise, kind friend, instead of just a gossiping acquaintance that I've

---

[1] Scene 33 is missing from the original.

known for years casually and never particularly cared for … I
wish … I wish …

CUT TO

Scene 36

CLOSE SHOT of **Dolly** *over* **Laura***'s shoulder.*

Dolly   Fancy him going all the way to South Africa. Is he
married?

Laura   Yes.

Dolly   Any children?

CUT TO

Scene 37

CLOSE UP of **Laura**.

Laura   Yes – two boys. He's very proud of them.

Dolly   (*off*) Is he taking them with him, his wife and children?

Laura   Yes – yes, he is.

CUT TO

Scene 38

CLOSE UP of **Dolly**.

Dolly   I suppose it's sensible in a way – rushing off to start life
anew in the wide open spaces and all that sort of thing, but I must
say wild horses wouldn't drag me away from England …

CUT TO

Scene 39

CLOSE UP of **Laura**.

Dolly   (*off*) ... and home and all the things I'm used to – I mean, one has one's roots after all, hasn't one?

Laura   Yes, one has one's roots.

CUT TO

Scene 40

BIG CLOSE UP of **Dolly**'s *MOUTH*.

Dolly   A girl I knew years ago went out to Africa you know – her husband had something to do with engineering or something, and my dear ...

CUT TO

Scene 41

CLOSE UP of **Laura**.

Dolly   (*off*) She really had the most dreadful time – she got some awful kind of germ through going out on a picnic and she was ill for months and months ...

Dolly's *voice has gradually faded away and we hear* **Laura**'s *thoughts – her lips do not move.*

Laura's voice   I wish you'd stop talking – I wish you'd stop prying and trying to find out things – I wish you were dead. No – I don't mean that – that was unkind and silly – but I wish you'd stop talking ...

Dolly's *voice fades in again –*

Dolly   (*off*) ... all her hair came out and she said the social life was quite, quite horrid – provincial, you know, and very nouveau riche ...

Laura (*wearily*) Oh, Dolly ...

CUT TO

Scene 42

CLOSE SHOT of **Dolly** *over* **Laura**'s *shoulder.*

Dolly What's the matter, dear – are you feeling ill again?

Laura No, not really ill, but a bit dizzy – I think I'll close my eyes for a little.

Dolly Poor darling – what a shame and here am I talking away nineteen to the dozen. I won't say another word and if you drop off I'll wake you just as we get to the level crossing. That'll give you time to pull yourself together and powder your nose before we get out.

CUT TO

Scene 43

CLOSE UP of **Laura**.

Laura Thanks, Dolly.

Scene 44

CLOSE UP of **Laura**

She leans her head back and closes her eyes. The background of the railway compartment darkens out and becomes a misty movement. (This is a Double Exposure Trick Shot. Slow motion picture to be taken of black smoke swirling past and away from both sides of camera – scene 44.) The noise of the train fades away and MUSIC takes its place.

Laura's voice   This can't last – this misery can't last – I must remember that and try to control myself. Nothing lasts, really – neither happiness nor despair – not even life lasts very long – there will come a time in the future when I shan't mind about this any more – when I can look back and say quite peacefully and cheerfully 'How silly I was' – No, No – I don't want that time to come ever – I want to remember every minute – always – always – to the end of my days …

Laura's *head gives a sudden jerk as the train comes to a standstill.*

Dolly   (*off*) Wake up, Laura! We're here!

Simultaneously the background of the compartment comes back to normal. Station lights flash past on to **Laura**'s *face. The MUSIC stops, and the screech of brakes takes its place. A* **Porter**'s *voice is heard calling:*

Porter   (*off*) Ketchworth – Ketchworth – Ketchworth.

DISSOLVE

Scene 45

MEDIUM SHOT, TRACKING. **Laura** *and* **Dolly** *are walking along the platform at Ketchworth. The lights from the stationary train illuminate their faces.*

Dolly   I could come to the house with you quite easily, you know – it really isn't very much out of my way – all I have to do is to cut through Elmore Lane – past the Grammar School and I shall be home in two minutes.

Laura   It's sweet of you, Dolly, but I really feel perfectly all right now. That little nap in the train did wonders.

Dolly   You're quite sure?

Laura   Absolutely positive.

The camera PANS with them to the barrier, where they give up their tickets. A whistle blows and the train can be heard leaving the station. **Dolly** *and* **Laura** *stop in the station yard beyond.*

CUT TO

Scene 46

CLOSE SHOT of **Laura** *and* **Dolly**.

Laura   Thank you for being so kind.

Dolly   Nonsense, dear. Well – I shall telephone in the morning to see if you've had a relapse.

Laura   I shall disappoint you.

She kisses **Dolly**.

Laura   Goodnight.

Dolly   Goodnight – give my love to Fred and the children.

DISSOLVE

Scene 47

EXT. LAURA'S HOUSE. NIGHT.

MEDIUM SHOT of **Laura** *as she approaches the gate of a solid, comfortable-looking house. The camera PANS with her as she enters the gate. She feels in her handbag for her latchkey, finds it and opens the front door and goes inside the house.*

CUT TO

Scene 48

INT. LAURA'S HOUSE. HALLWAY. NIGHT.

MEDIUM SHOT of **Laura** *as she enters the front door, gives a* *glance round the hall, shuts the door quietly and moves out of picture towards the stairs.*

CUT TO

Scene 49

LONG SHOT. The foreground of the picture is framed by a man's hat and coat on a hat-stand. Beyond is the stairway and an open door leading to the sitting room. **Laura** *enters picture and starts to go up the stairs.*

Fred   (*off, from the sitting room*) Is that you, Laura?

Laura   (*stopping on the stairs*) Yes, dear.

Fred   (*off*) Thank goodness you're back, the house has been in an uproar.

Laura   Why – what's the matter?

Fred   (*off*) Bobbie and Margaret have been fighting again, and they won't go to sleep until you go in and talk to them about it.

Margaret   (*off*) Mummy – Mummy! Is that you, Mummy?

Laura   Yes, dear.

Bobbie   (*off, from upstairs*) Come upstairs at once, Mummy – I want to talk to you.

Laura   (*on the way upstairs again*) All right. I'm coming – but you're both very naughty. You should be fast asleep by now.

CUT TO

Scene 50

INT. LAURA'S HOUSE. UPSTAIRS LANDING. NIGHT.

MEDIUM SHOT. **Laura** *crosses the landing to the half open door of the children's Night Nursery.*

CUT TO

Scene 51

INT. CHILDREN'S NIGHT NURSERY. LAURA'S HOUSE.
NIGHT.

*LONG SHOT. The foreground of the picture is framed by two
small twin beds. The room is in darkness and* **Laura** *is silhouetted
in the doorway.*

Laura   Now what is it, you two?

Bobbie   Well, Mummy, tomorrow's *my* birthday and I want to
go to the Circus, and tomorrow's *not* Margaret's birthday, and she
wants to go to the Pantomime, and I don't think it's fair.

Margaret   I don't see why we've got to do everything Bobbie
wants, just because it's his silly old birthday. Besides, my birthday
is in June, and there aren't any pantomimes in June.

Bobbie   (*persuasively*) Mummy, why don't you come and sit
down on my bed?

Margaret   No, Bobbie. Mummy's going to sit on my bed. She
sat with you last night.

Laura   I'm not going to sit with either of you. In fact I'm not
going to come into the room. It's far too late to discuss it tonight,
and if you don't go to sleep at once I shall tell Daddy not to let
you go to either.

Bobbie and Margaret   (*together*) Oh, Mummy!

DISSOLVE

Scene 52

INT. DINING ROOM. LAURA'S HOUSE. NIGHT.

CLOSE SHOT of **Laura** *and her husband* **Fred**, *who is a pleasant
looking man in his forties. They are seated at a round dining room
table and are just finishing their meal.* **Laura** *is officiating at*

the Cona coffee machine. The dining room is well furnished and comfortable without being in any way spectacular.

Fred   Why not take them to both? One in the afternoon and one in the evening?

Laura   You know that's impossible. We shouldn't get home to bed until all hours – and they'd be tired and fractious.

Fred   One on one day, then, and the other on the other.

Laura   (*handing him a cup of coffee*) Here you are, dear. You're always accusing me of spoiling the children. Their characters would be ruined in a month if I left them to your over tender mercies.

Fred   (*cheerfully*) All right – have it your own way.

CUT TO

Scene 53

CLOSE UP of **Laura**.

Laura   Circus or pantomime?

Fred   (*off*) Neither. We'll thrash them both soundly and lock them in the attic, and go to the cinema by ourselves.

Laura'*s eyes suddenly fill with tears.*

Laura   Oh, Fred.

CUT TO

Scene 54

CLOSE UP of **Fred**.

Fred   What on earth's the matter?

CUT TO

Scene 55

MEDIUM SHOT, **Fred** *and* **Laura**.

Laura   (*frantically dabbing her eyes*) Nothing – really it's nothing.

Fred *rises and crosses over to her. He puts his arms round her.*

CUT TO

Scene 56

CLOSE SHOT, **Fred** *and* **Laura**.

Fred   Darling – what's wrong? Please tell me …

Laura   Really and truly it's nothing – I'm just a little run-down. I had a sort of fainting spell in the Refreshment Room at Milford – wasn't it idiotic? Dolly Messiter was with me and talked and talked and talked until I wanted to strangle her – but still she meant to be kind – isn't it awful about people wanting to be kind? …

Fred   (*gently*) Would you like to go up to bed?

Laura   No, Fred – really … …

Fred   Come and sit by the fire in the library and relax – you can help me with the *Times* crossword.

Laura   (*forcing a smile*) You have the most peculiar ideas of relaxation.

Fred   That's better.

Laura *rises with his arms still round her.*

DISSOLVE

Scene 57

INT. LIBRARY. LAURA'S HOUSE. NIGHT.

Fred *and* **Laura** *are sitting on either side of the fire.* **Fred** *is in the foreground of the picture. On his lap is the* Times, *opened at the crossword puzzle. He holds a pencil in his hand.* **Laura** *has some sewing. The library is cosy and intimate.*

Fred But why a fainting spell? I can't understand it.

Laura Don't be so silly, darling – I've often had fainting spells and you know it. Don't you remember Bobbie's school concert and Eileen's wedding, and that time you insisted on taking me to that Symphony Concert in the Town Hall?

Fred That was a nose bleed.

Laura I suppose I must just be that type of woman. It's very humiliating.

Fred I still maintain that there'd be no harm in you seeing Doctor Graves.

Laura (*a little tremulously*) It would be a waste of time.

He looks at her.

Laura Do shut up about it, dear – you're making a fuss about nothing. I'd been shopping and I was tired and the Refreshment Room was very hot and I suddenly felt sick. Nothing more than that – really nothing more than that. Now get on with your old puzzle and leave me in peace.

Fred All right – have it your own way. (*after a pause*) You're a poetry addict – help me over this – it's Keats – 'When I behold upon the night-starred face, Huge cloudy symbols of a high' – something – in seven letters.

Laura (*with an effort*) Romance, I think – yes I'm almost sure it is. 'Huge cloudy symbols of a high romance' – It'll be in the *Oxford Book of English Verse*.

Fred   No, that's right, I'm certain – it fits in with 'delirium' and 'Baluchistan'.

Laura   Will some music throw you off your stride?

Fred   No, dear – I like it.

The camera PANS with **Laura** *as she crosses the room, turns on the radio and returns to her chair. She has tuned in to the opening movement of the Rachmaninoff Concerto in C minor.*

Scene 58

CLOSE UP of **Laura** *to cover above scene.*

Scene 59

CLOSE UP of **Fred** *to cover above scene.*

CUT TO

Scene 60

CLOSE UP of **Laura**. *She takes up her sewing, then puts it down again and looks at her husband.*

CUT TO

Scene 61

CLOSE UP of **Fred**. *He is concentrating hard and scratching his head thoughtfully with the pencil.*

CUT TO

Scene 62

CLOSE UP of **Laura**.

Her eyes fill with tears again. The camera slowly MOVES INTO A BIG CLOSE UP of **Laura**. *Her mouth remains closed but we hear her thoughts ...*

Laura's voice   Fred – Fred – dear Fred. There's so much that I want to say to you. You are the only one in the world with enough wisdom and gentleness to understand – if only it were somebody else's story and not mine. As it is you are the only one in the world that I can never tell – never – never – because even if I waited until we were old, old people and told you then, you would be bound to look back over the years ... and be hurt and oh, my dear, I don't want you to be hurt. You see, we are a happily married couple, and must never forget that. This is my home ...

CUT TO

Scene 63

MEDIUM SHOT of **Fred** *over* **Laura**'s *shoulder. He is engrossed in his crossword puzzle.*

Laura's voice   ... you are my husband – and my children are upstairs in bed. I am a happily married woman – or rather, I was, until a few weeks ago. This is my whole world and it is enough – or rather, it <u>was</u>, until a few weeks ago.

CUT TO

Scene 64

CLOSE UP of **Laura**.

Laura's voice   ... But, oh, Fred, I've been so foolish. I've fallen in love! I'm an ordinary woman – I didn't think such violent things could happen to ordinary people.

CUT TO

Scene 65

INT. LIBRARY. NIGHT AND INT. MILFORD JUNCTION REFRESHMENT ROOM.

MEDIUM SHOT of **Fred** *over* **Laura***'s shoulder.*

Laura's voice   … and it all started on an ordinary day, in the most ordinary place in the world.

The scene, with the exception of **Laura***, slowly starts to dim out.* **Laura** *remains a solid figure in the foreground. As the room fades away the station refreshment room takes its place.* **Laura***, as well as being in the foreground of the picture, is also seated at one of the tables in the refreshment room, thus giving the impression that she is watching herself.*

DISSOLVE

Scene 66

INT. MILFORD JUNCTION STATION. REFRESHMENT ROOM. NIGHT.

LONG SHOT. The time is 5.30. There are only two or three other people in the room. **Myrtle** *and* **Beryl** *are behind the counter, against which* **Albert** *is lolling, sipping a cup of tea.*

Laura's voice   … the Refreshment Room at Milford Junction. I was having a cup of tea and reading a book that I'd got that morning from Boot's – my train wasn't due for ten minutes … I looked up and saw a man come in from the platform. He had on an ordinary mac with a belt. His hat was turned down and I didn't even see his face. He got his tea at the counter and turned – then I did see his face. It was rather a nice face. He passed my table on the way to his. The woman at the counter was going on as usual. You know, I told you about her the other day – the one with the refined voice …

CUT TO

Scene 67

MEDIUM SHOT. **Myrtle,** **Beryl** *and* **Albert** *at the counter.*

Beryl   Minnie hasn't touched her milk.

Myrtle   Did you put it down for her?

Beryl   Yes, but she never came in for it.

Albert   (*conversationally*) Fond of animals?

Myrtle   In their place.

Albert   My landlady's got a positive mania for animals – she's got two cats, one Manx and one ordinary; three rabbits in a hutch in the kitchen, they belong to her little boy by rights; and one of them foolish-looking dogs with hair over his eyes.

Myrtle   I don't know to what breed you refer.

Albert   I don't think it knows itself …

Scene 68

CLOSE UP of **Albert** *to cover above scene.*

CUT TO

Scene 69

MEDIUM SHOT. The door from the platform is kicked open by **Stanley**. *He wears a seedy green uniform and carries a tray strapped to his shoulders. The camera PANS with him as he crosses the Refreshment Room to the counter, into a shot with* **Myrtle** *and* **Beryl**.

Stanley   Two buns and an apple.

Myrtle   What for?

Stanley   Party on the up platform.

Myrtle   Why can't they come in here for them?

Stanley   Ask me another.

He winks at **Beryl**.

Myrtle   Got something in your eye?

Stanley   Nothing beyond a bit of a twinkle every now and again.

Beryl   (*giggling*) Oh, you are awful!

Myrtle   You learn to behave yourself, my lad. Here are your buns. Beryl, stop sniggering and give me an apple off the stand.

The camera PANS with **Beryl** *as she takes an apple from the front of the stand.*

Scene 70

CLOSE UP of **Stanley** *to cover above scene.*

CUT TO

Scene 71

CLOSE SHOT of **Myrtle** *and* **Stanley**. *The camera PANS with* **Myrtle** *into a TWO SHOT with* **Beryl**.

Myrtle   Not off the front, silly, haven't you got any sense?

She takes one from the back of the stand so as to leave the symmetry undisturbed. There is the sound of a distant train whistle and the platform bell rings.

Myrtle   There's the boat train.

CUT TO

Scene 72

MEDIUM SHOT of **Laura**. *She glances at the clock, and collects her parcels in a leisurely manner.*

Myrtle   (*off*) Go and clean Number Three, Beryl. I can see the crumbs on it from here.

Beryl   (*off*) It's them rock-cakes.

Myrtle   (*off*) Never you mind about the rock-cakes. Just you do as you're told and don't argue.

The camera PANS with **Laura** *as she walks over to the door leading to platform Number 2.*

Albert   (*off*) What about my other cup. I shall have to be moving – the five-forty will be in in a minute.

Myrtle   (*off*) Who's on the gate?

Albert   (*off*) Young William.

Myrtle   (*off*) You're neglecting your duty, you know – that's what you're doing.

Albert   (*off*) – a bit of relaxation never did anyone any harm.

CUT TO

Scene 73

EXT. MILFORD JUNCTION STATION. NIGHT. (LOCATION)

LONG SHOT of the Express roaring into the Station.

CUT TO

Scene 74

EXT. MILFORD JUNCTION STATION. NIGHT. (STUDIO)

MEDIUM SHOT of **Laura**. *She is standing on the platform with the windows of the Refreshment Room behind her. The lights from the Express flash across her face as it streaks through Number 2 platform. She suddenly puts her hand to her face as a piece of grit gets into her eye. She takes out a handkerchief and rubs her eye for a few moments then turns and walks back into the Refreshment Room.*

CUT TO

Scene 75

INT. REFRESHMENT ROOM. NIGHT.

MEDIUM SHOT, from behind the counter. **Myrtle** *is in the foreground of the picture.* **Laura** *enters through the door, comes over to the counter and stands beside* **Albert**, *who is drinking his second cup of tea.*

Laura   Please, could you give me a glass of water? I've got something in my eye and I want to bathe it.

Myrtle   Would you like me to have a look?

Laura   Please don't trouble. I think the water will do it.

Myrtle   (*handing her a glass of water*) Here.

Myrtle *and* **Albert** *watch in silence as* **Laura** *bathes her eye.*

Albert   Bit of coal-dust, I expect.

Myrtle   A man I knew lost the sight of one eye through getting a bit of grit in it.

Albert   Nasty thing – very nasty.

Myrtle   (*as* **Laura** *lifts her head*) Better?

Laura   (*obviously in pain*) I'm afraid not – oh!

Alec *enters picture.*

Alec   Can I help you?

Laura   Oh, no please – it's only something in my eye.

Myrtle   Try pulling down your eyelid as far as it'll go.

Albert   And then blowing your nose.

Alec   Please let me look. I happen to be a doctor.

Laura   It's very kind of you.

Alec   Turn round to the light, please.

CUT TO

Scene 76

CLOSE TWO SHOT of **Laura** *and* **Alec**.

Alec   Now – look up – now look down – I can see it. Keep still …

He twists up the corner of his handkerchief and rapidly operates with it.

Alec   There …

Laura   (*blinking*) Oh, dear – what a relief – it was agonising.

Alec   It looks like a bit of grit.

Laura   It was when the express went through. Thank you very much indeed.

Alec   Not at all.

There is the sound of a bell on the platform.

Albert   (*off*) There we go – I must run.

Laura   How lucky for me that you happened to be here.

Alec   Anybody could have done it.

Laura   Never mind, you did, and I'm most grateful.

Alec   There's my train – Goodbye.

The camera follows **Alec** *as he leaves the buffet and goes out of the door to Number 3 platform.*

CUT TO

Scene 77

EXT. MILFORD JUNCTION STATION. NIGHT. (STUDIO)

MEDIUM SHOT. The camera PANS with **Alec** *as he comes out of the refreshment room and hurries along the platform and down the subway.*

CUT TO

Scene 78

EXT. MILFORD JUNCTION STATION. NIGHT. (STUDIO)

MEDIUM SHOT of **Laura** *as she comes out of the refreshment room door on to Number 3 platform. She idly glances across at the opposite platform and sees:*

CUT TO

Scene 79

EXT. MILFORD JUNCTION STATION. NIGHT. (LOCATION)

MEDIUM SHOT of the subway entrance on Number 4 platform from **Laura**'s *view-point.* **Alec** *walks on to the platform. After he has taken a few steps his train pulls into the station thus hiding him from view.*

CUT TO

Scene 80

EXT. MILFORD JUNCTION STATION. NIGHT. (STUDIO)

CLOSE UP of **Laura**. She watches the train as it draws to a standstill.

Laura's voice   … That's how it all began – just through me getting a little piece of grit in my eye.

Laura *looks up as she hears her own train approaching.*

CUT TO

Scene 81

EXT. MILFORD JUNCTION STATION. NIGHT. (LOCATION)

LONG SHOT of Number 3 and 4 platforms. The engine of **Alec**'s *train is in the background.* **Laura**'s *train steams into Number 3 platform, hiding it from view.*

DISSOLVE

Scene 82

EXT. MILFORD JUNCTION STATION. RAILWAY CARRIAGE. NIGHT. (STUDIO)

MEDIUM SHOT, taken from outside the window of **Laura**'s *compartment.* **Laura** *sits down, opens her book and starts to read.*

Laura's voice   I completely forgot the whole incident – it didn't mean anything to me at all, at least I didn't think it did.

There is the sound of a Guard's whistle and the train starts to move off (*track the camera*).

FADE OUT

As the screen goes black, we hear **Laura**'s *voice.*

Laura's voice   The next Thursday I went into Milford again as usual …

FADE IN:

Scene 83

EXT. MILFORD HIGH STREET. DAY. (LOCATION)

MEDIUM SHOT of **Laura**. *The camera is TRACKING with* **Laura** *as she walks along the High Street, carrying a shopping basket. She checks the contents of the basket with a shopping list and having decided on her next port of call, she quickens her step.*

DISSOLVE

Scene 84

INT. BOOTS CHEMIST. DAY.

MEDIUM SHOT. **Laura** *is walking away from the library section and goes over to a counter with soaps, toothbrushes, etc.*

Laura's voice   I changed my book at Boot's – Miss Lewis had at last managed to get the new Kate O'Brien for me – I believe she'd kept it hidden under the counter for two days. On the way out I bought two new toothbrushes for the children – I like the smell of a chemist's better than any other shop – it's such a mixture of nice things – herbs and scent and soap …

CUT TO

Scene 85

CLOSE SHOT of **Mrs. Leftwich** *at the end of the counter.*

Laura's voice   … that awful Mrs. Leftwich was at the other end of the counter, wearing one of the silliest hats I've ever seen.

CUT TO

Scene 86

MEDIUM SHOT of **Laura**. *She places the toothbrushes in her shopping bag and leaves the counter.*

Laura's voice   ... fortunately she didn't look up, so I got out without her buttonholing me. Just as I stepped out on to the pavement ...

DISSOLVE

Scene 87

EXT. MILFORD HIGH STREET. DAY. (LOCATION)

MEDIUM SHOT of **Laura** *as she comes out of Boots.* **Alec** *comes by walking rather quickly. He is wearing a turned-down hat and a mackintosh. He recognises her – stops – and raises his hat.*

Alec   Good morning.

Laura   *(jumping slightly)* Oh – good morning.

Alec   How's the eye?

Laura   Perfectly all right. How kind it was of you to take so much trouble.

Alec   It was no trouble at all.

After a slight pause.

Alec   It's clearing up, I think.

Laura   Yes – the sky looks much lighter, doesn't it?

Alec   Well, I must be getting along to the hospital.

Laura   And I must be getting along to the grocer's.

Alec   *(with a smile)* What exciting lives we lead, don't we? Goodbye.

Scene 88

INT. SUBWAY. NIGHT.

MEDIUM SHOT of **Laura** *walking along the subway. She is a little out of breath.*

Laura's voice   That afternoon I had been to the Palladium as usual, but it was a terribly long film and when I came out I had had to run nearly all the way to the station.

Laura *starts to go up the steps leading to platform Number 3.*

CUT TO

Scene 89

EXT. MILFORD JUNCTION STATION. NIGHT. (STUDIO)

MEDIUM SHOT of **Laura** *as she comes up the subway steps on to platform Number 3.*

Laura's voice   As I came up on to the platform the Churley train was just puffing out.

CUT TO

Scene 90

EXT. MILFORD JUNCTION STATION. NIGHT. (LOCATION)

LONG SHOT of the train leaving platform Number 4.

CUT TO

Scene 91

EXT. MILFORD JUNCTION STATION. NIGHT. (STUDIO)

CLOSE SHOT of **Laura**, *watching the Churley train.*

Laura's voice   I looked up idly as the windows of the carriages went by, wondering if he was there ... I remember this crossing my mind but it was quite unimportant – and I was really thinking of other things – the present for your birthday was worrying me rather. It was terribly expensive, but I knew you wanted it and I'd sort of half taken the plunge and left a deposit on it at Spink and Robson's until the next Thursday. The next Thursday ...

DISSOLVE

Scene 92

INT. SPINK & ROBSON'S. DAY.

CLOSE UP of a travelling clock with a barometer, and dates all in one. It is standing on a glass show case.

CUT TO

Scene 93

CLOSE UP of **Laura**. (*show case in background*). *She is looking down at the clock admiringly.*

Laura's voice   ... Well – I squared my conscience by thinking how pleased you would be, and bought it – it was wildly extravagant I know, but having committed the crime, I suddenly felt reckless and gay ...

DISSOLVE

Scene 94

EXT. MILFORD HIGH STREET. DAY. (LOCATION)

LONG SHOT. The camera PANS with **Laura** *as she walks along the street, carrying a small parcel in her hand. It is a sunny day and she is smiling. A barrel organ is playing.*

Laura's voice   The sun was out and everybody in the street looked more cheerful than usual – and there was a barrel organ at the corner by Harris's, and you know how I love barrel organs – it was playing 'Let the Great Big World Keep Turning', and I gave the man sixpence and went to the Kardomah for lunch.

DISSOLVE

Scene 95

INT. KARDOMAH CAFÉ. DAY.

MEDIUM SHOT of **Laura***, who is sitting at an alcove table in the Kardomah. A* **waitress** *is just finishing taking her order.*

Laura's voice   It was very full, but two people had got up from the table just as I had come in – that was a bit of luck, wasn't it? Or was it? Just after I had given my order, I saw him come in. He looked a little tired, I thought, and there was nowhere for him to sit, so I smiled and said …

Laura   Good morning.

CUT TO

Scene 96

CLOSE UP of **Alec**.

Alec   Good morning. Are you all alone?

CUT TO

Scene 97

MEDIUM SHOT, **Laura** *and* **Alec**.

Laura   Yes, I am.

Alec   Would you mind very much if I shared your table – it's very full and there doesn't seem to be anywhere else?

Laura   (*moving a couple of parcels and her bag*) Of course not.

Alec *hangs up his hat and mackintosh and sits down next to her.*

CUT TO

Scene 98

TWO SHOT, **Alec** *and* **Laura**.

Alec   I'm afraid we haven't been properly introduced – my name's Alec Harvey.

Laura   (*shaking hands*) How do you do – mine's Laura Jesson.

Alec   Mrs. or Miss?

Laura   Yes. You're a doctor, aren't you? I remember you said you were that day in the refreshment room.

Alec   Yes – not a very interesting doctor – just an ordinary G.P. My practice is in Churley.

A **waitress** *comes to the table.*

Waitress   Can I take your order?

Alec   (*to* **Laura**) What did you plump for?

Laura   The soup and the fried sole.

Alec   (*to* **waitress**) The same for me, please.

Waitress   Anything to drink?

Alec   No, thank you.

Alec *pauses and looks at* **Laura**.

Alec   That is – would you like anything to drink?

Laura   No, thank you – just plain water.

Alec   (*to* **waitress**) Plain water please.

As the **waitress** *goes away a* **Ladies Orchestra** *starts to play very loudly.* **Laura** *jumps.*

CUT TO

Scene 99

LONG SHOT of the **Ladies Orchestra**. *They are playing with enthusiasm.*

CUT TO

Scene 100

CLOSE SHOT of **Laura** *and* **Alec**. *They both laugh.* **Alec** *catches* **Laura**'s *eye and nods towards the* **cellist**.

CUT TO

Scene 101

CLOSE SHOT of the **cellist**. *She is a particularly industrious member of the orchestra.*

Laura's voice   I'd seen that woman playing the cello hundreds of times, but I'd never noticed how funny she looked.

CUT TO

Scene 102

CLOSE SHOT, **Laura** *and* **Alec**.

Laura   It really is dreadful, isn't it – but we shouldn't laugh – they might see us.

Alec   There should be a society for the prevention of cruelty to musical instruments – you don't play the piano, I hope?

Laura   I was forced to as a child.

Alec   You haven't kept it up?

Laura   (*smiling*) No – my husband isn't musical at all.

Alec   Bless him!

Laura   For all you know, I might have a tremendous, burning professional talent.

Alec   (*shaking his head*) Oh dear, no.

Laura   Why are you so sure?

Alec   You're too sane – and uncomplicated.

Laura   (*fishing in her bag for her powder puff*) I suppose it's a good thing to be so uncomplicated – but it does sound a little dull.

Alec   You could never be dull.

Laura   Do you come here every Thursday?

Alec   Yes, to spend a day in the hospital. Stephen Lynn – he's the chief physician here – graduated with me. I take over from him once a week – it gives him a chance to go up to London and me a chance to study the hospital patients.

Laura   I see.

Alec   Do you?

Laura   Do I what?

Alec   Come here every Thursday?

Laura   Yes – I do the week's shopping, change my library book, have a little lunch, and generally go to the pictures. Not a very exciting routine, really, but it makes a change.

Alec   Are you going to the pictures this afternoon?

Laura   Yes.

Alec   How extraordinary – so am I.

Laura   But I thought you had to work all day in the hospital.

Alec   Well, between ourselves, I killed two patients this morning by accident and the Matron's very displeased with me. I simply daren't go back…

Laura   How can you be so silly?

Alec   Seriously – I really did get through most of my work this morning – it won't matter a bit if I play truant. Would you mind very much if I came to the pictures with you?

Laura   (*hesitating*) Well – I …

Alec   I could sit downstairs and you could sit upstairs.

Laura   Upstairs is too expensive.

She smiles. The **Orchestra** *stops playing.*

Laura's voice   The orchestra stopped as abruptly as it had started and we began to laugh again, and I suddenly realised that I was enjoying myself so very much.

A **waitress** *arrives back with the soup.*

Laura's voice   I had no premonitions, although I suppose I should have had. It all seemed so natural – and so – so innocent.

Scene 103

CLOSE UP of **Alec** *over* **Laura***'s shoulder to cover above scene.*

Scene 104

CLOSE UP of **Laura** *over* **Alec***'s shoulder to cover above scene.*

DISSOLVE

Scene 105

CLOSE UP of the LUNCHEON BILL on a plate. **Alec***'s hand comes into picture and picks it up.* **Laura***'s hand comes into picture and tries to take it from him.*

Laura's voice   We finished lunch, and the idiot of a waitress had put the bill all on one.

CUT TO

Scene 106

CLOSE SHOT of **Laura** *and* **Alec**.

Alec   I really must insist.

Laura   I couldn't possibly.

Alec   Having forced my company on you, it's only fair that I should pay through the nose for it.

Laura   Please don't insist – I would so much rather we halved it, really I would – please.

Alec   I shall give in gracefully.

Laura's voice   We halved it meticulously – we even halved the tip.

CUT TO

Scene 107

MEDIUM SHOT, **Laura**, **Alec** *and the* **waitress**. *They get up from the table and the orchestra starts again. They start laughing again. The camera PANS with them as they start to leave the restaurant.*

DISSOLVE

Scene 108

EXT. MILFORD HIGH STREET. DAY. (LOCATION)

MEDIUM SHOT, TRACKING with **Laura** *and* **Alec** *as they walk along the High Street.*

Laura We have two choices – *'The Loves of Cardinal Richelieu'* at the Palace, and *'Love in a Mist'* at the Palladium.

Alec You're very knowledgeable.

Laura There must be no argument about buying the tickets – we each pay for ourselves.

Alec You must think me a very poor doctor if I can't afford a couple of one-and-ninepennies.

Laura I insist.

Alec I *had* hoped that you were going to treat me!

Laura Which is it to be – Palace or Palladium?

Alec (*with decision*) Palladium, I was once very sick on a Channel steamer called *'Cardinal Richelieu'*.

DISSOLVE

Scene 109

INT. CINEMA. DAY. (B.P. – MINIATURE)

LONG SHOT of the Palladium proscenium. On the screen a trailer is being shown, advertising a coming attraction. Superimposed over four spectacular SHOTS (library) in ever increasing sizes, are the following words, which zoom up towards the audience:

STUPENDOUS! COLOSSAL!! GIGANTIC!!! EPOCH-MAKING!!!!!

A burst of flame appears, followed by the title of the picture

'Flames of Passion'. The trailer ends abruptly and the first of a series of advertisements is flashed on the screen. It is a drawing of a pram with the words:

'BUY YOUR PRAM AT BURTON'S

22, MILFORD HIGH STREET'.

CUT TO

XXXXXXXXX

XXXXXXXXX

XXXXXXXXX

Scene 116

INT. REFRESHMENT ROOM. NIGHT.

MEDIUM SHOT, from behind the counter. **Myrtle** *and* **Beryl** *are gossiping in the foreground of the picture.* **Alec** *and* **Laura** *enter through the door in background.* **Laura** *goes over to a table out of picture.* **Alec** *comes forward to the counter.*

Myrtle   And for the third time in one week he brought that common man and his wife to the house without so much as a by your leave. (*to* **Alec**) Yes?

Alec   Two teas, please.

Myrtle   Cakes or pastry?

Alec   (*to* **Laura**) Cakes or pastry?

Laura   (*off*) No, thank you.

Alec   Are those Bath buns fresh?

Myrtle   Certainly they are – made this morning.

Alec   Two please.

Myrtle *puts two Bath buns on a plate. Meanwhile* **Beryl** *has drawn two cups of tea.*

Myrtle   That'll be tenpence.

Alec   All right. (*he pays her*)

Myrtle   Take the tea to the table, Beryl.

Alec   I'll carry the buns.

CUT TO

Scene 117

MEDIUM SHOT of **Laura**, *who has seated herself at a table.*
Beryl *brings the tea to the table.* **Alec** *follows with the buns.*

Alec   You must eat one of these – fresh this morning.

Laura   Very fattening.

Alec   I don't hold with such foolishness.

Beryl *goes out of picture towards the counter.*

Beryl   (*off*) What happened then, Mrs. Bagot?

Laura *gives* **Alec** *a nudge to draw his attention to* **Myrtle** *and*
Beryl.

CUT TO

Scene 118

CLOSE SHOT of **Myrtle** *and* **Beryl** *behind the counter.*

Myrtle   (*slightly relaxed in manner*) Well – it's all very fine, I
said, expecting me to do this, that and the other, but what do I get
out of it? You can't expect me to be a cook, housekeeper and char
rolled into one during the day, and a loving wife in the evening,
just because you feel like it. Oh, dear, no. There are just as good
fish in the sea, I said, as ever came out of it, and I packed my
boxes there and then and left him.

Beryl   Didn't you ever go back?

Myrtle   Never. I went to my sister's place at Folkestone for a bit, and then I went in with a friend of mine and we opened a tea-shop in Hythe.

Beryl   And what happened to him?

Myrtle   Dead as a doornail inside three years.

Beryl   Well, I never!

Myrtle   So you see, every single thing she told me came true – first, them clubs coming together, an unexpected journey; then the Queen of Diamonds and the ten – that was my friend and the tea-shop business; then the Ace of Spades three times running.

Scene 119

CLOSE UP of **Myrtle** *to cover above scene.*

CUT TO

Scene 120

CLOSE SHOT of **Laura** *and* **Alec**.

Alec   The gipsy obviously warned her.

Laura   Is tea bad for one? Worse than coffee, I mean?

Alec   If this is a professional interview, my fee is a guinea.

Laura   Why did you become a doctor?

Alec   That's a long story. Perhaps because I'm a bit of an idealist.

Laura   I suppose all doctors ought to have ideals, really – otherwise I should think their work would be unbearable.

Alec   Surely you're not encouraging me to talk shop?

Laura   Why shouldn't you talk shop? It's what interests you most, isn't it?

Alec   Yes – it is. I'm terribly ambitious, really – not ambitious for myself so much as for my special pigeon.

Laura   What is your special pigeon?

Alec   Preventative medicine.

Laura   Oh, I see.

Alec   (*laughing*) I'm afraid you don't.

Laura   I was trying to be intelligent.

Alec   Most good doctors, especially when they're young, have private dreams – that's the best part of them; sometimes, though, those get over-professionalised and strangulated and – am I boring you?

Laura   No – I don't quite understand – but you're not boring me.

Alec   What I mean is this – all good doctors must be primarily enthusiasts. They must have, like writers and painters and priests, a sense of vocation – a deep-rooted, unsentimental desire to do good.

Laura   Yes – I see that.

Alec   Well, obviously one way of preventing disease is worth fifty ways of curing it – that's where my ideal comes in – preventative medicine isn't anything to do with medicine at all, really – it's concerned with conditions, living conditions and common sense and hygiene. For instance, my speciality is pneumoconiosis.

Laura   Oh, dear.

Alec   Don't be alarmed, it's simpler than it sounds – it's nothing but a slow process of fibrosis of the lung due to the inhalation of particles of dust. In the hospital here there are splendid opportunities for observing cures and making notes, because of the coal mines.

Laura   You suddenly look much younger.

Alec   (*brought up short*) Do I?

Laura   Almost like a little boy.

Alec   What made you say that?

Laura   (*staring at him*) I don't know – yes, I do.

Alec   (*gently*) Tell me.

Laura   (*with panic in her voice*) Oh, no – I couldn't really. You were saying about the coal mines.

Alec   (*looking into her eyes*) Yes – the inhalation of coal dust – that's one specific form of the disease – it's called anthrocosis.

Laura   (*hypnotized*) What are the others?

Alec   Chalicosis – that comes from metal dust – steel-works, you know …

Laura   Yes, of course. Steel-works.

Alec   And silicosis – stone dust – that's gold mines.

Laura   (*almost in a whisper*) I see.

There is a sound of a bell.

Laura   That's your train.

Alec   (*looking down*) Yes.

Laura   You mustn't miss it.

Alec   No.

Laura   (*again with panic in her voice*) What's the matter?

Alec   (*with an effort*) Nothing – nothing at all.

Laura   (*socially*) It's been so very nice – I've enjoyed my afternoon enormously.

Alec   I'm so glad – so have I. I apologise for boring you with those long medical words.

Laura   I feel dull and stupid, not to be able to understand more.

Alec   Shall I see you again?

There is the sound of a train approaching.

Laura   It's the other platform, isn't it? You'll have to run. Don't worry about me – mine's due in a few minutes.

Alec   Shall I see you again?

Laura   Of course – perhaps you could come over to Ketchworth one Sunday. It's rather far, I know, but we should be delighted to see you.

Alec   (*intensely*) Please – please …

The train is heard drawing to a standstill …

Laura   What is it?

Alec   Next Thursday – the same time.

Laura   No – I can't possibly – I –

Alec   Please – I ask you most humbly …

Laura   You'll miss your train.

Alec   All right.

He gets up.

Scene 121

CLOSE TWO SHOT, **Alec** *and* **Laura** *to cover above scene.*

Scene 122

CLOSE SHOT of **Laura** *over* **Alec***'s shoulder to cover above scene.*

Scene 123

CLOSE SHOT of **Alec** *over* **Laura***'s shoulder to cover above scene.*

Scene 124

CLOSE UP of **Laura** *to cover above scene.*

Scene 125

CLOSE UP of **Alec** *to cover above scene.*

CUT TO

Scene 126

MEDIUM SHOT, **Laura** *and* **Alec**.

Laura   Run …

Alec   (*taking her hand*) Goodbye.

Laura   (*breathlessly*) I'll be there.

Alec   Thank you, my dear.

CUT TO

Scene 127

CLOSE SHOT of **Beryl** *and* **Myrtle** *behind the counter. They are watching* **Laura** *and* **Alec**. **Myrtle** *gives* **Beryl** *a nudge.*

CUT TO

Scene 128

MEDIUM SHOT, **Laura** *and* **Alec**. *The camera PANS with* **Alec** *as he runs to the door leading to Number 3 platform. He collides with* **Albert Godby**, *who is on his way in.*

Albert   'Ere – 'ere – take it easy now – take it easy.

CUT TO

Scene 129

MEDIUM SHOT of **Laura**. *She collects her shopping basket and the camera PANS with her as she goes over to the door to Number 3 platform.*

CUT TO

Scene 130

EXT. MILFORD JUNCTION STATION. NIGHT (STUDIO)

MEDIUM SHOT of **Laura** *as she comes out of the Refreshment Room door on to the platform. She looks up past camera, at* **Alec***'s train, which can be heard pulling out of the station.*

CUT TO

Scene 131

EXT. MILFORD JUNCTION STATION. NIGHT. (STUDIO)

MEDIUM SHOT of **Alec**, *from* **Laura***'s viewpoint. He is leaning out of a carriage window. He waves to her as the train starts to pull out of the station* (*track the camera*).

CUT TO

Scene 132

EXT. MILFORD JUNCTION STATION. NIGHT. (STUDIO)

CLOSE UP of **Laura**. *She waves back, and her eyes follow the departing train.*

Laura's voice   I stood there and watched his train draw out of the station. I stared after it until its little red taillight had vanished into the darkness. I imagined him arriving at Churley and giving up his ticket and walking through the streets and letting himself into his house with his latchkey. Madeleine, his wife, would probably be in the hall to meet him – or perhaps upstairs in her room – not feeling very well – small, dark and rather delicate – I wondered if he'd say 'I met such a nice woman in the Kardomah – we had lunch and went to the pictures' –

We hear **Alec**'s *voice repeating:*

Laura's voice   – then suddenly I knew that he wouldn't – I knew beyond a shadow of doubt that he wouldn't say a word, and at that moment the first awful feeling of danger swept over me.

On the words: 'first awful feeling ...' a cloud of steam from an incoming engine blows across the picture, almost obscuring **Laura**. *The grinding of brakes and hiss of steam as her train draws to a standstill interrupts her thoughts. She walks out of picture towards the train.*

CUT TO

Scene 133

EXT. MILFORD JUNCTION STATION. NIGHT. (STUDIO)

MEDIUM SHOT of **Laura** *as she walks through the clearing steam and enters a Third Class compartment.*

CUT TO

Scene 134

INT. RAILWAY COMPARTMENT. NIGHT. (B.P. NOT
NECESSARY)

MEDIUM SHOT. **Laura** *enters the door at the far end of the
fairly crowded compartment. The camera PANS with her as she
walks into a CLOSE SHOT and sits down between two other*
passengers*. She glances around the carriage.*

Laura's voice I looked hurriedly around the carriage to see if
anyone was looking at me.

CUT TO

Scene 135

MEDIUM SHOT. The camera PANS along the **passengers** *seated
on the opposite side of the carriage.*

Laura's voice … as though they could read my secret thoughts.
Nobody was looking at me except a clergyman in the opposite
corner.

The **clergyman** *catches her eye and turns his head away.*

CUT TO

Scene 136

CLOSE UP of **Laura***. She opens her library book.*

Laura's voice I felt myself blushing and opened my library
book and pretended to read.

The train gives a jerk as it starts to move off.

DISSOLVE

Scene 137

EXT. KETCHWORTH STATION. NIGHT. (STUDIO)

MEDIUM SHOT of **Laura**. *The camera TRACKS with her as she walks along the Ketchworth platform towards the barrier. There are several other passengers around her.*

Laura's voice   By the time we got to Ketchworth, I had made up my mind definitely that I wouldn't see Alec any more.

A woman's voice   Good evening, Mrs. Jesson.

Laura *does not hear her.*

Laura's voice   It was silly and undignified flirting like that with a complete stranger.

She walks on a pace or two then turns.

Laura   Oh – oh – good evening.

DISSOLVE

Scene 138

EXT. LAURA'S HOUSE. NIGHT.

MEDIUM SHOT of **Laura** *as she walks up the path to the front door.*

Laura's voice   I walked up to the house quite briskly and cheerfully. I had been behaving like an idiot, admittedly, but after all no harm had been done.

Laura *opens the front door.*

CUT TO

Scene 139

INT. HALL. LAURA'S HOUSE. NIGHT.

MEDIUM SHOT of **Laura** *as she enters the Hall. She looks up past camera towards the stairs.*

Laura's voice   You met me in the hall. Your face was strained and worried and my heart sank.

Laura   Fred! What's the matter?

CUT TO

Scene 140

MEDIUM SHOT of **Fred** *as he moves down the last two stairs into the Hall. The camera PANS with him into a TWO SHOT with* **Laura**.

Fred   It's all right, old girl, but you've got to keep calm and not be upset.

Laura   What is it? What's wrong?

Fred   It's Bobbie – he was knocked down by a car on the way home from school …

Laura *gives a little cry.*

Fred   It's not serious – he was just grazed by the mudguard but it knocked him against the kerb and he's got slight concussion – the doctor's upstairs with him now …

The camera PANS with **Laura** *as she flings down her parcels and book and goes upstairs at a run, tearing off her coat as she goes.* **Fred** *follows.*

CUT TO

Scene 141

INT. CHILDREN'S NIGHT NURSERY AND LANDING.
NIGHT.

*MEDIUM SHOT. The camera is shooting through the open door
of the Night Nursery on to the landing beyond.* **Laura** *arrives
on the landing and hurries towards camera and into the nursery
door.*

She stops in the doorway as she sees:

CUT TO

Scene 142

INT. NIGHT NURSERY. NIGHT.

MEDIUM SHOT of the **doctor** *standing beside* **Bobbie**'s *bed.*
Bobbie *is lying in the bed with his eyes shut, and his head and
right arm bandaged. The* **doctor** *puts his fingers to his lips.*

Doctor   It's all right, Mrs. Jesson – nothing to worry about –
he'll be as right as rain in a few hours.

CUT TO

Scene 143

CLOSE SHOT of **Laura**. *The camera TRACKS and PANS with her
as she goes across the room and kneels into a CLOSE SHOT with*
Bobbie *at the bed. The* **doctor** *now becomes an unimportant part
of the picture; his legs only being visible.*

Laura   (*whispering*) You're sure – you're sure it's not serious?

Doctor   (*smiling*) Quite sure – but it was certainly a very lucky
escape.

The **doctor** *moves off out of picture.*

Doctor (*off*) I've given him a little sedative and I should advise keeping him at home for a couple of days. It must have been a bit of a shock and his right arm is rather badly bruised.

*The **doctor**'s voice has gradually faded away ...*

Laura's voice   I felt so dreadful, Fred – looking at him lying there with that bandage round his head. I tried not to show it but I was quite hysterical inside as though the whole thing were my fault – a sort of punishment – an awful, sinister warning.

DISSOLVE

Scene 144

MEDIUM SHOT, **Laura** *and* **Bobbie**. **Laura** *is seated on* **Bobbie**'*s bed. The* **maid** *comes into picture and hands* **Bobbie** *a plate of bread and milk.*

Laura's voice   An hour or two later, of course, everything became quite normal again. He began to enjoy the whole thing thoroughly, and revelled in the fact that he was the centre of attraction. Do you remember how we spent the whole evening planning his future?

DISSOLVE

Scene 145

INT. LIBRARY. NIGHT.

MEDIUM SHOT, **Fred** *and* **Laura**. *They are seated on either side of the fire.* **Fred** *is on the sofa with a crossword puzzle and* **Laura** *is smoking a cigarette.*

Laura   But he's much too young to decide really.

Fred   It's a good life – and if the boy has a feeling for it ...

Laura   How can we possibly really know that he has a feeling for it. He'll probably want to be an engine driver next week.

Fred   It was last week that he wanted to be an engine driver.

Laura   But it seems so final somehow, entering a child of that age for the Navy.

Fred   It's a healthy life.

Laura   (*with slight exasperation*) I know it's a good life, dear, and I know it's a healthy life, and I know that he'll be able to see the world and have a wife in every port and keep on calling everybody 'sir' – but what about us?

Fred   How do you mean? 'What about us'?

Laura   We shall hardly ever see him …

Fred   Nonsense.

Laura   It isn't nonsense. He'll be sent away to sea as a smooth-faced boy and the next thing we know he'll be walking in with a long beard and a parrot.

Fred   I think you take rather a Victorian view of the Navy, my dear.

Laura   He's our only son and I should like to be there while he's growing up.

Fred   All right, old girl. We'll put him into an office and you can see him off on the eight-fifty every morning.

Laura   (*crushing her cigarette out*) You really are very annoying – you know perfectly well that I should hate that.

Laura *rises and goes round to the sofa table behind* **Fred**. *On the table is a work basket out of which she starts to take some wool, etc.*

Fred   All right – all right, have it your own way.

Scene 146

CLOSE UP of **Laura** *to cover above scene.*

Scene 147

CLOSE UP of **Fred** *to cover above scene.*

CUT TO

Scene 148

MEDIUM SHOT of **Fred** *and* **Laura**.

Laura   (*suddenly*) Fred …

Fred   (*busily counting spaces*) Yes –

Laura   I had lunch with a strange man today and he took me to the movies.

Fred   Good for you.

Laura   He's awfully nice – he's a doctor …

Fred   (*rather abstractedly filling in a word*) A – very – noble – profession …

Laura   (*helplessly*) Oh dear.

Fred   It was Richard the Third who said 'My Kingdom for a horse', wasn't it?

Laura   Yes, dear.

Fred   Well, all I can say is that I wish he hadn't – it ruins everything.

Laura   I thought perhaps we might ask him over to dine one evening …

Fred   By all means – (*he looks up*) Who?

Laura   Doctor Harvey. The one I was telling you about.

Fred   Must it be dinner?

Laura   You're never at home for lunch.

Fred   Exactly.

Laura *leaves the table and goes over and sits beside Fred.*

Laura   (*starting to laugh, almost hysterically*) Oh, Fred!

Scene 149

CLOSE UP of **Laura** *to cover above scene.*

Scene 150

CLOSE UP of **Fred** *to cover above scene.*

CUT TO

Scene 151

CLOSE SHOT, **Fred** *and* **Laura**.

Fred   (*looking up*) What on earth's the matter?

Laura   (*laughing more*) It's nothing – it's only that …

She breaks off and goes on laughing helplessly until she has to wipe her eyes.

Laura   Oh, Fred …

Fred   I really don't see what's so terribly funny.

Laura   I do – it's all right, darling, I'm not laughing at you – I'm laughing at me, I'm the one that's funny – I'm an absolute idiot – worrying myself about things that don't really exist – making mountains out of molehills …

Fred   I told you when you came in that it wasn't anything serious – there was no need for you to get into such a state …

Laura   No – I see that now – I really do …

She goes on laughing.

DISSOLVE

Scene 152

INT. KARDOMAH CAFÉ. DAY.

MEDIUM SHOT of **Laura**. *She is sitting at her same table. She is alone. The* **Ladies Orchestra** *is playing away as usual.*

Laura's voice   I went to the Kardomah and managed to get the same table. I waited a bit but he didn't come. … The ladies orchestra was playing away as usual – I looked at the cellist – she had seemed to be so funny last week, but today she didn't seem funny any more – she looked pathetic, poor thing.

DISSOLVE

Scene 153

EXT. HOSPITAL. DAY.

LONG SHOT of **Laura**, *walking past the hospital.*

Laura's voice   After lunch I happened to pass by the Hospital. I remember looking up at the windows and wondering if he were there and whether something awful had happened to prevent him turning up.

DISSOLVE

Scene 154

INT. REFRESHMENT ROOM. NIGHT.

LONG SHOT. **Laura** *is leaving the counter, carrying a cup of tea, which* **Myrtle** *has just poured out for her. She walks over to* *a table and sits down in the foreground of the picture, back to camera.*

Laura's voice   I got to the station earlier than usual. I hadn't enjoyed the pictures much – it was one of those noisy musicals things and I'm so sick of them – I had come out before it was over.

Myrtle *comes over to the stove in the centre of the room. She bends down to put more coal into it.* **Albert Godby** *enters and perceiving her slightly vulnerable position, he tiptoes towards her.*

CUT TO

Scene 155

CLOSE SHOT of **Laura**. *She watches* **Albert**. *After a moment there is a loud smack, off.* **Laura** *smiles.*

CUT TO

Scene 156

CLOSE SHOT, **Myrtle** *and* **Albert**. **Myrtle** *springs to an upright position.*

Myrtle   Albert Godby, how dare you.

Albert   I couldn't resist it.

Myrtle   I'll trouble you to keep your hands to yourself.

Myrtle *walks out of picture towards the counter.*

Albert   You're blushing – you look wonderful when you're angry – like an avenging angel.

Albert *walks out of picture towards the counter.*

CUT TO

Scene 157

MEDIUM SHOT of **Myrtle** *as she arrives at the counter.*

Myrtle   I'll give you avenging angel – coming in here taking liberties …

Albert   (*entering picture*) I didn't think after what you said last Monday you'd object to a friendly little slap.

Myrtle   Never you mind about last Monday – I'm on duty now. A nice thing if Mr. Saunders had happened to be looking through the window.

Albert   If Mr. Saunders is in the 'abit of looking through windows, it's time he saw something worth looking at.

Myrtle   You ought to be ashamed of yourself.

Albert   It's just high spirits – don't be mad at me.

Myrtle   High spirits, indeed. Here, take your tea and be quiet.

Albert   It's all your fault, anyway.

Myrtle   I don't know to what you're referring, I'm sure.

Albert   I was thinking of tonight.

Myrtle   If you don't learn to behave yourself there won't be a tonight – or any other night, either …

Albert   Give us a kiss.

Myrtle   I'll do no such thing. The lady might see us.

Albert   Just a quick one – across the counter.

He grabs her arm across the counter.

Myrtle   Albert, stop it.

Albert   Come on – there's a love.

Myrtle   Let go of me this minute.

Albert   Come on, just one …

They scuffle for a moment, upsetting a neat pile of cakes on to the floor.

Myrtle   Now look at me Banburys – all over the floor.

Albert *bends down to pick them up.*

Scene 158

CLOSE UP of **Myrtle** *to cover above scene.*

Scene 159

CLOSE UP of **Albert** *to cover above scene.*

CUT TO

Scene 160

MEDIUM SHOT of **Stanley** *as he enters the door.*

Stanley   Just in time – or born in the vestry.

CUT TO

Scene 161

MEDIUM SHOT of **Laura**. *She glances up at the clock, takes up her shopping basket, and during the following dialogue, the camera PANS with her to the door leading to platform Number 3.*

Myrtle   (*off*) You shut your mouth and help Mr. Godby pick up them cakes. Come along, what are you standing there gaping at?

Stanley   (*off*) Where's Beryl?

Myrtle   (*off*) Never you mind about Beryl; you ought to be on Number Two, and well you know it.

Albert   (*off, reflectively*) Love's young dream!

CUT TO

Scene 162

EXT. MILFORD JUNCTION STATION. NIGHT. (STUDIO)

*MEDIUM SHOT of **Laura** as she comes out of the refreshment
room door on to Number 3 platform.*

Laura's voice   As I left the refreshment room I saw a train
coming in – his train. He wasn't on the platform, and I suddenly
felt panic stricken at the thought of not seeing him again.

CUT TO

Scene 163

*MEDIUM SHOT of the Subway entrance, to Number 2 and 3
platforms.* **Alec** *dashes up the Subway steps on to the platform,
and the camera PANS with him as he runs into a TWO SHOT with*
Laura.

Alec   (*breathlessly*) Oh, my dear, I'm so sorry – so terribly sorry.

Laura   Quick – your train – you'll miss it.

*The camera TRACKS with them as they both rush along the
platform towards the subway steps.*

Alec   (*as they go*) I'd no way of letting you know – the house
surgeon had to operate suddenly – it wasn't anything really
serious, but I had to stand by, as it was one of my special patients.

CUT TO

Scene 164

INT. SUBWAY. NIGHT.

MEDIUM SHOT. **Laura** *and* **Alec** *are running down the subway steps towards the camera.*

Alec   ... You do understand, don't you?

Laura   (*now rather breathless*) Of course – it doesn't matter a bit.

They turn the corner at the foot of the steps, and the camera TRACKS with them as they run along the subway towards the steps leading up to Number 4 platform.

Alec   I thought of sending a note along to the Kardomah but I thought they would probably never find you, or keep on shouting your name out and embarrass you, and I ...

They start running up the steps leading to platform Number 4 – the camera PANS with them.

Laura   Please don't say any more – I really do understand ...

CUT TO

Scene 165

EXT. MILFORD JUNCTION STATION. NIGHT. (STUDIO)

MEDIUM SHOT. The camera is shooting on to the subway entrance to Number 4 platform. A whistle blows. **Laura** *and* **Alec** *hurry on to the platform.*

Laura   Quickly – oh, quickly. The whistle's gone.

The camera PANS with them across the platform to the waiting train. **Alec** *opens the door of a Third Class compartment and turns to* **Laura**.

CUT TO

Scene 166

CLOSE SHOT, **Laura** and **Alec**. (*moving train.*)

Alec   I'm so relieved that I had a chance to explain – I didn't think I should ever see you again.

Laura   How absurd of you.

The train starts to move off.

Laura   Quickly – quickly …

CUT TO

Scene 167

MEDIUM SHOT of **Laura** *and* **Alec**. (*moving train.*)

Alec *jumps into the train as it is moving off. He leans out of the window.* **Laura** *walks along a few paces with the train.*

Alec   Next Thursday.

Laura   Yes. Next Thursday.

The train gradually gains on **Laura***, and* **Alec** *goes out of picture.*

CUT TO

Scene 168

CLOSE UP of **Laura**. *She watches* **Alec***'s departing train, waves after it and stands quite still until the sound of it has died away in the distance. A strident VOICE from the Loud Speakers breaks in:*

'THE TRAIN FOR CHURLEY, LEE GREEN, LANGDON AND BANTHORPE IS STANDING AT NUMBER 3 PLATFORM.'

Laura *suddenly realises that she is about to miss her own train*

and the camera PANS with her as she makes a dash for the
subway steps.

DISSOLVE

Scene 169

INT. PALLADIUM CINEMA. DAY. (STUDIO)

CLOSE SHOT of **Laura** *and* **Alec** *sitting in the front row of the*
Circle at the Palladium. They are both laughing and obviously
very happy. The lights go up.

Alec   The stars can change in their courses, the universe go up
in flames and the world crash around us, but there'll always be
Donald Duck.

Laura   I do love him so, his dreadful energy, his blind frustrated
rages …

The lights begin to dim.

Alec   It's the big picture now – here we go – no more laughter –
prepare for tears.

CUT TO

Scene 170

INT. CINEMA. DAY. (*Miniature.*)

LONG SHOT, the proscenium. The main title of the big picture is
flashed on to the screen. It is the film advertised in the trailer of
two weeks ago, 'FLAMES OF PASSION.'

Laura's voice   It was a terribly bad picture.

DISSOLVE

Scene 171

INT. CINEMA. DAY. (LOCATION)

MEDIUM SHOT of **Laura** *and* **Alec** *walking up the last few steps of the Circle towards the exit. The back of an* **usherette** *forms the foreground of the picture.*

Laura's voice   We crept out before the end, rather furtively, as though we were committing a crime. The usherette at the door looked at us with stony contempt.

DISSOLVE

Scene 172

EXT. CINEMA and STREET. DAY. (LOCATION)

MEDIUM SHOT of **Laura** *and* **Alec** *coming out of the Cinema.* **Alec** *takes* **Laura***'s arm, and the camera TRACKS with them as they walk along the street. (Cinema posters advertising 'Flames of Passion' to be designed.)*

Laura's voice   It really was a lovely afternoon and it was a relief to be in the fresh air. Do you know, I believe we should all behave quite differently if we lived in a warm, sunny climate all the time. We shouldn't be so withdrawn and shy and difficult.

DISSOLVE

Scene 173

EXT. BOTANICAL GARDENS. DAY. (LOCATION)

A PICTORIAL LONG SHOT of **Alec** *and* **Laura** *as they walk along by the side of a lake.*

Laura's voice   Oh, Fred, it really was a lovely afternoon. There were some little boys sailing their boats – one of them looked awfully like Bobbie – that should have given me a pang

of conscience I know, but it didn't … I was enjoying myself –
enjoying every single minute.

CUT TO

Scene 174

MEDIUM SHOT, TRACKING with **Alec** *and* **Laura**. *After a few
moments* **Alec** *stops walking and turns to* **Laura**.

Laura's voice   Alec suddenly said that he was sick of staring at
the water and that he wanted to be <u>on</u> it.

DISSOLVE

Scene 175

*LONG SHOT. The foreground of the picture is composed of one or
two rowing boats, which have been covered up for the winter. On
the landing stage in the background a* **boatman** *is pushing* **Alec**
and **Laura** *away from the shore.*

Laura's voice   All the boats were covered up but we managed to
persuade the old man to let us have one.

CUT TO

Scene 176

CLOSE SHOT of the **boatman**.

Laura's voice   He thought we were raving mad. Perhaps he was
right.

CUT TO

Scene 177

LONG SHOT, with the **boatman** *in the foreground.*

Laura's voice   … Alec rowed off at a great rate, and I trailed my hand in the water – it was very cold but a lovely feeling.

CUT TO

Scene 178

MEDIUM SHOT, **Alec** *and* **Laura** *in the boat. The camera TRACKING with them.* **Laura** *is in the foreground of the picture.* **Alec** *catches a crab and an oar slips out of its rowlock.*

Laura   You don't row very well, do you?

Alec   (*putting the oar back in the rowlock*) I'm going to be perfectly honest with you. I don't row at all, and unless you want to go round and round in ever narrowing circles, you had better start steering.

CUT TO

Scene 179

CLOSE SHOT of **Laura**. She laughs and picks up the steering ropes. They start off again.

DISSOLVE

Scene 180

LONG SHOT of **Laura** *and* **Alec** *in the boat, which is following a somewhat erratic course.*

Laura's voice   We had such fun, Fred. I felt gay and happy and sort of released – that's what's so shameful about it all – that's what would hurt you so much if you knew – that I could feel as intensely as that – away from you – with a stranger.

DISSOLVE

Scene 181

MEDIUM SHOT, **Laura** *and* **Alec**. *The camera is TRACKING with the boat.* **Laura** *is in the foreground of the picture. They are approaching a very low bridge.*

Laura's voice   Presently we came to a bridge and Alec said:

Alec   For heaven's sake steer to the left or we will hit it.

As the bridge looms nearer and nearer **Alec** *rises to his feet.*

CUT TO

Scene 182

CLOSE UP of **Laura**. *She pulls the wrong rope and looks up enquiringly at* **Alec**. *There is a crash and a shudder as the boat hits the bridge.*

Laura's voice   I never *could* tell left from right.

The boat rocks violently and there is a loud splash. **Laura** *looks towards the water and begins to laugh.*

CUT TO

Scene 183

MEDIUM SHOT of **Alec**. *He is standing in the lake. The water only comes up to his knees – he is very wet.*

CUT TO

Scene 184

EXT. BOTANICAL GARDENS. DAY. (LOCATION)

CLOSE UP of **Laura**. *She is roaring with laughter.*

DISSOLVE

Scene 185

INT. BOATHOUSE. DUSK.

CLOSE SHOT of **Alec**'s *trousers, hanging over a line in front of an open 'Ideal' boiler. The camera PULLS BACK to reveal several more articles of clothing, and then PANS over to* **Alec** *who is seated on an upturned dinghy. He is wearing an overcoat, which is obviously not his own, and is smoking a cigarette. He looks past camera at:*

CUT TO

Scene 186

MEDIUM SHOT of **Laura**, *from* **Alec**'s *viewpoint. She is kneeling by the boiler, laying out* **Alec**'s *shoes and socks to dry.*

CUT TO

Scene 187

MEDIUM SHOT, **Laura** *and* **Alec**. **Laura** *gets up and goes over to a carpenter's bench, upon which a kettle is boiling on a gas ring. Beside the ring is a bottle of milk and two cups. In the background of the picture are a collection of punts, boats, oars, etc.* **Laura** *starts to make the tea.*

Laura   The British have always been nice to mad people. That boatman thinks we are quite dotty, but just look how sweet he has been: overcoat, tea, milk – even sugar.

CUT TO

Scene 188

CLOSE SHOT of **Alec**. *He watches her prepare the tea. After a moment we hear the sound of* **Laura** *walking across the Boathouse towards* **Alec**. *He follows her with his eyes. Her hand comes into picture and gives him a cup of tea.*

Alec   Thank you.

CUT TO

Scene 189

MEDIUM SHOT, **Laura** *and* **Alec**. **Laura** *sits down on an old wooden chair. They both begin to stir their tea.*

Alec   (*quietly*) You know what's happened, don't you?

Laura   Yes – yes, I do.

Alec   I've fallen in love with you.

Laura   Yes – I know.

Alec   Tell me honestly – my dear – please tell me honestly if what I believe is true …

Laura   (*in a whisper*) What do you believe?

Alec   That it's the same with you – that you've fallen in love too.

Laura   (*near tears*) It sounds so silly.

Alec   Why?

Laura   I know you so little.

Alec   It is true, though – isn't it?

Laura   (*with a sigh*) Yes – it's true.

Alec   (*making a slight movement towards her*) Laura …

Laura   No please … we must be sensible – please help me to be sensible – we mustn't behave like this – we must forget that we've said what we've said.

Alec   Not yet – not quite yet.

Laura   (*panic in her voice*) But we must – don't you see!

Alec   (*leaning forward and taking her hand*) Listen – it's too late now to be as sensible as all that – it's too late to forget what we've said – and anyway, whether we'd said it or not couldn't have mattered – we know – we've both of us known for a long time.

Laura   How can you say that – I've only known you for four weeks – we only talked for the first time last Thursday week?

Alec   Last Thursday week. Hasn't it been a long time since then – for you? Answer me truly.

Laura   Yes.

Alec   How often did you decide that you were never going to see me again?

Laura   Several times a day.

Alec   So did I.

Laura   Oh, Alec.

Alec   I love you – I love your wide eyes and the way you smile and your shyness, and the way you laugh at my jokes.

Laura   Please don't …

Alec   I love you – I love you – you love me too – it's no use pretending that it hasn't happened because it has.

Laura   (*with tremendous effort*) Yes, it has. I don't want to pretend anything either to you or to anyone else …but from now on I shall have to. That's – that's wrong – don't you see? That's what spoils everything. That's why we must stop here and now talking like this. We are neither of us free to love each other, there is too much in the way. There's still time, if we control ourselves and behave like sensible human beings, there's still time to – to …

She puts her head down and bursts into tears.

Alec   There's no time at all.

Alec *goes over to her, takes her in his arms and kisses her.*

Scene 190

CLOSE SHOT, **Laura** *and* **Alec** *to cover above scene.*

Scene 191

CLOSE UP of **Laura** *to cover above scene.*

Scene 192

CLOSE UP of **Alec** *to cover above scene.*

CUT TO

Scene 193

EXT. MILFORD JUNCTION STATION. NIGHT. (STUDIO)

CLOSE UP of the station bell, which rings loudly.

CUT TO

Scene 194

INT. BOOKING HALL and NUMBER 1. PLATFORM. NIGHT. (STUDIO)

MEDIUM SHOT of **Laura** *and* **Alec** *as they come on to Number 1 platform from the booking hall.*

Laura   There's your train.

Alec   Yes.

Laura   I'll come with you – over to the other platform.

The camera PANS with them as they go along the platform and down the subway steps.

CUT TO

Scene 195

INT. SUBWAY. NIGHT.

MEDIUM SHOT of **Laura** *and* **Alec**. *They come down the steps and start to walk along the subway.*

Alec *stops and takes her in his arms. She struggles a little.*

Laura   No, dear – please ... not here – someone will see.

Alec   (*kissing her*) I love you so.

They are interrupted by the sound of feet coming down the subway steps. A SHADOW appears on the wall behind them. They hurry off through the subway.

CUT TO

Scene 196

INT. SUBWAY. NIGHT.

LONG SHOT. In the foreground of the picture the dim outline of **Laura** *can be seen, watching herself and* **Alec** *as they walk along the subway towards Number 4 Platform. The sound of an express train roaring overhead, becomes the sound of loud MUSIC.* **Fred**'s *voice is heard:*

Fred's voice   Don't you think we might have that down a bit, darling?

After a slight pause.

Fred's voice   Hoi – Laura.

DISSOLVE

Scene 197

INT. LIBRARY. NIGHT.

*LONG SHOT, over **Laura**'s shoulder. The Subway has suddenly disappeared and **Fred** and the library have taken its place.*

Laura   (*jumping*) Yes, dear?

Fred   You were miles away.

Laura   Was I? Yes, I suppose I was.

Fred   (*rising*) Do you mind if I turn it down a little – it really is deafening …

He goes over towards the radio.

Laura   (*with an effort*) Of course not.

*She bends down and starts sewing. **Fred** turns down the radio and returns to his place.*

Fred   I shan't be long over this and then we'll go up to bed. You look a bit tired, you know …

Laura   Don't hurry – I'm perfectly happy.

*She continues her sewing for a moment or two, then she looks up again. **Fred**'s head is down, concentrating on the paper.*

Scene 198

*CLOSE UP of **Fred** to cover above scene.*

Scene 199

CLOSE UP of **Laura** *to cover above scene.*

CUT TO

Scene 200

CLOSE SHOT of **Laura**. *She passes her hand across her forehead wearily.*

Laura's voice   How can I possibly say that? 'Don't hurry, I'm perfectly happy'. If only it were true. Not, I suppose, that anybody is ever perfectly happy, really, but just to be ordinarily contented – to be at peace. It's such a little while ago really, but it seems an eternity since that train went out of the station – taking him away into the darkness.

DISSOLVE

Scene 201

INT. SUBWAY. NIGHT.

CLOSE SHOT of **Laura**. *The camera is TRACKING with her as she walks back through the subway. The sound of her train is heard pulling in overhead.*

Laura's voice   I went over to the other platform and got into my train as usual.

DISSOLVE

Scene 202

INT. RAILWAY COMPARTMENT. NIGHT.

CLOSE SHOT of **Laura**. *She is seated in the corner of a railway compartment. The back projection plate is moving left to right.*

Scene 237

CLOSE SHOT, **Albert**, **Myrtle** *and* **Beryl**.

Myrtle   Thank you, Albert.

Beryl   What a nerve, talking to you like that.

Myrtle   Be quiet, Beryl – pour me out a nip of Three Star – I'm feeling quite upset.

Albert   I've got to get back to the gate.

Myrtle   (*graciously*) I'll be seeing you later, Albert.

Albert   (*with a wink*) Okay.

Albert *goes out of picture.* **Beryl** *brings* **Myrtle** *a glass of brandy.*

Myrtle   (*sipping it*) I will say one thing for Albert **Godby**, he may be on the saucy side but he's a gentleman.

CUT TO

Scene 238

CLOSE SHOT of **Laura**. *A train bell goes. She fumbles in her bag and finds a cigarette. She lights it. There is the sound of her train approaching.*

Myrtle   (*off*) There's the five forty-three.

Beryl   (*off*) We ought to have another Huntley and Palmers to put in the middle, really.

Myrtle   (*off*) There are some more on the shelf.

Laura *sits, puffing her cigarette, listening to her train draw into the station. Suddenly she rises, crushes out her cigarette, grabs her bag, and the camera PANS with her to the door leading to Number 3 platform.*

CUT TO

Scene 239

EXT. MILFORD JUNCTION STATION. NIGHT. (STUDIO)

MEDIUM SHOT of **Laura**. *The camera PANS with her as she runs across Number 3 platform and gets into her train.*

CUT TO

Scene 240

INT. THIRD CLASS RAILWAY CARRIAGE. NIGHT.

MEDIUM SHOT of **Laura** *as she enters the compartment and sits down next to two* **women**.

CUT TO

Scene 241

CLOSE UP of **Laura**. *She is in a nervous state of indecision. The* **Guard***'s whistle blows. After a second or two she suddenly jumps up.*

CUT TO

Scene 242

MEDIUM SHOT of **Laura**. *She stumbles over the* **women** *sitting next to her.*

Laura   (*muttering*) Excuse me, I have forgotten something.

CUT TO

Scene 243

EXT. MILFORD JUNCTION STATION. NIGHT. (LOCATION)

MEDIUM SHOT of **Laura** *as she gets out of the train, just as it begins to move off. The camera PANS with her as she runs along the platform with the train gathering speed behind her. She runs out of the picture towards the barrier leaving a SHOT of the train as it steams away from the station.*

DISSOLVE

Scene 244

INT. MAIN ENTRANCE HALLWAY AND STAIRCASE OF A BLOCK OF FLATS. NIGHT.

LONG SHOT of the main entrance and hallway of a block of flats. **Laura** *enters from the street. It is raining. She walks towards camera and pauses for a moment to examine a board, upon which are listed the names of the tenants and their flat numbers. During the following narrative, the camera FOLLOWS her up the stairs to the door of Stephen Lynn's flat on the second floor.*

Laura's voice   Stephen Lynn lived in that newish rather ugly Block in Acacia Road just behind the hospital. The flat was on the second floor. I didn't want to wait to ring for the lift so I went up the stairs. I felt quite calm and detached as though all feeling had died in me. I deceived myself, too. I explained to myself that I really had to see him again, just once, to make clear to him that it couldn't be as he wanted – that it could never be as he wanted – that we should have to say goodbye – finally and for ever. When I arrived at the door I paused a minute to get my breath, then I rang the bell – I noticed that my hand was shaking.

Alec *opens the door. She goes quickly past him into the hall almost without looking at him.*

CUT TO

Scene 245

INT. FLAT. NIGHT.

MEDIUM SHOT, **Alec** *and* **Laura**.

Alec   (*softly*) Oh, darling. I didn't dare to hope.

The camera PANS with **Alec** *and* **Laura** *as he leads her gently through to the sitting-room into a LONG SHOT. It is rather a bleak little room. The furniture looks impersonal. He has lit the fire, but it hasn't had time to get under way and is smoking. They stand quite still for a moment, looking at each other.*

Laura   It's raining.

Alec   (*his eyes never moving from her face*) Is it?

Laura   It started just as I turned out of the High Street.

Alec   You had no umbrella and your coat's wet …

He gently helps her off with her coat.

Alec   You mustn't catch cold – that would never do.

Laura   (*looking at herself in the glass over the mantelpiece, and slowly taking off her hat*) I look an absolute fright.

Alec   (*taking her hat and her scarf*) Let me put them down.

Laura   Thank you.

Alec   (*putting them on a chair near the writing desk with the coat*) I hope the fire will perk up in a few minutes …

Laura   I expect the wood was damp.

Alec   (*ruefully*) Yes – I expect it was.

There is a silence.

Alec   Do sit down, darling …

Laura *sits down on the sofa.*

CUT TO

Scene 246

CLOSE SHOT of **Laura**.

Laura   (*with an attempt at gaiety*) I got right into the train and then got out again – wasn't it idiotic?

Alec   (*sitting down next to her and taking her in his arms*) We're both very very foolish … . (*he kisses her*)

Laura   (*weakly*) Alec – I can't stay you know – really, I can't.

Alec   Just a little while – just a little while.

There is the sound of the lift gates clanking. They both break apart and look up past camera at:

CUT TO

Scene 247

MEDIUM SHOT, the flat hallway, from their eye line. There is the sound of a step outside on the landing and then the sound of a key being fitted into the front door.

CUT TO

Scene 248

MEDIUM SHOT, **Laura** *and* **Alec**. *They jump to their feet.*

Laura   (*in a frantic whisper*) Quickly – quickly – I must go …

Alec *snatches up her hat and coat and pushes them into her hand.*

Alec   Here – through the kitchen – there's a tradesman's staircase …

The camera PANS with them as they rush into the small kitchen.

CUT TO

Scene 249

INT. KITCHENETTE. NIGHT.

MEDIUM SHOT. There is a door opening on to the fire escape. **Alec** *tears it open,* **Laura** *runs through it on to a metal staircase, without even looking back. She disappears down the stairs.* **Alec** *shuts the door quietly after her and leans against it for a moment with his eyes closed.*

A man's voice   (*from the sitting-room*) Is that you, Alec?

Alec   (*as casually as he can*) Yes.

He starts to walk back into the sitting-room.

CUT TO

Scene 250

INT. SITTING ROOM. NIGHT.

MEDIUM SHOT over **Alec**'*s shoulder. The camera TRACKS with him as he walks through into the sitting room, where* **Stephen Lynn** *is standing by the entrance to the hall. He is a thin, rather ascetic-looking man.* **Alec** *walks towards him into a TWO SHOT.*

Alec   You are back early.

Stephen   I felt a cold coming on so I denied myself the always questionable pleasure of dining with that arch arguer Roger Hinchley and decided to come back to bed. (*walking over to the chair by the writing desk*) Inflamed membranes are unsympathetic to dialectic –

Alec   What will you do about food?

Stephen   (*smiling*) I can ring down to the restaurant later on if I want anything – we live in a modern age and this is a service flat.

Alec   (*with a forced laugh*) Yes – yes – I know.

Stephen   (*still smiling*) It caters for all tastes.

He lightly flicks **Laura***'s scarf off the chair and hands it to* **Alec***.*

Stephen   You know Alec, my dear, you have hidden depths that I never even suspected.

Alec   Look here, Stephen, I really …

Stephen   (*holding up his hand*) For heaven's sake, Alec, no explanations or apologies – I am the one who should apologise for having returned so inopportunely – it is quite obvious to me that you were interviewing a patient privately – women are frequently neurotic creatures and the hospital atmosphere upsets them. From the rather undignified scuffling I heard when I came into the hall I gather that she beat a hurried retreat down the backstairs. I'm surprised at this farcical streak in your nature, Alec – such carryings on were quite unnecessary – after all, we have known each other for years and I am the most broad-minded of men.

Alec   (*stiffly*) I'm really very sorry, Stephen. I'm sure that the whole situation must seem inexpressibly vulgar to you. Actually it isn't in the least. However, you are perfectly right – explanations are unnecessary – particularly between old friends. I must go now.

Stephen   (*still smiling*) Very well.

Alec   I'll collect my hat and coat in the hall. Goodbye.

Stephen   Perhaps you'd let me have my latch key back? I only have two and I'm so afraid of losing them – you know how absent minded I am.

Alec   (*giving him the key*) You're very angry, aren't you.

Stephen   No, Alec – not angry – just disappointed.

Alec *goes out without another word.*

Scene 251

CLOSE UP of **Alec** *to cover above scene.*

Scene 252

CLOSE UP of **Stephen** *to cover above scene.*

CUT TO

Scene 253

EXT. STREET. NIGHT.

The camera is TRACKING on a CLOSE SHOT of **Laura**'*s legs and feet. She is running fast along the pavement. It is pouring with rain.*

CUT TO

Scene 254

EXT. STREET. NIGHT.

CLOSE UP of **Laura** *from a low angle. She is still running. The background of the picture is composed of the tops of houses. As she approaches a lamp post the light increases on her face and dies away quickly as she passes it.*

CUT TO

Scene 255

EXT. STREET. NIGHT.

CLOSE SHOT, TRACKING of the pavement from **Laura**'*s angle. Her shadow becomes large and elongated as she moves further away from the lamp post.*

CUT TO

Scene 256

EXT. STREET. NIGHT.

MEDIUIM LONG SHOT of **Laura** *as she approaches another lamp post. She is out of breath and slows down to a walk.*

Laura's voice   I ran until I couldn't run any longer – I leant against a lamp post to try to get my breath – it was in one of those side roads that lead out of the High Street. I know it was stupid to run but I couldn't help myself.

CUT TO

Scene 257

CLOSE SHOT of **Laura** *as she leans against the lamp post.*

Laura's voice   I felt so utterly humiliated and defeated and so dreadfully, dreadfully ashamed. After a moment or two I pulled myself together and walked on in the direction of the station.

The camera starts to TRACK with her along the street.

Laura's voice   It was still raining but not very much. I suddenly realised that I couldn't go home, not until I had got myself under more control and had a little time to think. Then I thought of you waiting at home for me and the dinner being spoilt.

DISSOLVE

Scene 258

INT. TOBACCONIST'S SHOP. NIGHT.

CLOSE SHOT of **Laura** *at the telephone in a tobacconist's shop. She looks pale and bedraggled.*

Laura's voice   So I went into the High Street and found a tobacconist and telephoned to you – do you remember – ?

Laura   (*at the telephone*) Fred – is that you? (*with a tremendous effort she makes her voice sound ordinary*) Yes, dear – it's me – Laura – Yes – of course everything's perfectly all right but I shan't be home to dinner – I'm with Miss Lewis. Miss Lewis, dear – the librarian at Boot's I told you about – I can't explain in any detail now because she's just outside the telephone box – but I met her a little while ago in the High Street in the most awful state, her mother has just been taken ill and I've promised to stay with her until the doctor comes – Yes, dear, I know, but she's always been tremendously kind to me and I'm desperately sorry for her – No – I'll get a sandwich – tell Ethel to leave a little soup for me in a saucepan in the Kitchen – Yes, of course – as soon as I can. Goodbye.

She hangs up the telephone.

Laura's voice   It's awfully easy to lie – when you know that you're trusted implicitly – so very easy, and so very degrading.

She walks slowly out of the box.

DISSOLVE

Scene 259

EXT. STREET. NIGHT. (UXBRIDGE LOCATION.)

LONG SHOT. The camera is shooting from a high angle on to a road leading off the High Street. It has stopped raining but the pavement is still wet and glistening. **Laura** *is slowly walking towards the camera.*

Laura's voice   I started walking without much purpose – I turned out of the High Street almost immediately – I was terrified that I might run into Alec – I was pretty certain that he'd come after me to the station.

DISSOLVE

Scene 260

EXT. STREET. NIGHT. (UXBRIDGE LOCATION.)

LONG SHOT. The camera is shooting down on to another street.
Laura *is still walking.*

Laura's voice   I walked for a long while ...

DISSOLVE

Scene 261

EXT. WAR MEMORIAL. NIGHT. (STUDIO).

*LONG SHOT. The foreground of the picture is composed of part of
the War Memorial Statue: a soldier's hand gripping a bayoneted
service rifle. Beyond it* **Laura** *is seen as a tiny figure walking
towards a seat near the base of the Memorial.*

Laura's voice   Finally, I found myself at the War Memorial –
you know it's right at the other end of the town. It had stopped
raining altogether and I felt stiflingly hot so I sat down on one of
the seats.

CUT TO

Scene 262

CLOSE SHOT of **Laura** *on the seat.*

Laura's voice   There was nobody about and I lit a cigarette – I
know how you disapprove of women smoking in the street – I do
too, really – but I wanted to calm my nerves and I thought it might
help.

DISSOLVE

Scene 263

EXT. WAR MEMORIAL. NIGHT. (STUDIO)

CLOSE SHOT of **Laura**. *She is profile to camera and has finished her cigarette.*

Laura's voice   I sat there for ages – I don't know how long – then I noticed a policeman walking up and down a little way off – he was looking at me rather suspiciously. Presently he came up to me.

The **Policeman** *walks up into a MEDIUM SHOT over* **Laura**'s *shoulder.*

Policeman   Feeling all right, Miss?

Laura   (*faintly*) Yes, thank you.

Policeman   Waiting for someone?

Laura   No – I'm not waiting for anyone.

Policeman   You don't want to go and catch cold you know – that would never do.

Laura   I don't feel in the least cold, thank you.

Policeman   It's a damp night to be sitting about on seats, you know.

Laura   (*rising*) I'm going now anyhow – I have a train to catch.

CUT TO

Scene 264

CLOSE SHOT, **Laura** *and the* **Policeman**.

Policeman   You're sure you feel quite all right?

Laura   Yes – quite sure – Goodnight.

Policeman   Goodnight, Miss.

As **Laura** *walks off the camera PANS and TRACKS with her, shooting on to her back.*

Laura's voice   I walked away – trying to look casual – knowing that he was watching me. I felt like a criminal. I walked rather quickly back in the direction of the High Street.

DISSOLVE

Scene 265

EXT. MILFORD JUNCTION STATION. NIGHT. (STUDIO)

LONG SHOT. The clock on Platforms 2 and 3 forms the foreground of the picture. The time is six minutes to ten. **Laura** *comes up out of the subway in the background and walks along the platform towards camera. The station is not very well lit and there is hardly anybody about.*

Laura's voice   I got to the station fifteen minutes before the last train to Ketchworth, and then I realised that I had been wandering about for over three hours, but it didn't seem to be any time at all.

Laura *enters the refreshment room.*

CUT TO

Scene 266

INT. REFRESHMENT ROOM. NIGHT.

LONG SHOT. It is nearly closing time. The room is half-lighted. There is the melancholy noise of a goods train chugging through the station. **Beryl** *is draping the things on the counter with muslin clothes while* **Stanley**, *wearing his ordinary clothes, stands gossiping with her.* **Laura** *enters through the door in the background.*

Stanley   Be a sport, Beryl, shut down five minutes early and tell your mother you was kept ten minutes late – that gives us a quarter of an hour.

Beryl   What happens if Mrs. Bagot comes back?

Stanley   She won't – she's out having a bit of slap and tickle with our **Albert**.

Beryl   Stan, you are awful!

Stanley   I'll wait for you in the yard.

Beryl   Oh, all right.

Stanley *goes out.*

Laura   I'd like a glass of brandy, please.

Beryl   We're just closing.

Laura   I see you are, but you're not quite closed yet, are you?

Beryl   (*sullenly*) Three Star?

Laura   Yes, that'll do.

Beryl   (*getting it*) Tenpence, please.

Laura   (*taking money from her bag*) Here – and – have you a piece of paper and an envelope?

Beryl   I'm afraid you'll have to get that at the bookstall.

Laura   The bookstall's shut – please – it's very important – I should be so much obliged…

Beryl   Oh, all right – wait a minute.

She exits.

CUT TO

Scene 267

CLOSE UP of **Laura**. *She sips the brandy at the counter; she is obviously trying to control her nerves. After a moment* **Beryl** *can*

*be heard walking back across the Refreshment Room. She enters
picture and puts down some notepaper and an envelope.*

Laura   Thank you so much.

Beryl   We close in a few minutes, you know.

Laura   Yes, I know.

Beryl *exits picture and the camera PANS with* **Laura** *as she takes
a few paces along the counter in order to be under the light.*

*She stares at the paper for a moment, takes another sip of brandy
and then begins to write.*

CUT TO

Scene 266

CLOSE SHOT of **Beryl**. *She looks at* **Laura** *with exasperation
and goes out of picture.*

CUT TO

Scene 269

CLOSE SHOT of **Laura**. **Beryl** *can be heard walking away across
the refreshment room and slamming the door at the other end.*
Laura *falters in her writing, then breaks down and buries her face
in her hands. In the background the door to the platform opens
and* **Alec** *enters. He looks hopelessly round for a moment, then
seeing her, and walks forward into a CLOSE TWO SHOT.*

Alec   Thank God – Oh, darling …

Laura   Please go away – please don't say anything …

Alec   I've been looking for you everywhere – I've watched every
train.

Laura   Please go away …

Alec   You're being dreadfully cruel. It was just a beastly accident that he came back early – he doesn't know who you are – he never even saw you.

Laura   I suppose he laughed, didn't he? (*bitterly*) I suppose you spoke of me together as men of the world?

Alec   We didn't speak of you – we spoke of a nameless creature who had no reality at all.

Laura   Why didn't you tell him who I was? Why didn't you tell him we were cheap and low and without courage – why didn't you ...

Alec   Stop it, Laura – pull yourself together.

Laura   It's true. Don't you see? It's true ...

Alec   We know we really love each other – that's true – that's all that really matters.

Laura   It isn't all that matters – other things matter too, self-respect matters, and decency – I can't go on any longer.

Alec   Could you really say goodbye – not see me any more?

Laura   Yes – if you'd help me.

Alec   (*after a pause*) I love you, Laura – I shall love you always until the end of my life – all the shame that the world might force on us couldn't touch the real truth of it. I can't look at you now because I know something – I know that this is the beginning of the end – not the end of my loving you – but the end of our being together. But not quite yet, darling – please, not quite yet.

Laura   (*in a dead voice*) Very well – not quite yet.

Alec   I know what you feel about this evening – I mean about the beastliness of it. I know about the strain of our different lives; our lives apart from each other. The feeling of guilt, of doing wrong is a little too strong, isn't it? Too persistent? Perhaps too great a price to pay for the few hours of happiness we get out of it. I know all this because it's the same for me too.

Laura   You can look at me now – I'm all right.

Alec   (*looking at her*) Let's be careful – let's prepare ourselves – a sudden break now, however brave and admirable, would be too cruel. We can't do such violence to our hearts and minds.

Laura   Very well.

Alec   I'm going away.

Laura   I see.

Alec   But not quite yet.

Laura   Please – not quite yet.

A train bell goes.

CUT TO

Scene 270

CLOSE SHOT of the door leading to the Staff Room. It opens and **Beryl** *comes in.*

Beryl   That's the ten ten. It's after closing time.

CUT TO

Scene 271

MEDIUM SHOT, **Alec**, **Laura** *and* **Beryl**.

Alec   Oh, is it?

Beryl   I shall have to lock up.

Alec   All right.

The camera PANS with **Laura** *and* **Alec** *as* **Beryl** *escorts them to the door of Number 3 platform.* **Laura** *and* **Alec** *go out and the camera remains on* **Beryl** *as she slams the door after them and bolts up.*

CUT TO

Scene 272

EXT. MILFORD JUNCTION STATION. NIGHT. (STUDIO)

CLOSE SHOT, TRACKING with **Laura** *and* **Alec** *as they walk up and down the platform.*

Alec   I want you to promise me something.

Laura   What is it?

Alec   Promise me that however unhappy you are, and however much you think things over, that you'll meet me next Thursday.

Laura   Where?

Alec   Outside the hospital – twelve thirty?

Laura   All right – I promise.

Alec   I've got to talk to you – I've got to explain.

Laura   About going away?

Alec   Yes.

Laura   Where are you going? Where can you go? You can't give up your practice.

Alec   I've had a job offered me. I wasn't going to tell you – I wasn't going to take it – but I know now, that it's the only way out.

Laura   Where?

Alec   A long way away – Johannesburg.

Laura   (*stopping still*) Oh, Alec …

Alec   My brother's out there. They're opening a new hospital – they want me in it – it's a fine opportunity really. I'll take Madeleine and the boys. It's been torturing me – the necessity of making a decision one way or the other. I haven't told anybody – not even Madeleine. I couldn't bear the idea of leaving you – but now I see, it's got to happen soon anyway – it's almost happening already.

Laura   When will you go?

Alec   Almost immediately – in about two weeks time.

Laura   It's quite near, isn't it?

Alec   Do you want me to stay? Do you want me to turn down the offer?

Laura   Don't be foolish, Alec.

Alec   I'll do whatever you say.

Laura   (*her eyes filling with tears*) That's unkind of you, my darling.

Scene 273

CLOSE UP of **Alec** *to cover above scene.*

Scene 274

CLOSE UP of **Laura** *to cover above scene.*

CUT TO

Scene 275

CLOSE UP of the Station LOUD SPEAKER, which announces:

'THE TRAIN FOR KETCHWORTH, LONGDEAN and PETERFORD IS NOW ENTERING NUMBER 3 PLATFORM'.

A train can be heard entering the Station.

DISSOLVE

Scene 276

EXT. MILFORD JUNCTION STATION. NIGHT. (STUDIO)

MEDIUM SHOT, **Laura** *and* **Alec**. **Alec** *opens the door of an empty Third Class Compartment and* **Laura** *gets in.* **Alec** *shuts the door after her and* **Laura** *leans out of the open window.*

Alec   You're not angry with me, are you?

Laura   No, I'm not angry – I don't think I'm anything, really – I just feel tired.

Alec   Forgive me.

Laura   Forgive you for what?

CUT TO

Scene 277

CLOSE UP of **Alec** *over* **Laura**'s *shoulder.*

Alec   For everything – for having met you in the first place – for taking the piece of grit out of your eye – for loving you – for bringing you so much misery.

CUT TO

Scene 278

CLOSE UP of **Laura** *over* **Alec**'s *shoulder.*

Laura   (*trying to smile*) I'll forgive you – if you'll forgive me.

CUT TO

Scene 279

CLOSE UP of **Alec** *over* **Laura**'s *shoulder. There is the sound of* *the Guard's whistle and the train starts to move. The camera and* **Laura** *TRACK away from* **Alec** *as he stands staring after the train as it pulls out of the station.*

FADE OUT

Laura's voice   All that was a week ago – it is hardly credible that it should be so short a time.

FADE IN

Scene 280

EXT. HOSPITAL. DAY.

LONG SHOT of the hospital entrance from the opposite side of the road. **Laura** *is standing by a lamp post in the foreground of the picture. After a moment* **Alec** *comes down the hospital steps and joins her.*

Laura's voice   Today was our last day together. Our very last altogether in all our lives. I met him outside the hospital as I had promised at 12.30 – this morning – at 12.30 this morning – that was only this morning.

DISSOLVE

Scene 281

INT. CAR. DAY.

CLOSE SHOT, **Laura** *and* **Alec**.

Laura's voice   We drove into the country again, but this time he hired a car. I lit cigarettes for him every now and then as we went along. We didn't talk much – I felt numbed and hardly alive at all. We had lunch in a village pub.

DISSOLVE

Scene 282

EXT. COUNTRY BRIDGE. DAY. (LOCATION)

LONG SHOT. **Alec** *and* **Laura** *are leaning over the bridge. The car is parked near by.*

Laura's voice   Afterwards we went to the same bridge over the … stream – the bridge that we had been to before.

CUT TO

Scene 283

EXT. COUNTRY BRIDGE. DAY. (STUDIO)

CLOSE SHOT, **Laura** *and* **Alec** *as they lean over the bridge looking down into the water.* **Laura** *shivers.* **Alec** *puts his arm round her.*

Alec   Please know this – please know that you'll be with me for ages and ages yet – far away into the future. Time will wear down the agony of not seeing you, bit by bit the pain will go – but the loving you and the memory of you won't ever go – please know that.

Laura   I know it.

Alec   It's easier for me than for you. I do realise that, really I do. I at least will have different shapes to look at, and new work to do – you have to go on among familiar things – my heart aches for you so.

Laura   I'll be all right.

DISSOLVE

Scene 284

EXT. MILFORD JUNCTION STATION AND YARD. NIGHT. (STUDIO)

LONG SHOT. **Laura** *and* **Alec** *are crossing the Station Yard towards the booking hall.*

Laura's voice   Those last few hours together went by so quickly. We walked across the station yard in silence and went into the refreshment room.

DISSOLVE

Scene 285

INT. REFRESHMENT ROOM. NIGHT.

MEDIUM SHOT, **Albert** *and* **Myrtle** *at the counter.* (*This is exactly the same SET UP as Scene 9.*)

Albert   Hullo! – Hullo! – Hullo!

Myrtle   Quite a stranger, aren't you?

Albert   I couldn't get in yesterday.

Myrtle   (*bridling*) I wondered what had happened to you.

Albert   I 'ad a bit of a dust up.

Myrtle   (*preparing his tea*) What about?

Albert   Saw a chap getting out of a first class compartment.

The camera PANS off **Albert** *and* **Myrtle** *as it did in the first sequence, but this time it TRACKS in to a CLOSE SHOT of* **Alec** *and* **Laura** *at their table. The voices of* **Albert** *and* **Myrtle** *fade away to a murmur in the background.*

Alec   Are you all right, darling?

Laura   Yes, I'm all right.

Alec   I wish I could think of something to say.

Laura   It doesn't matter – not saying anything, I mean.

Alec   I'll miss my train and wait to see you into yours.

Laura   No – No – please don't. I'll come over to your platform with you – I'd rather.

Alec   Very well.

Laura   Do you think we shall ever see each other again?

Alec   I don't know. (*his voice breaks*) Not for years anyway.

Laura   The children will all be grown up – I wonder if they'll ever meet and know each other.

Alec   Couldn't I write to you – just once in a while?

Laura   No – please not – we promised we wouldn't.

Alec   Laura, dear, I do love you so very much. I love you with all my heart and soul.

Laura   (*without emotion*) I want to die – if only I could die.

Alec   If you died you'd forget me – I want to be remembered.

Laura   Yes, I know – I do too.

Alec   (*glancing at the clock*) We've still got a few minutes.

Dolly   (*off*) Laura! What a lovely surprise!

Laura   (*dazed*) Oh, Dolly.

Scene 286

CLOSE UP of **Laura** *to cover above scene.*

Scene 287

CLOSE UP of **Alec** *to cover above scene.*

CUT TO

Scene 288

MEDIUM SHOT, **Laura**, **Alec** and **Dolly**.

Dolly My dear! I've been shopping 'till I'm dropping. My feet are nearly falling off, and my throat's parched. I thought of having tea in Spindle's, but I was terrified of losing the train.

Laura's voice It was cruel of Fate to be against us right up to the last minute. Dolly Messiter – poor, well-meaning, irritating Dolly Messiter …

The camera is SLOWING TRACKING IN TO A V. CLOSE UP of **Laura**.

Dolly I'm always missing trains and being late for meals, and Bob gets disagreeable for days at a time. (*her voice is fading away*) He's been getting those dreadful headaches, you know. I've tried to make him see a Doctor but he won't. (*her voice fades out*)

Laura's voice … crashing into those few precious minutes we had together. She chattered and fussed, but I didn't hear what she said. I was dazed and bewildered. Alec behaved so beautifully – with such perfect politeness. Nobody could have guessed what he was really feeling – then the bell went for his train.

THE PLATFORM BELL RINGS.

CUT TO

Scene 289

MEDIUM SHOT, **Laura**, **Alec** *and* **Dolly**.

Laura There's your train.

Alec Yes, I know.

Dolly Aren't you coming with us?

Alec   No, I go in the opposite direction. My practice is in Churley.

Dolly   Oh, I see.

Alec   I'm a general practitioner at the moment.

Laura   (*dully*) Doctor Harvey is going out to Africa next week.

Dolly   Oh, how thrilling.

There is the sound of **Alec***'s train approaching.*

Alec   I must go.

Laura   Yes, you must.

Alec   Goodbye.

Dolly   Goodbye.

He shakes hands with Dolly and looks at **Laura** *swiftly once.*

CUT TO

Scene 290

CLOSE UP of **Laura***.* **Alec***'s hand comes into picture and gives her shoulder a little squeeze.*

Laura's voice   I felt the touch of his hand for a moment and then he walked away …

CUT TO

Scene 291

MEDIUM SHOT of **Alec** *from* **Laura***'s view-point, as he crosses the refreshment room and goes out of the door on to the platform.*

Laura's voice   … away – out of my life forever.

CUT TO

Scene 292

CLOSE SHOT, **Laura** *and* **Dolly**. **Laura** *is gazing out of the door through which* **Alec** *has just passed. She seems almost unaware of the chattering* **Dolly** *at her side, who proceeds to fumble in her handbag for lipstick and a mirror.* **Dolly** *is chattering, but we do not hear her voice. The camera starts to TRACK SLOWLY FORWARD into a CLOSE UP of* **Laura**.

Laura's voice   Dolly still went on talking, but I wasn't listening to her – I was listening for the sound of his train starting – then it did …

CUT TO

Scene 293

MEDIUM SHOT of the door on to the platform from **Laura**'s *eye-line. The sound of* **Alec**'s *train is heard as it starts to move out of the station.*

CUT TO

Scene 294

CLOSE UP of **Laura**.

Laura's voice   I said to myself – 'He didn't go – at the last minute his courage failed him – he couldn't have gone – at any moment now he'll come into the refreshment room again pretending that he'd forgotten something'. I prayed for him to do that – just so that I could see him once more – for an instant – but the minutes went by …

There is the sound of the Station Bell.

CUT TO

Scene 295

CLOSE SHOT of **Laura** *and* **Dolly**.

Dolly   Is that the train?

She addresses **Myrtle**.

Dolly   Can you tell me, is that the Ketchworth train?

Myrtle   (*off*) No, that's the express.

Laura   The boat train.

Dolly   Oh yes – that doesn't stop, does it?

She gets up and moves out of picture towards the counter.

CUT TO

Scene 296

CLOSE UP of **Laura**.

The echo of Dolly's voice   Yes – that doesn't stop, does it? ... It doesn't stop, does it?

The echo of Myrtle's voice   That's the express ...

The echo of Dolly's voice   It doesn't stop ... It doesn't stop ...

The echo of Myrtle's voice   That's the EXPRESS ...

Laura's voice   ... It Doesn't stop ... Doesn't STOP ... DOESN'T STOP ... DOESN'T STOP ... DOESN'T STOP ...

The words begin to merge into the roar of the approaching express.

Laura's voice   ... DOESN'T STOP. DOESN'T STOP. DOESN'T STOP. DOESN'T STOP.

Laura *jumps to her feet and the camera PANS with her as she rushes blindly out of the door, leading to platform Number 2.*

(*As the camera PANS to the door it goes off level giving the effect of* **Laura** *running uphill.*)

CUT TO

Scene 297

EXT. MILFORD JUNCTION STATION. NIGHT. (STUDIO … CAMERA TILTED)

Scene 297

MEDIUM SHOT of **Laura** *as she runs out of the refreshment room towards the camera and the railway lines.*

CUT TO

Scene 298

EXT. MILFORD JUNCTION STATION. NIGHT. (LOCATION … CAMERA TILTED)

MEDIUM SHOT of the railway lines from above. The express hurtles through the picture.

CUT TO

Scene 299

EXT. MILFORD JUNCTION STATION. NIGHT. (STUDIO … CAMERA TILTED)

CLOSE UP of **Laura** *from a low angle. She is swaying on the edge of the platform. The lights from the express streak past her face. The noise is deafening. She stands quite still. The lights stop flashing across her face and the sound of the train dies away* *rapidly. SLOWLY THE CAMERA RETURNS TO A NORMAL ANGLE.*

Laura's voice   I meant to do it, Fred, I really meant to do it. I stood there trembling – right on the edge – but then, just in time I stepped back – I couldn't – I wasn't brave enough – I should like to be able to say that it was the thought of you and the children that prevented me – but it wasn't – I had no thoughts at all – only an overwhelming desire not to be unhappy any more – not to feel anything ever again. I turned and went back into the refreshment room – that's when I nearly fainted …

DISSOLVE

Scene 300

INT. LIBRARY. NIGHT. LAURA'S HOUSE.

CLOSE UP of **Laura***, who is sitting with her sewing in her lap – she is staring straight in front of her.*

CUT TO

Scene 301

CLOSE UP of **Fred***, who is looking at her. He continues to look at her in silence for a moment or two.*

Fred   (*gently*) Laura.

She doesn't answer. He gets up.

CUT TO

Scene 302

CLOSE SHOT of **Laura***.* **Fred** *enters picture and kneels beside her and softly touches her hand.*

Fred   Laura …

Laura   (*turning her head slowly and looking at him – her voice sounds dead*) Yes, dear?

Fred   Whatever your dream was – it wasn't a very happy one, was it?

Laura   (*in a whisper*) No.

Fred   Is there anything I can help with?

Laura   Yes, my dear – you always help …

Fred   You've been a long way away?

Laura   (*nodding – her eyes fill with tears*) Yes, Fred.

Fred *moves a little closer to her and quietly rests his face against her hand.*

Fred   (*with a catch in his voice*) Thank you for coming back to me.

FADE OUT

THE END

The Astonished Heart

Introduction to *The Astonished Heart*

Noël had great success on both the West End and Broadway stages in 1936 with *Tonight at 8.30* – a sequence of nine one act plays in which he and Gertrude Lawrence played all the leads.

He had mixed results with the films that were subsequently made of the individual plays.

Encouraged by the success they'd enjoyed with *Private Lives* in 1931, MGM filmed *We Were Dancing* in 1942, which was described publicly as 'based in part on a play by Noël Coward'. The best the *New York Times* could say was that 'it does have a brittle quality characteristic of his work'.

They might well have noted that whereas *Private Lives* had been personally supervised by the formidable Irving Thalberg, this outing was produced and directed by the more mundane talent of Robert Z. Leonard. Thalberg had died without seeing *Tonight at 8.30*.

His widow, Norma Shearer, died in a professional sense. Offered the lead in *Mrs. Miniver* – for which Greer Garson was to win the Oscar – she turned it down in favour of *We Were Dancing*, obviously anticipating a repetition of the success she had enjoyed as Amanda in *Private Lives*. But whereas she had had Coward dialogue to deliver then, now she had only Hollywood pastiche Coward, which it apparently took three scriptwriters to concoct.

The results so disenchanted the studio that somewhere along the line they sold the remaining rights in *Tonight at 8.30* to British producer, Sidney Box, who over the next few years proceeded to sell the individual plays off on an ad hoc basis.

***

The next one to be filmed in 1945 was *Still Life*, which – as *Brief Encounter* – became and has remained one of the screen's enduring love stories. But then, it did have the considerable talents of David Lean to direct what Noël himself had written in the screenplay.

***

In 1952 came *Meet Me Tonight*, which Noël adapted from three more of his *Tonight at 8.30* plays. *Red Peppers* ('An Interlude with

Music'), *Fumed Oak* ('An Unpleasant Comedy in Two Scenes') and
Ways and Means ('A Comedy in Three Scenes').

In prospect the idea seemed to make sense. British 'anthology'
films made under the imprimatur of J. Arthur Rank had enjoyed
considerable commercial success in the early 1950s, particularly
Quartet (1948), *Trio* (1950) and *Encore* (1951), all based on short
stories by Somerset Maugham.

By 1952 perhaps the vogue was over anyway. In any case, *Meet Me
Tonight* was apathetically received – except by Noël, who confided to
his *Diary* – 'Absolutely awful – vilely directed and, with one or two
minor exceptions, abominably acted. Came home and rested'.

In retrospect he may have remembered his own earlier verdict
on the *Tonight at 8.30* canon – 'The whole point of *Red Peppers*
is to spend an evening seeing Noël Coward and Gertie Lawrence
not playing Noël Coward and Gertie Lawrence, that is the fun. The
moment you do one of these little plays for real, they don't exist'.

***

He would prove that with the 1950 *The Astonished Heart*.

It was the third and last time Noël played a leading role on film
– and it was a happenstance.

Michael Redgrave was cast as the psychiatrist, Christian Faber,
and shooting was under way in June 1949. Noël went to see the
rushes and was not happy with what he saw.

Since Redgrave was an old friend, he agonized about what he
should do. Finally, he decided that he would play the part himself
and talked to Redgrave, who was only too glad to agree. He had
found the role uncomfortable. 'He behaved really truly superbly,
and I will always respect him for it', Noël recorded in his *Diary*.

Having created and played the character, Noël knew Faber well
and – as was his habit – had written a character description – 'about
40 years old, tall and thin. He moves quickly and decisively, as
though there was never enough time for what he had to do'.

He was more than happy with the two women he would play
opposite.

The elegant, somewhat neurotic Margaret Leighton would make
a perfect Leonora. He would play with her again in the West End a
little later in Shaw's *The Apple Cart*. Leonora was 'a lovely creature

of about 30, exquisitely dressed and with great charm of manner.' Celia Johnson was an obvious choice as Christian's wife, Barbara. She had already appeared in three Coward films – *In Which We Serve*, *This Happy Breed* and her role as Laura in *Brief Encounter* had won her an Oscar nomination. Barbara was 'a tranquil, intelligent woman of about 36'.

When asked to define the difference between his two leading ladies, Noël replied – 'Margaret is so *chic*. Celia is so – *understanding*! The only thing that keeps Celia from becoming the greatest actress of her time is her monotonous habit of having babies'. The whole enterprise was something of a 'family' affair.

Joyce Carey plays his secretary, Susan. She would play Coward on stage and screen. Bernard Miles's wife, Kath, in *In Which We Serve*, Mrs. Bradman in *Blithe Spirit* ... Myrtle Bagot, the genteel proprietress of the station buffet in *Brief Encounter*. Susan was, somewhere between thirty and forty ... plainly and efficiently dressed as befits a secretary,.

Tim Verney, Christian's assistant, was his life companion, Graham Payn. ('A nice looking man in his early thirties'.)

In retrospect, it can be seen that there were three problems. Material that may work in the theatrical atmosphere of the stage as a brief one set play can often appear overly melodramatic on the big cinema screen. Perhaps David Lean – who knew Noël's work so well – could have found a way to make the material work. But there was the second problem. David Lean didn't direct it. He'd moved from Coward to Dickens.

The film was co-directed by Terence Fisher and Anthony Darnborough and they were definitely not in the Lean league.

The third problem was that Noël did not make a convincing Christian Faber. There was a sense of camaraderie in the scenes with Joyce, Graham and Celia but the sense of a tortured affair with Margaret Leighton was just not there. Tortured, yes, but mainly because credibility was absent. The critics were lukewarm at best.

Towards the end of his life Noël would often refer to 'Poor old *Astonished Heart*. I should love to see it again, just to find out if it is really as bad as they said it was'. But he never did. Although he would undoubtedly have enjoyed the satisfaction of seeing it become a minor 'cult' film. In historical context it happened to come at a time when Coward was out of favour in England with the critics. 'Dad's Renaissance' as he called it, was some years ahead. But, as so often, Noël had a way of getting the last word.

In a late short story, *Star Quality*, two of the characters go to the cinema, where they see 'an exquisitely acted but rather tedious picture about a psychiatrist who commits suicide'.

The film was produced by Gainsborough Pictures in 1949/50 and was first shown at the Odeon, Leicester Square, in March 1950.

Credits

Producer	Anthony Darnborough
Directors	Terence Fisher and
	Anthony Darnborough
Screenplay	Noël Coward
Photography	Jack Asher
Editor	V. Sagovsky
Artistic Supervisor for Mr Coward	Gladys Calthrop
Music	Noël Coward

Cast

Christian Faber	Noël Coward
Barbara Faber	Celia Johnson
Leonora Vail	Margaret Leighton
Susan Birch	Joyce Carey
Tim Verney	Graham Payn
Alice Smith	Amy Veness
Philip Lucas	Ralph Michael
Ernest	Michael Hordern
Helen	Patricia Glyn
Sir Reginald	Alan Webb
Miss Harper	Everley Gregg
Soames	John Salew
Waiter	Gerald Anderson
Barman	John Warren

Mary Ellis made a short anonymous appearance as a patient of Faber's.

FADE IN

TITLES AND OPENING SHOT. EARLY MORNING.

*LONG SHOT of CHESTER HOUSE. It is on the right of screen
and the park is in the background. An expensive car stands outside
the doorway – if possible no other traffic.*

DISSOLVE TO

Scene 1

INT. FABERS' FLAT. HALL. DAY.

The door at the far end of the hall opens and **Barbara** *comes
out. She closes the door quietly behind her and hurries along
the hall and into the drawing room. She is dressed and looks
strained and tired, as though she has been up all night – as indeed
she has.*

Scene 2

INT. DRAWING ROOM. FABERS' FLAT. DAY.

Barbara *goes to the telephone and dials a number. She waits,
drumming her fingers nervously on the table, until the call is
answered. Then...*

Barbara   Could I speak to Mrs. Vail, please? (*pause*)
Mrs. Faber ...

Scene 3

INT. HALL OF LEONORA'S HOUSE. DAY.

A rather superior maidservant (**Helen**) *is answering the
telephone.*

Helen   Mrs. Vail's still asleep, madam. (*pause*) I don't like to disturb her, madam. She's never called before nine o'clock. Shall I ask her to ring you back?

Scene 4

INT. DRAWING ROOM. FABERS' FLAT. DAY.

Barbara *at the telephone.*

Barbara   But I tell you – this is urgent. I'll take the responsibility. (*pause*) You can tell Mrs. Vail it's a matter of life and death. Now please hurry and call her …

Scene 5

INT. HALL OF LEONORA'S HOUSE. DAY.

Helen *at the telephone.*

Helen   Very well, madam. If you'll just hold the line …

She puts down the receiver and goes upstairs.

Scene 6

INT. DRAWING ROOM. FABERS' FLAT. DAY.

Barbara *takes a cigarette from the box on the table. Her hand trembles a little as she lights it. Then she picks up the telephone again quickly as she hears the crackle of a voice at the other end.*

Barbara   Leonora? I'm sorry to disturb you like this, but something's happened. Chris –

Scene 7

INT. BEDROOM. LEONORA'S HOUSE. DAY.

Leonora *is in bed, with the telephone in her hand. As she hears Chris's name mentioned, she breaks in, wearily –*

Leonora   I don't want to talk about this, Barbara – please! (*pause*) Oh, very well. What is it? (*pause*)

Leonora *suddenly sits bolt upright and her expression changes completely.*

Leonora   No! Oh, my dear! (*pause*) Of course I'll come – if you want me to … it'll take me half an hour, I'm afraid. (*pause*) All right. I'll be as quick as I can.

She replaces the receiver, throws back the clothes and gets out of bed. Slipping her feet into the slippers which are waiting at the bedside, she runs across to the door, opens it and calls –

Leonora   Helen! I've got to go out at once. Ring for a taxi, will you?

Scene 8

INT. DRAWING ROOM AND HALL. FABERS' FLAT. DAY.

Barbara *stubs out her cigarette and goes into the hall. She crosses to the consulting room suite. This consists of three rooms – an office in which* **Susan** *and* **Tim** *work, with a waiting room on one side of it and* **Christian Faber***'s consulting room on the other.* **Barbara** *goes into the office.*

Scene 9

INT. OFFICE. FABERS' FLAT. DAY.

Barbara *crosses the office towards the consulting room.*

Scene 10

INT. CONSULTING ROOM. FABERS' FLAT. DAY.

As **Barbara** *comes in,* **Ernest** *is drawing the curtains. He turns and says –*

Ernest   Good morning, madam.

Barbara   Good morning, Ernest.

Ernest   Is there any – news?

Barbara   Not yet.

She opens **Christian***'s engagement book and starts to flick through the pages.*

Scene 11

INT. CONSULTING ROOM. FABERS' FLAT. DAY.

Engagement book. **Barbara***'s hand turns the pages. Under the date, March 10th, written in* **Chris***'s hand are the words 'Lecture. Birmingham. Meet* **Tim** *9.30 Paddington'. The rest of the day is crossed through in pencil.* **Barbara** *puts down the book and reaches for the telephone. As she does so, we ...*

CUT TO

Scene 12

EXT. CHESTER HOUSE. DAY.

A taxi draws up and **Susan Birch** *gets out. She pays her fare and hurries into the building.*

Scene 13

INT. FOYER. CHESTER HOUSE. DAY.

Susan *half runs towards the lift, passing the* **hall porter**.

Porter   Morning, miss.

She doesn't answer. She savagely presses the lift bell several times. When the lift arrives, she is through the gates like a flash. The lift quickly ascends.

Scene 14

INT. LIFT. DAY.

Susan *in lift.*

Scene 15

INT. CORRIDOR. CHESTER HOUSE. DAY.

Susan *comes out of the lift on the top floor and hurries to the Fabers' front door. She opens it with a key and goes inside.*

Scene 16

INT. HALL. FABERS' FLAT. DAY.

Susan *closes the front door and crosses to the drawing room. As she does so,* **Ernest** *comes out of the office.*

Ernest   She's not in there, Miss Birch.

Susan   (*turning quickly*) Oh? Where then?

Ernest   In the consulting room. She's terribly upset, miss. We all are.

Susan   Yes. Of course.

She goes into the office.

Scene 17

INT. OFFICE. FABERS' FLAT. DAY.

Susan *starts to pull off her coat and gloves. As she does so,* **Barbara** *comes to the consulting room door.*

Barbara   Susan. Don't take your things off just yet, please.

Susan   (*turning swiftly*) Oh! My dear! (*she comes over to her*) I came as quickly as I could.

Barbara   Yes. I didn't expect you so soon.

Susan   Is there anything I can do?

Barbara   You could help me by going to Paddington.

Susan   Paddington?

Barbara   I've just been looking at Chris's appointments. He was due to meet Tim there at nine-thirty. That lecture in Birmingham.

Susan   I'll telephone and put him off.

Scene 18

INT. OFFICE. FABERS' FLAT. DAY.

Barbara *and* **Susan** *walk towards the door.*

Barbara   I've tried that. He'd just left for the station.

Susan   All right. Leave it to me … How is he?

This as they pass out into the hall together.

Scene 19

INT. HALL. FABERS' FLAT. DAY.

They walk to the front door.

Barbara   Just the same.

Susan   I've been feeling numb inside ever since you telephoned … does *she* know?

Barbara   I talked to her a few minutes ago.

She opens the front door, and stands there while **Susan** *rings for the lift.*

Scene 20

INT. CORRIDOR. CHESTER HOUSE. DAY.

This is played while **Susan** *is waiting for the lift.*

Susan   (*bitterly*) I hope she's satisfied.

Barbara   It's awful for her too, you know.

Susan   She'll get over it.

Barbara   So shall we, I expect – in time.

Susan   It doesn't matter to her, not really, not like it matters to me. She'll cry a lot and be beautifully heartbroken.

Barbara   Don't be unkind.

Susan   I hate her.

Barbara   Oh, don't Susan! Looking back on it all now, I believe it's as much my fault as hers – and what's the use of hating her?

Susan   I don't care whether it's any use or not – I hate her more than I've ever hated anyone in my whole life.

Barbara   You might as well hate a piece of notepaper because someone's written something cruel on it.

Before **Susan** *can reply, the lift arrives. She hurries inside after pressing* **Barbara**'*s arm comfortingly.*

Susan   I'll be back as quickly as I can.

Scene 21

INT. CORRIDOR. CHESTER HOUSE. DAY.

CLOSE UP of **Barbara**, *covering scene 20.*

Scene 22

INT. CORRIDOR. CHESTER HOUSE. DAY.

CLOSE UP of **Susan** – *covering scene 20 – at the end, the CAMERA TRACKS BACK as she enters lift and* **Barbara** *turns to go back to the flat.*

Scene 23

INT. HALL. FABERS' FLAT. DAY.

Barbara *makes her way back along the hall. As she does so, the bedroom door opens and* **Sir Reginald** *comes out.*

Sir Reginald   You sent for her?

Barbara   Yes. She's coming.

Sir Reginald   Good.

Barbara   How much time is there?

Sir Reginald   It's hard to say. It may be an hour – perhaps two.

Barbara   Is he conscious?

Sir Reginald   Only for a brief moment, every now and then.

Barbara   And he still asks for her? In those brief moments?

Sir Reginald   Yes.

Barbara   I'll send her straight in when she comes.

Sir Reginald   Do, my dear. Meanwhile I suggest you have some brandy and rest for a bit.

Barbara   I can't rest.

Sir Reginald   Then take the brandy – it'll make the waiting easier.

Barbara   Nothing could do that.

She turns away as he goes back into the bedroom.

Scene 24

INT. HALL. FABERS' FLAT. DAY.

CLOSE SHOT of **Barbara**, *covering scene 23.*

Scene 25

INT. HALL. FABERS' FLAT. DAY.

CLOSE SHOT of SIR REGINALD, covering scene 23.

DISSOLVE TO

Scene 26

EXT. PADDINGTON STATION. DAY.

Susan *gets out of a taxi outside the station.*

Scene 27

EXT. PADDINGTON STATION. DAY.

Susan *makes her way into the station, pushing through crowds, looking towards the barrier.*

Scene 28

EXT. PADDINGTON STATION. DAY

Tim *is waiting at the barrier,* **Susan** *walks to him.*

Scene 29

EXT. PADDINGTON STATION. DAY.

Susan *reaches* **Tim**.

Susan   Tim!

Tim   (*surprised*) Oh, hello, Susan! What's up?

Susan   Barbara sent me.

Tim   Where's Chris? Isn't he coming?

Susan   No

Tim   Why not?

Susan   He can't.

Tim   (*seeing her agitated expression*) What's happened?

Susan   He's –

As she starts to tell him, a train begins to let off steam and drowns any further dialogue. We cannot hear what they are saying, but the look on **Tim**'*s face is that of blank misery.*

Scene 30

EXT. PADDINGTON STATION. DAY.

CLOSE SHOT of **Susan**, *covering scene 29.*

Scene 31

EXT. PADDINGTON STATION. DAY

CLOSE SHOT of **Tim**, *covering scene 29.*

DISSOLVE TO

Scene 32

EXT. WINDOWS OF DRAWING ROOM. FABERS' FLAT. DAY.

Barbara *is looking through the window at the rain.*

Scene 33

INT. DRAWING ROOM. FABERS' FLAT. DAY.

Susan *is sitting on the edge of a chair not far from the door, while* **Tim** *is at the fireplace, smoking a cigarette.* **Barbara** *stands at the window looking out. It has begun to rain heavily and the sound of it driving against the panes seems unnaturally loud in the still room. There is an air of strain, as though any of them might cry out at any moment. The silence is broken by* **Barbara**.

Barbara   It's raining quite hard now. But it's only what one expects at this time of the year, isn't it?

Tim   Yes.

Barbara   The traffic seems slower than usual – I expect that's my imagination.

Tim   Don't you think you'd better come away from the window now?

Barbara   (*turning to speak to them*) Don't worry. I'm all right.

Susan   She answered the telephone herself, didn't she?

Barbara   Yes.

Susan   She ought to be here by now.

Barbara   Yes – yes, she ought.

Susan *glances desperately at* **Tim**, *then rises and makes for the door.* **Barbara** *turns and looks at her.*

Barbara   What is it?

Susan   I thought perhaps I'd better go into the office.

Barbara   No don't. Stay with us.

Susan   It's no use – I shall only cry and make a fool of myself.

Barbara   I'd rather you cried here with us than all by yourself in there.

Susan   (*dabbing her eyes*) I'm all right now.

Barbara   Don't make too much of an effort – I'd cry if I could –

She turns back to the window again, staring out with unseeing eyes.

Scene 34

INT. DRAWING ROOM. FABERS' FLAT. DAY.

CLOSE SHOT of **Barbara**, *covering scene 33.*

Scene 35

INT. DRAWING ROOM. FABERS' FLAT. DAY.

MEDIUM CLOSE SHOT of **Susan** *when she looks at* **Tim** *in scene 33.*

Scene 36

INT. DRAWING ROOM. FABERS' FLAT. DAY.

VERY CLOSE SHOT of **Susan** *when she looks at* **Tim** *in scene 33.*

Scene 37

INT. DRAWING ROOM. FABERS' FLAT. DAY.

MEDIUM CLOSE SHOT of **Tim** *when he looks at* **Susan** *in scene 33.*

Scene 38

INT. DRAWING ROOM. FABERS' FLAT. DAY.

VERY CLOSE SHOT of **Tim** *when he looks at* **Susan** *in scene 33.*

Scene 39

INT. DRAWING ROOM. FABERS' FLAT. DAY.

CLOSE SHOT of **Barbara**.

Barbara   … tears are a little relief. They let the grief out for a minute or two. I envy them.

Tim   You won't be able to see her from there, you know.

Barbara   (*suddenly*) How extraordinary!

Tim   What?

Barbara   I've just remembered. It was exactly like this the day I met her again and it's exactly a year ago. I was standing looking out of the window at the rain – only it wasn't this window. It was Darlington's in Fulham Road …

As she says these last six words, we …

DISSOLVE TO

Scene 40

INT. DARLINGTON'S ANTIQUE SHOP. DAY.

Barbara *is standing inside the shop and looking out of the window at the rain. The set-up is so contrived that her position is exactly similar to that at the end of the previous scene. The only difference is that* **Barbara** *now wears outdoor clothes.*

Barbara's *voice continues through the DISSOLVE, and as narrative behind the opening of this scene.*

Barbara's voice   ... I'd been doing some shopping and I was waiting for my change and staring out of the window at the rain, when suddenly – there was Leonora?

As **Barbara**'s *voice says these words, outside the window appears a woman, carrying an open umbrella. It is blowing hard and she is having some difficulty holding it. When she gets to the shelter of Darlington's shop-blind, she decides to give up the struggle and lets down her umbrella. The action of doing this brings her face to face with* **Barbara**, *only the window separating them.* **Barbara** *taps on the window and says ...*

Barbara   Leonora!

Leonora *looks up and says something which we cannot hear.* **Barbara** *crosses to the door, opens it and says ...*

Barbara   It *is* Leonora Amos, isn't it?

Leonora   Barbara! Barbara Forbes! Don't believe it ... after all these years!

Barbara   Do come in out of that awful rain.

Leonora   My dear, I daren't. Once I get inside one of these places, I buy everything.

Barbara   Then let's have some tea somewhere, shall we? At least we can sit down.

Leonora   Yes, let's ... I'd like that.

Barbara   There's a little place just here ... (*she pauses as the shop assistant appears and give her some change*) ... Thank you. You'll send them this week, won't you? (*to* **Leonora**) We'll have to make a dash for it. Ready?

They both open their umbrellas and hurry off down the road, into the café.

Scene 41

INT. CAFÉ. DAY.

Barbara *and* **Leonora** *discard their dripping umbrellas and seat themselves at one of the little tables.*

Leonora   Ah. That's better.

She catches **Barbara***'s appraising glance across the table, and laughs.*

Leonora   I know what you're thinking!

Barbara   I can't possibly say you haven't changed more thoroughly than anyone I have ever seen.

Leonora   It might be not wearing those school hats.

Barbara   Those hats!

A **waitress** *comes to their table.*

Barbara   Tea, please.

Waitress   Anything to eat?

Leonora   Not for me. I really daren't.

Barbara   Just some biscuits, please.

Waitress   No biscuits, madam.

Barbara   Just the tea, then.

Waitress   Yes madam.

She goes.

Leonora   Dear Barbara, how pleasant this is. How long ago is it?

Barbara   Seventeen – no, eighteen years. I'm thirty-four now. I left school long before you did –

Leonora   I remember missing you dreadfully.

Barbara   (*lighting her cigarette*) You went to America, didn't you?

Leonora   Yes. Father left Brazil in nineteen-thirty and soon after, we went to Washington.

Barbara   I heard you were married.

Leonora   Oh, did you? That was much later.

The **waitress** *brings the tea.*

Barbara   (*to* **waitress**) Thank you.

Leonora   (*watching her pour out the tea*) You do that with tremendous authority. I always lose my head and put in the milk first or afterwards or whatever I oughtn't to do. Which should it be?

Barbara   There are several schools of thought – personally I always leave it to the inspiration of the moment.

Leonora   On the other hand, I have no indecision at all with Dry Martinis.

Barbara   You were dreadfully sophisticated at school. Myrtle Reed said you were fast and would come to a bad end.

Leonora   She was the large spotty one wasn't she? – with the over developed kneecaps?

Barbara   (*reprovingly*) She was Captain of the hockey team, dear, and we were very, very proud of her.

Leonora   What's your name now?

Barbara   Faber. Mrs. Christian Faber.

Leonora   What does your husband do?

Barbara   He's only one of the most famous psychiatrists in the world, dear.

Leonora   How impressive. Is he terribly old?

Barbara   Terribly. What's your name?

Leonora   Vail.

Barbara   Leonora Vail – very euphonious. What does <u>your</u> husband do?

Leonora   Drinks like a fish.

Barbara   Oh dear!

Leonora   I haven't seen him for years – I'll tell you the whole sordid story another time – this atmosphere's too genteel – I shouldn't be able to let myself go. I've just taken a sweet little house – you must come and see it.

Barbara   I should love to.

Leonora   And your husband, of course.

Barbara   I'm sure he'd like to, but it all depends. You can never count on him. His work comes first, you see.

Leonora   I should be jealous, I think.

Barbara   Jealous?

Leonora   But you're better balanced than I am – less emotional – you always were.

Barbara   It would be tiresome to go on being emotional after twelve years of marriage.

Leonora   Yes, I suppose so. I'm longing to see him.

Barbara   Why not come tomorrow?

Leonora *takes out an address book from her handbag and opens it.*

Leonora   All right. Where?

Barbara   Seventeen, Chester House. It's that big block by the park. You can't mistake it …

Leonora *writes this down in her book.*

Scene 42

INT. CAFÉ. DAY.

CLOSE SHOT of **Barbara**, *covering scene 41.*

Scene 43

INT. CAFÉ. DAY.

VERY CLOSE SHOT of **Barbara**, *covering scene 41.*

Scene 44

INT. CAFÉ. DAY.

CLOSE SHOT OF **Leonora**, *covering scene 41.*

Scene 45

INT. CAFÉ. DAY.

VERY CLOSE SHOT of **Leonora**, *covering scene 41.*

FADE OUT.

FADE IN.

Scene 46

EXT. CHESTER HOUSE. DAY.

Leonora*'s taxi draws up and she gets out, making her way into the building.*

Scene 47

INT. DRAWING ROOM. FABERS' FLAT. DAY.

Ernest *has just finished mixing some cocktails and is about to leave the room when* **Barbara** *takes the cigarette box and finds that it is almost empty.*

Barbara   We'll want some more cigarettes, Ernest. This is nearly empty.

She puts the box down.

Ernest   Very good, madam.

He moves towards the hall as **Susan Birch** *comes in, papers in hand.*

Barbara   When Mrs. Vail arrives – I'm expecting her.

Ernest   Yes, Madam.

He goes out.

Barbara   (*to* **Susan**) Is Chris coming?

Susan   Unlikely. He's got Soames in there.

Barbara   Soames?

Susan   The very depressed one that goes on for hours – anxiety complex and mother fixation and a disgruntled wife.

Barbara   I should think she has every reason to be disgruntled.

There is a ring at the bell. **Susan** *looks at* **Barbara**.

Susan   May I stay?

Barbara   Of course (*smiling*).

Tim *enters.*

Barbara   Now, what do *you* want?

Tim   A drink.

Scene 48

INT. HALL. FABERS' FLAT. DAY.

Ernest *is opening the door to* **Leonora**.

Leonora   Mrs. Faber? Mrs. Vail.

Ernest   Will you come in, madam?

Leonora   Thank you.

Ernest *enters the lounge, leaving* **Leonora** *glancing around.*

Scene 29

INT. DRAWING ROOM. FABERS' FLAT. DAY.

Barbara *goes towards* **Leonora**, *while* **Tim** *takes a drink. He and* **Susan** *look at this exquisitely dressed visitor with some interest.*

Leonora   My dear (*she and* **Barbara** *kiss*) isn't that lift rather bad for your husband's patients? It shoots up like a rocket.

Barbara   We have the more serious cases carried up the stairs on stretcher. This is Susan Birch – Chris's right hand.

Leonora *shakes hands with* **Susan**.

Barbara   And this is Tim Verney, Chris's left hand – or perhaps it's the other way round – settle it among yourselves – Leonora Vail – Amos that was.

Leonora *shakes hands with* **Tim**.

Leonora   Leonora Amos, terrible at games! Do you remember?

Barbara *and* **Leonora** *sit down.*

Barbara   Of course I do.

Leonora   I think Barbara wrote that beastly little rhyme herself.

Tim   (*moving to table and smiling*) Was it true?

Leonora   Absolutely.

Tim   How about a cocktail?

Leonora   Please.

He brings two drinks. **Leonora** *takes hers and holds it up towards* **Barbara**.

Scene 50

INT. FABERS' FLAT. DRAWING ROOM. DAY.

MEDIUM LONG SHOT of **Tim** *at the fireplace.*

Leonora   The nastiest girl in the school.

Barbara   (*laughing*) But the best King Lear.

Leonora   (*also laughing*) Oh, of course, I'd forgotten that.

Scene 51

INT. DRAWING ROOM. FABERS' FLAT. DAY.

CLOSE SHOT of **Susan**.

Susan   I foresee a flood of reminiscence.

Scene 52

INT. DRAWING ROOM. FABERS' FLAT. DAY.

REVERSE SHOT of scene 50.

Tim   So do I – come along, Susan, we'd better go.

Barbara   No, don't go – you can bear it, Tim, you'll probably discover a lot of useful little psychological echoes from my childhood.

Scene 53

INT. DRAWING ROOM. FABERS' FLAT. DAY.

MEDIUM CLOSE SHOT of **Susan**.

Susan   (*rising*) I must go anyhow – all these have to be dealt with.

The camera PANS RIGHT with her to group.

Tim   And I'll have to see if Chris wants rescuing from Soames.

Susan   (*glancing at her watch*) Yes, his time's nearly up.

She starts to walk towards the door and **Tim** *moves behind the couch.*

Leonora   (*to* **Barbara**) Does he work all day long, your husband?

Barbara   Yes, most of the night as well, sometimes.

Leonora   What's he like?

Barbara   Horrible.

Leonora   I sympathise. Mine was an absolute darling. So much so that I divorced him after eighteen months –

Scene 54

INT. DRAWING ROOM. FABERS' FLAT. DAY.

CLOSE SHOT of **Susan** *at the door.*

Susan   Goodbye, Mrs. Vail.

Scene 55

INT. DRAWING ROOM. FABERS' FLAT. DAY.

MEDIUM CLOSE SHOT – **Leonora**, **Barbara** *and* **Tim**.

Leonora   Goodbye.

Susan *disappears into the hall.*

Tim   Goodbye. We shall probably meet again very soon.

Leonora   I hope so.

Barbara   Ask Chris to come in for a second if he can when he's got rid of his patient.

Tim   All right.

Tim *goes out.*

Leonora   What a nice man.

Barbara   Tim's a dear (*offering her a cigarette*) … he's extremely brilliant too. Chris thinks the world of him.

Leonora   I have a feeling I shall be a little frightened of Chris.

Barbara   (*lighting a cigarette*) Oh no, he's not in the least frightening – he gets a bit abstracted every now and then – when he's working too hard.

Leonora   I see.

Barbara   And yours – was he really such a – a darling?

Leonora   Oh, it was all horrid. He was much older than me, very rich – fortunately – that's all there was to it, really.

Barbara   And you never wanted to marry again?

Leonora   I wanted to once, but it wasn't possible. Everything went wrong –

Barbara   I'm so sorry.

Leonora   I minded horribly at the time, but I travelled a bit and got over it. It's a long while ago, anyhow.

Barbara   (*holding up her glass*) Another cocktail?

Leonora   Please.

Barbara *gets the shaker and refills their glasses.*

Leonora   What does your husband do exactly? (*laughing*) I know that you told me he was a psychiatrist – but is he one of the kind that 'sublimates' – or one of the kind that 'determines'?

Barbara   I've absolutely *no* idea! Chris just says he's a plain, straightforward alienist.

Leonora   Alienist! What a funny word! I always thought that an alienist was some kind of immigration official.

Barbara   You'd better not mention that to Chris. He once had a most dreadful scene with an immigration official.

They laugh again.

Scene 56

INT. DRAWING ROOM. FABERS' FLAT. DAY.

MEDIUM CLOSE SHOT of **Leonora**. (*Before* **Barbara** *rises to re-fill their glasses in scene 55*)

Scene 57

INT. DRAWING ROOM. FABERS' FLAT. DAY.

MEDIUM CLOSE SHOT of **Barbara**. (*Before she rises to re-fill their glasses in scene 55*)

Scene 58

INT. DRAWING ROOM. FABERS' FLAT. DAY.

MEDIUM CLOSE SHOT of **Leonora**. (*After* **Barbara** *sits down again in scene 55.*)

Scene 59

INT. DRAWING ROOM. FABERS' FLAT. DAY.

MEDIUM CLOSE SHOT of **Barbara**. (*After she sits down again in scene 55.*)

Scene 60

INT. OFFICE. FABERS' FLAT. DAY.

Susan *is just talking to one of the patients –* **Mr Soames**. *She makes a note in her diary, as she says –*

Susan   Next Thursday then. Goodbye Mr. Soames.

Ernest *appears in the doorway and ushers* **Soames** *out.* **Susan** *crosses to the waiting room and calls into it –*

Susan   Miss Harper, please.

Scene 61

INT. OFFICE. FABERS' FLAT. DAY.

A woman of uncertain age comes from the waiting room and **Susan** *ushers her into the consulting room. As she announces her,* **Tim** *comes from the consulting room. He has some notes in his hand. As the door closes, we hear –*

Miss Harper   Good afternoon, Dr. Faber.

Susan   Isn't she lovely?

Tim   Who? Miss Harper?

Susan   No, don't be so silly, Mrs. Vail.

Tim   Very smooth and shiny.

Susan   Didn't you like her?

Tim   Yes, I suppose so, I only saw her for a moment.

Susan   I thought she looked you over fairly thoroughly.

Tim   Rubbish!

Susan   It's all right. I'm here to protect you.

Tim   (*now sitting at his desk*) Thanks.

He starts working at his notes.

Scene 62

INT. HALL. FABERS' FLAT. DAY.

Barbara *is about to take* **Leonora** *on a tour of the flat. As they come from the drawing room and walk towards the bedroom ...*

Leonora   I suppose he'd know all about me in a minute, wouldn't he? The very first second he clapped eyes on me?

Barbara   Certainly.

Leonora   How terrifying.

Barbara   Don't pretend! I'm perfectly sure you're not terrified of anyone.

Leonora   Do his patients fall in love with him?

Barbara   Practically always.

Leonora   Don't you hate that?

Barbara   You are funny, Leonora.

Leonora   Am I? Nicely funny, or nastily funny?

Barbara   Certainly funny.

She leads the way into the bedroom and **Leonora** *follows her. As they come inside,* **Leonora** *exclaims ...*

Leonora   How very nice – except for one thing.

Barbara   What's that?

Leonora   No photograph of Chris.

She goes over to the dressing table, sits down and begins to powder her nose.

Barbara   Do you mind?

Scene 63

INT. BEDROOM. FABERS' FLAT. DAY.

Leonora *is seated at the dressing table, with* **Barbara** *standing.*

Leonora   Of course I mind – dreadfully. I want to see what he's like. I don't even know whether he's got a moustache or not. Has he?

Barbara   No.

Leonora   Beard?

Barbara   No beard.

Leonora   Tall or short?

Barbara   Short.

Leonora   Fat?

Barbara   Not exactly fat, let's say a little podgy.

Leonora   Oh, Barbara!

Barbara   He has very little chance of getting exercise, you see. Still, he does his best with these things in the bedroom.

Leonora   What things?

Barbara   You know, they're attached to the wall and you gasp and strain and they snap back again. He has a rowing machine, too.

Scene 64

INT. BEDROOM. FABERS' FLAT. DAY.

Leonora *moves towards the half open door.*

Leonora   Is this the bathroom?

Barbara   Yes.

Leonora *pops her head into the bathroom – she turns back from the bathroom to face* **Barbara**.

Leonora   What a dreadful liar you are! I suppose he's eight feet high and absolutely bewitching.

Barbara   If you care for long black moustaches, yes.

They begin to move out of the bedroom once more, talking as they go, into the hall.

Scene 65

INT. BATHROOM. FABERS' FLAT. DAY. (TRANSPARENCY)

A flash of the bathroom, which is empty of all the paraphernalia which **Barbara** *has described. This is the view from the door as* **Leonora** *sees it when she looks into the bathroom in scene 64*

Scene 66

INT. HALL. FABERS' FLAT. DAY.

Leonora *and* **Barbara**.

Leonora   I've made up my mind to fall in love with him on sight.

Barbara   He's quite used to that.

Leonora   You're positively smug about him, Barbara. Tell me, seriously – do you really adore him?

Barbara   I love him very much.

Leonora   How marvellous. And does he really love you?

Barbara   Really, Leonora.

They go into the drawing room.

Scene 67

INT. DRAWING ROOM. FABERS' FLAT. DAY.

Leonora *is still talking as they come through into the drawing room.*

Leonora   I know I'm behaving badly – do forgive me –

She breaks off suddenly and, from her viewpoint, we see that **Christian Faber** *is already in the room, standing by the fireplace. He has a book in his hand and has looked up from it as they entered.*

Barbara   Oh, Chris –

Leonora   At last!

Scene 68

INT. DRAWING ROOM. FABERS' FLAT. DAY.

Christian *at the fireplace,* **Leonora** *and* **Barbara** *walk to him.*

Christian   (*surprised*) What?

Barbara   This is Mrs. Vail, Chris, one of my oldest friends. We were at school together –

Christian   (*absently*) Oh, how do you do.

Barbara   Do you want a drink?

Christian   No, I've got some more work to do.

Leonora   I think it only fair that you should know that until Barbara disillusioned me, I thought you were an immigration official.

Christian   (*smiling perfunctorily*) Did you really? (*to* **Barbara**) Listen, dear, we are dining with Mary tonight, aren't we?

Barbara   Yes.

Christian   Well, you go without me and tell her I'll come in for coffee.

Barbara   (*laughing*) She knows that already, darling, she told me on the telephone this morning.

Christian   (*reaching the table in foreground*) Mary is one of the most intelligent women I know.

Scene 69

INT. DRAWING ROOM. FABERS' FLAT. DAY.

MEDIUM CLOSE SHOT of **Barbara**, *camera left and* **Leonora**, *camera right, over* **Christian***'s left shoulder, covering scene 68.*

Scene 70

INT. DRAWING ROOM. FABERS' FLAT. DAY.

MEDIUM CLOSE SHOT of **Leonora**, *camera left and* **Christian**, *camera right, over* **Barbara***'s left shoulder, covering scene 68.*

Scene 71

INT. DRAWING ROOM. FABERS' FLAT. DAY.

Christian *at the table.* **Barbara** *and* **Leonora** *in the background.*

Leonora   (*with slightly forced impudence*) I also thought you had a long moustache!

Christian   (*not quite understanding*) What – ?

Barbara   (*quickly*) Moustache, dear. Leonora thought you had a moustache.

Christian   (*with a completely empty smile*) No, I haven't a moustache.

He exits to the door.

Scene 72

INT. DRAWING ROOM. FABERS' FLAT. DAY.

MEDIUM CLOSE SHOT of **Barbara** *and* **Leonora**, *covering scene 71.*

Scene 73

INT. DRAWING ROOM. FABERS' FLAT. DAY.

MEDIUM CLOSE SHOT of **Christian**, *covering scene 71.*

Scene 74

INT. DRAWING ROOM. FABERS' FLAT. DAY.

Barbara *and* **Leonora**.

Leonora   I'd rather he were an immigration official.

Barbara   Never mind.

Leonora   He didn't even see me. I do think it's a shame.

Barbara   He saw you all right.

Leonora   I was going to ask him to my house-warming next week … now I'm not so sure.

Barbara   You mean you'd like me to come alone?

Leonora   No – bring the other young man with you, Tim whatever his name was. I like him much better. Next Wednesday!

Barbara   That'll be lovely.

Leonora   That's settled them. Now I really must go.

They start towards the hall.

Barbara   You're sure you wouldn't like to stay and have your passport examined or anything?

Leonora   No. I've given up the whole idea.

We follow them into the hall, shooting behind them.

Barbara   What whole idea?

Leonora   About falling madly in love with your husband, and his falling madly in love with me, and then me having a lovely 'old friends together' scene with you and everyone behaving beautifully and making sacrifices all round.

Scene 75

INT. HALL. FABERS' FLAT. DAY.

MEDIUM CLOSE SHOT of **Barbara** *and* **Leonora**.

Barbara   What's your telephone number?

She picks up the telephone book from the hall table.

Leonora   You're not going to put me off are you?

Barbara   Don't be silly, of course not.

Leonora   Mayfair 0540.

Barbara   (*scribbling it down*) Mayfair 0540.

Leonora   I'll expect you on Wednesday, about eight?

Barbara *opens the door.*

Barbara   Do you really want me to ask Tim?

Leonora   Of course, he's an angel, and bring your old alienist too, if he'll come.

She goes out through the front door.

Barbara   (*laughingly*) I'll try to persuade him.

She closes the door.

Scene 76

INT. OFFICE. FABERS' FLAT. DAY.

Susan *is sitting at her desk, and is finishing a telephone conversation with a patient.*

Susan   (*into phone*) … the 15th at three-thirty. Yes, that's a Friday. Right, Miss Foster.

While she has been speaking, **Tim** *has come quietly from the consulting room. He has walked to the bookcase. As he opens one of its glass doors, it clicks sharply.* **Susan** *starts and looks round quickly as she puts down the telephone.*

Susan   Oh, Tim, you made me jump. What are you doing?

Tim   Is there a Bible in the house?

Susan   (*leaving her desk and joining him*) I suppose there must be somewhere. What do you want it for?

Tim   Chris wants a quotation to use in his lecture on Friday.

Susan   Does he know a special one – ?

Tim   Vaguely – something in Deuteronomy –

They both continue looking over the shelves.

Scene 77

INT. OFFICE. FABERS' FLAT. DAY.

MEDIUM CLOSE SHOT of **Barbara** *and* **Susan**. **Barbara** *comes in with some letters and* **Susan** *moves to her.*

Susan   I say, Barbara, is there a Bible in the house?

Barbara   I should think so. Why – who wants one?

Susan   Chris. Tim and I have searched everywhere, but we've drawn a blank.

Barbara   Funny – we should have one somewhere …

She breaks off as **Ernest** *passes the open door and calls to him.*

Barbara   Oh, Ernest, is there a Bible in the house?

Ernest   (*coming into the doorway*) I think cook has one, madam.

Barbara   Ask her if she'll lend it to me for a minute, will you?

Ernest   Very good, madam.

He goes back the way he came, closing the door.

Scene 78

INT. KITCHEN. FABERS' FLAT. DAY.

The cook is busy with pastry patterns when **Ernest** *comes in.*

Ernest   Got your Bible handy, Alice?

Alice   (*showing floury hands*) Looks like it, doesn't it?

Ernest   The missus wants one.

Alice   Whatever for?

Ernest   I don't know.

He goes out with the Bible into the hall.

Scene 79

INT. HALL. FABERS' FLAT. DAY.

Ernest *comes from the kitchen and makes his way towards the office and goes inside, carrying the Bible.*

Scene 80

INT. OFFICE. FABERS' FLAT. DAY.

Ernest *brings in the Bible and hands it to* **Barbara**.

Ernest   The Bible, madam.

Barbara   Thank you, Ernest.

Ernest *exits and* **Barbara** *puts the BIBLE down on the desk.* **Tim** *and* **Susan** *look over at it.*

Scene 81

INT. OFFICE. FABERS' FLAT. DAY.

Tim, **Barbara** *and* **Susan**.

Tim   It's Moses, Deuteronomy twenty something – it starts with 'The Lord shall smite thee –'

Barbara *turns the pages.*

Tim   It's for his paper on 'The Inferior Function'.

Barbara   This must be it – (*she reads*) 'The Lord shall smite thee with madness, and blindness and astonishment of the heart'.

Tim   Yes, that's it.

He takes the Bible and goes back into the consulting room as we ...

FADE OUT.

Scene 82

INT. OFFICE. FABERS' FLAT. DAY.

CLOSE SHOT of **Barbara** *reading lines in scene 81 (for American version).*

FADE IN

Scene 83

INT. DINING ROOM. FABERS' FLAT. NIGHT.

Barbara, **Christian** *and* **Tim** *are drinking coffee after dinner.* **Tim** *looks at his wrist watch and says ...*

Tim   We've exactly half an hour. I'd better get the car round.

He finishes his coffee and gets up.

Christian   All right – I'll be down in five minutes.

Tim   Goodnight, Barbara.

Barbara   Goodnight, Tim.

Tim *goes out.*

Christian   (*sighing*) Oh dear.

Barbara   Tired, darling?

Christian   No – just wishing that I needn't go.

Barbara   You always say that before a lecture – it's nerves I expect – like a great prima donna trembling before the overture.

Scene 84

INT. DRAWING ROOM. FABERS' FLAT. NIGHT.

Pick up **Barbara** *and* **Christian** *to the dining room doorway.*

Christian   I should be a great deal more nervous than this if I thought I was about to boom my way through *Tristan and Isolde*.

Barbara   So should I. I should be nervous if I thought you were going to sing one of the smaller *Indian Love Lyrics*.

Christian *picks up his manuscript.*

Christian   Don't you care for my singing voice?

Barbara   No dear. Do you?

Christian   You used to love it. When I was trilling away in the bathroom, you used to stand outside the door for hours.

Barbara   We only had one bathroom, my love, and occasionally I wanted to use it for myself.

Christian   You'll be sorry when you give your next musical evening and ask me to sing *'Trees'* and I refuse.

Barbara   (*stricken*) Oh, Chris, wouldn't it be awful if I really had a next musical evening?

Christian   Absolutely horrible.

He kisses her lightly.

Christian   I suppose I'd better go. Tim will be waiting.

They go out into the hall.

Scene 85

INT. DRAWING ROOM. FABERS' FLAT. NIGHT.

TWO SHOTS of **Barbara** *and* **Christian**, *to cover scene 84.*

Scene 86

INT. DRAWING ROOM. FABERS' FLAT. NIGHT.

CLOSE SHOT of **Barbara**, *to cover scene 84.*

Scene 87

INT. DRAWING ROOM. FABERS' FLAT. NIGHT.

CLOSE SHOT of **Christian**, *to cover scene 84.*

Scene 88

INT. HALL. FABERS' FLAT. NIGHT.

Christian *and* **Barbara** *come into the hall from the dining room. She helps him on with his coat – he picks up his briefcase.*

Barbara   Sure you don't want me to come?

Christian   Quite sure. You'll put me off. I can't be pompous and important with you watching me like a sharp, critical lynx, waiting for me to split an infinitive.

Barbara   (*putting her arms round him*) Darling – you're very important to me whether I'm there or not. I just wanted to suddenly mention it.

She gives him a swift kiss and he goes.

DISSOLVE TO

Scene 89

EXT. KINGSWAY HALL. NIGHT.

It is early evening, about seven o'clock. A car pulls up outside the entrance to Kingsway Hall. **Christian** *gets out of the car, which is driven by* **Tim**.

Tim   Five minutes to park this and I'll be with you.

Christian   Right. Don't hurry.

He crosses the pavement and disappears into the hall. As he does so, we let him walk out of the shot and hold on a poster alongside

on the other side of the moon, as it were, are the causes of which
we can see but the superficial effects.

The forces which are released in moments of apparent
unimportance are far from slight or simple. When boy meets girl
for the first time and their eyes meet with a sudden recognition
across the space which seemingly divides them, then there may be
released a cataclysmic change in their two lives. In that innocent
moment of time, it is as if a world may turn in its sleep, revealing
the other side of the moon, and setting free new powers, new
patterns and new possibilities for good and ill.

Professor Jung has called this other unfamiliar undeveloped side
of the personality the 'inferior function'. He says …

Christian *suddenly fluffs his lecture, then recovers himself and
continues.*

… 'Sensitiveness is the symptom of the presence of inferiority. Thus the psychological conditions of division and misunderstanding arise, not only as between two people, but also in the form of division within oneself. The very essence of the inferior function is characterised by its autonomy. It is self-sufficient, it attacks, it fascinates, it entangles us, in such ways that we cease to be masters of ourselves and become incapable of fair judgement between ourselves and others. Yet it is necessary for the development of character that we should allow the other side, the inferior function, to find expression.'

When **Christian** *fluffs his lecture – he comes to a full stop, and stares for a split second at someone in the audience. Then he recovers himself and carries on.*

During the hesitation – which is only momentary – we have a CUT of **Leonora** *sitting in the audience a couple of rows from the front, gazing up at the speaker with perhaps just a shade more rapt attention than is really necessary. Back to* **Christian** *as he recovers himself and goes on with the lecture, and then a CUT of* **Tim**, *in the audience, leaning forward to see what caused* **Christian** *to fluff. He glances from* **Leonora** *to* **Christian** *and back again, frowning incredulously. Then he settles down to listen to the lecture.*

FADE OUT.

FADE IN.

Scene 99

INT. DINING ROOM. FABERS' FLAT. DAY.

Barbara *is pouring out coffee at breakfast next morning.*
Christian *is immersed in The Times.*

Barbara   How did it go last night?

Christian   (*glancing up from his newspaper*) Not too badly. Why?

Barbara   I just wondered. By the way, Leonora's expecting us at her house-warming tonight, in case you've forgotten.

Christian   I haven't forgotten, but I'm afraid I can't go. Mitchell's sending a case to me from Oxford – I'll have to take it.

Barbara   Oh, dear!

Christian   I'm not really sorry – I shouldn't know a soul anyway – I should only be bored to death.

Barbara   Maybe she feels that way about you. Her invitation was rather grudging, so I shouldn't worry.

Christian   I won't.

Outwardly placid, he continues to read the newspaper, and then he hears **Leonora***'s voice echo in his ear.*

Leonora's voice   I think it is only fair you should know that until Barbara disillusioned me, I thought you were an immigration official.

Barbara   Another cup of coffee, dear?

Christian   No thanks.

Scene 100

INT. DINING ROOM. FABERS' FLAT. DAY.

Abruptly, **Christian** *closes the paper and throws it down and leaves the table, muttering ...*

Christian   What on earth is she talking about?

Christian *exits and* **Barbara** *is left, looking puzzled.*

DISSOLVE TO

Scene 101

INT. FABERS' FLAT. CONSULTING ROOM. DAY.

Although this scene takes place during the day, the blinds of the consulting room are drawn and the only illumination comes from a lamp over the desk where **Christian** *is sitting. At the opposite side of the desk is an armchair and in it, sitting back, relaxed, is a rather precise little man of about fifty, wearing a black jacket and striped trousers. Throughout this scene, he speaks very simply and seriously in answer to* **Christian***'s questions.* **Christian***'s voice is a thought more caressing than usual. The little man's name is* **Mr. Burton**.

Burton   (*continuing something he has been saying before the scene opened*) ... and then my wife found out. I'd been to the pictures with Freda and I was just saying goodbye to her at the 'bus stop and I turned round to walk home – and there was Millie.

Christian   What did she do?

Burton   Nothing. She just looked at me – sort of hurt-like ... and said 'You'd better come home, hadn't you?'

Christian   And you did? (**Burton** *nods*) Have you seen Freda again since then?

Burton   No.

Christian   Why not? Didn't you want to? (**Burton** *shakes his head*) Aren't you in love with her any more? (**Burton** *shakes his head again*) You are really, aren't you?

Burton   (*nodding absently*) It's awful. It's like when you're hungry – starving. All you can think about is food – all the time – till it nearly drives you crazy. Only I keep thinking about Freda. I just can't get her out of my mind.

Christian   Then why don't you see her again?

Burton   Oh, I couldn't do that.

Christian   Why not?

Burton   Because of Millie.

Christian   You mean she'd be angry with you?

Burton   Oh no. Worse than that. Much worse.

Christian   What could she do?

Burton   You don't know Millie.

Christian   No – but you do. What would she do?

Burton   I can't tell you.

Christian   But you want me to help you, don't you? (**Burton** *nods*) Then *you* must help *me*. What are you afraid Millie might do?

Burton   It's so degrading.

Christian   You can tell me.

Burton   If I go on seeing Freda, she'll … she'll try to commit suicide. She's tried already. She put her head in the gas oven.

Christian   It wasn't really Millie who did that, was it?

Burton   (*reluctantly*) No.

Christian   Who was it?

Burton   It was me.

Christian   Why did you want to commit suicide?

Burton   Do I shouldn't think of Freda any more.

Christian   Are you going to do that again?

Burton   I don't know.

Christian   Suppose Freda were here now, you wouldn't want to commit suicide then, would you?

Burton   She isn't here, is she?

Christian   What would you say to her if she were?

Burton   I can't tell you.

Christian   Try! Tell me all the things you want to say to her.

Burton   No. No!

Christian   All right. Just as you like. (*he changes his tactics*) Why don't you write her a letter?

Burton   No! You'll show it to Millie.

Christian   I promise you I won't.

Christian *rises.*

Scene 102

INT. CONSULTING ROOM. FABERS' FLAT. DAY.

MEDIUM CLOSE SHOT of **Burton**, *covering scene 101.*

Scene 103

INT. CONSULTING ROOM. FABERS' FLAT. DAY.

MEDIUM CLOSE SHOT of **Christian**, *covering scene 101.*

Scene 104

INT. CONSULTING ROOM. FABERS' FLAT. DAY.

TWO SHOTS of **Christian** *and* **Burton**, *to cover scene 101.*

Scene 105

INT. CONSULTING ROOM. FABERS' FLAT. DAY.

Christian *and* **Burton**. **Christian** *goes round to* **Burton**.

Christian   Look. I'll leave you alone for five minutes while you write to her. Here's a pencil and pad. Now you sit down and write to Freda, eh?

Burton   All right … You won't look?

Christian   No. I won't look.

He goes out. The little man picks up the pad and begins to write.

Scene 106

INT. OFFICE. FABERS' FLAT. DAY.

Christian *comes out of the consulting room.* **Tim** *and* **Susan** *are at work in the office. As the door closes behind* **Christian**, **Tim** *looks enquiringly at him.*

Christian   He's doing a writing test. Don't let him go until I come back. Give him ten minutes.

Christian *exits.*

Tim   (*looking at wrist watch*) Right.

Scene 107

INT. HALL. FABERS' FLAT. DAY.

Christian *comes from the office and crosses to the drawing room.*

Scene 108

INT. DRAWING ROOM. FABERS' FLAT. DAY.

Barbara *is sitting in an armchair with a tray of tea things on a low table in front of her.* **Christian** *comes in.*

Christian   Any tea left?

Barbara   Yes, of course.

Christian   (*with a sigh*) I feel a bit battered.

Barbara   (*starting to pour the tea*) Difficult case?

Christian   (*walking to the window*) No – not really – just heartbreaking.

Barbara   Not poor Mrs. Frazer?

Christian   (*smiling*) No – poor Mrs. Frazer was a humbug

– all she wanted was to talk about how fascinating she was and
how everyone adored her and how, in spite of all that, she was
somehow lonely and could I please explain why?

Scene 109

INT. DRAWING ROOM. FABERS' FLAT. DAY.

Barbara *gets up and takes a cup of tea to* **Christian** *at the
window.*

Barbara   Did you?

Christian   Yes – I said it was probably liver and sent her to a
fortune teller.

Barbara   How heartless of you. What's this one?

Christian   Burton. He's a bank clerk. A gentle little man with a
nice wife and two grown up daughters. Leslie sent him to me.

Barbara   What's wrong with him?

Christian   He tried to commit suicide.

Barbara   Love affair?

They move back to the fireplace.

Christian   Yes. His wife knows and this, coupled with a sense
of guilt and a desire for respectability, plus his obsession with the
other woman, is tearing him to pieces.

Barbara   Is she being good about it, do you suppose, or nagging
at him?

Christian   I'm not quite sure yet. I suspect she's being fairly
self-righteous.

Barbara   Poor thing … she's probably miserable. And the other
woman? Does she really care for him?

Christian   I shouldn't think so.

Barbara   Oh, poor, poor man – what a cruel story.

Christian   My job is full of cruel stories. (*he puts down his cup*)
I must go back.

Christian *finishes drinking his tea, puts down the cup, kisses*
Barbara *on the forehead and moves forward.*

Scene 110

INT. DRAWING ROOM. FABERS' FLAT. DAY.

Christian *crosses the room, stops in front of the mirror on the
telephone table, and straightens his tie. And as he does so, we
hear* **Leonora**'s *voice off-screen ...*

Leonora's voice   I also thought you had a long moustache.

Christian *raises an eyebrow at his own thoughts, tentatively
fingers his bare upper lip and goes out.*

Scene 111

INT. DRAWING ROOM. FABERS' FLAT. DAY.

CLOSE SHOT of **Christian** – *his reflection in the mirror.*

DISSOLVE TO

Scene 112

EXT. LEONORA'S HOUSE. EVENING.

Shot of the exterior of **Leonora**'s *house with cars parked outside.*

DISSOLVE TO

Scene 113

INT. LEONORA'S HOUSE. NIGHT.

The house-warming is in full swing, as **Barbara** *and* **Tim** *thread their way through the throng towards* **Leonora**.

Leonora   Darling! How lovely to see you! And Tim – I never can remember people's surnames.

Tim   Verney.

Leonora   You'll have to write it down for me somewhere. Now you must have a drink, both of you.

She beckons to **Helen**, *and they take their cocktails.*

Leonora   That's better.

Barbara   I'm terribly sorry, darling, but Chris couldn't manage it. A case came up at the last minute.

Leonora   And now he's digging into someone's repressions and all that sort of thing.

Barbara   Yes, all that sort of thing.

Leonora   How exciting.

Tim   More interesting than exciting.

Leonora   You have a superior look in your eye and I resent it deeply.

Tim   (*laughing*) I'm sorry …

A **woman** *interrupts.*

Scene 114

INT. LEONORA'S LOUNGE. NIGHT.

After the interruption, **Leonora** *continues talking to* **Barbara** *and* **Tim**.

Leonora   It must be frustrating work, unearthing everybody's rattling little skeletons and fitting them together like Meccano. What about himself?

Barbara   What do you mean?

Leonora   Does he know all about himself, right from the beginning? Is everything cut and dried and accounted for?

Tim   I expect so.

Leonora   (*to* **Barbara**) And you? Has he a chart of you hanging up over his desk?

Barbara   He doesn't need a chart for me, Leonora.

Leonora   Something tells me I've gone too far – oh dear – I didn't mean to – don't be cross.

Barbara   (*smiling*) I'm not in the least cross.

Leonora   Do come and help me with Hilda Rockwell.

Barbara   The painter?

Leonora   How clever of you to know. She's the only lioness here – very abstract of course and never utters, just looks smoulderingly at people – she gives me the creeps.

Tim   I can't wait.

They go in search of her.

Scene 115

INT. LEONORA'S LOUNGE. NIGHT.

CLOSE SHOT of **Barbara** *and* **Leonora**, *covering scene 114.*

Scene 116

INT. LEONORA'S LOUNGE. NIGHT.

CLOSE SHOT of **Barbara** *and* **Tim**, *to cover scene 114.*

DISSOLVE TO

Scene 117

INT. BEDROOM. FABERS' FLAT. DAY.

The telephone bell is ringing in the Faber's bedroom the following morning. **Barbara** *answers it while in bed.*

Barbara   Hello – yes – this is Mrs. Faber. (*she listens for a moment or two with a slightly worried look*) Yes, Florence, I understand. When was this? I see ... tell her not to worry, I'll be down on the ten-thirty train. Is there anything she wants? All right, I'll remember. Goodbye.

As she replaces the receiver, **Christian**, *who has been finishing his dressing in another part of the room, turns and speaks to her.*

Christian   Trouble?

Barbara   Yes – Mother's ill. I'll have to go down.

Christian   Of course.

Barbara   It'll mean several days, I'm afraid.

Christian   Don't bother about me. You stay as long as you want to.

During these last few speeches, **Barbara** *has risen and put on her dressing gown and crossed to the window.*

Barbara   I'll be back as soon as possible, you know that. Oh, dear! ...

FADE OUT.

FADE IN TO

Scene 118

INT. CONSULTING ROOM. FABERS' FLAT. NIGHT.

Christian *is working at his desk several nights later, when* **Tim** *pauses on his way out at the door.*

Tim   Nothing else you want before I go, is there?

Christian   No, I've practically finished.

Tim   By the way, have you heard from Barbara?

Christian   Yes, I had a letter this morning. She hopes to be home in a day or two.

Tim   Good. The place doesn't seem the same without her.

Christian   (*smiling*) No need to tell me that.

Tim   (*as he exits*) Sorry. It's that obvious streak in me. Goodnight.

Christian   Goodnight, Tim.

As the door closes behind him the telephone rings on **Christian***'s desk, and he answers it.*

Christian   (*into the telephone*) Hello? Yes – Oh, it's you, darling. (*he laughs*) Yes, Tim was just asking me if you were ever coming back …

Christian *puts down the receiver and hurries over to the door. He opens it and goes into the office.*

Scene 119

INT. COUNTRY HOUSE. ('A'). NIGHT. LOUNGE

(*This is a corner of the lounge – a very small set, purely for a cut*). **Barbara** *is speaking from her mother's home in the country.*

Barbara   (*into the telephone*) … No – nothing serious, I've just remembered I had a date with Leonora to go to a theatre tonight. Can you possibly get Tim to take her – I know she likes him.

Christian   (*squeezed voice off*) I'll have to hurry, he may be gone. Anyway, I'll get someone. Where are the tickets?

Barbara   In the top drawer of my desk. Thank you, darling. I'll ring you tomorrow. Goodbye.

Scene 120

INT. OFFICE. FABERS' FLAT. NIGHT.

Susan *is just putting on her hat and coat to go for the evening.*

Christian   Has Tim left yet?

Susan   Yes. Do you want anything?

Christian   Barbara just telephoned. She wanted him to take Mrs. Vail to a play tonight.

Susan   Rather late in the day, isn't it?

Christian   Barbara never has got out of the habit of leaving things to the last minute.

He goes to **Barbara***'s desk, a small one in a corner, and rummages in the top drawer for the tickets.*

Christian   <u>You</u> wouldn't like to go, I suppose?

Susan   I'd love to, but I can't. I'm dining with Julian Macey and his new wife. It's ages since I saw a really good play, too.

Christian   It may be a very bad one. If it is, I hope you'll sympathise with me.

Susan   Why, are you going?

Christian   I don't see how I can get out of it.

Susan   Well, it'll do you good – take you out of yourself.

Christian   I don't want to be 'taken out of myself'.

Susan   I'm not so sure of that … Goodnight!

She goes, leaving **Christian** *wondering what she meant.*

DISSOLVE TO

Scene 121

EXT. THEATRE. NIGHT.

Christian *and* **Leonora Vail** *get out of a taxi and make their way into the theatre. They are both in evening dress.*

DISSOLVE TO

Scene 122

INT. THEATRE CORRIDOR. NIGHT.

Christian *and* **Leonora** *walk along the deserted theatre corridor.*

Scene 123

INT. THEATRE AUDITORIUM. NIGHT.

Leonora *and* **Christian** *take their programme from the attendant, and make for their seats in the stalls. The play has already begun and, naturally, the whole row has to get up to allow them to enter and reach their seats at the far end. They sit down quietly and, without glancing at each other, prepare to concentrate on the stage.*

DISSOLVE TO

Scene 124

INT. THEATRE AUDITORIUM. NIGHT.

Orchestra playing in foreground – the audience and theatre auditorium in background.

Scene 125

INT. THEATRE AUDITORIUM. NIGHT.

The curtain comes down at the end of the first act to spasmodic applause. The lights go up and **Christian** *is caught in the act of stifling a yawn.* **Leonora** *looks at him out of the corner of her eye and smiles.*

Christian   Would you like a drink?

Leonora   More than anything in this world.

They rise and murmur their excuses as the whole row is once again forced to its feet to allow them to pass.

Scene 126

INT. THEATRE CORRIDOR. NIGHT.

Leonora *and* **Christian** *trickle along with the crowd towards the bar which is thronged. They pause outside the blocked entrance.*

Leonora   Can you tell me what Act Two has in store for us?

Christian   I've a fair idea.

Leonora   Strange! So have I. And the third?

Christian   I wouldn't be surprised if they fell into each other's arms.

Leonora   You must have second sight.

Christian   No – just dismal anticipation.

Leonora   It would be quite shocking if we cut the rest of it, wouldn't it?

Christian   (*gravely*) Quite shocking.

Leonora   On the other hand, I might get a complex about bad plays or something.

Christian   My subconscious tells me we shan't be here.

Leonora   What a charming subconscious you must have.

Christian   It's not always so obliging – but it has its uses. Shall we go?

Leonora *nods. They both slip quietly through the exit door to the foyer.*

DISSOLVE TO

Scene 127

INT. WEST END CLUB. NIGHT.

This is a quiet West End Club with a restful atmosphere. **Leonora** *and* **Christian** *have just finished dinner and are at the liqueur stage. They are in a corner, secluded and a little remote from the rest of the other diners.*

Christian   Were you really angry – that first time we met?

Leonora   Yes – I think I was.

Christian   I didn't mean to be rude.

Leonora   You certainly did.

Christian   Yes – now I come to think of it, I did.

Leonora   Why?

Christian   You irritated me, you were so conscious of how absolutely beautiful you looked.

Leonora   I never thought that.

Christian   Your manner demanded attention insistently, like a child banging its spoon on the table, making a clamour, yelling for more –

Leonora   How horrid that sounds.

Christian   Quite natural, though. I expect you've always been spoilt.

Leonora   No, I haven't.

Christian   Have you had many lovers?

Leonora   No – not many.

Christian   … and the few – whoever they were – did you love them?

Leonora   (*turning away slightly*) Please don't be quite so clinical.

Christian   (*impulsively*) Forgive me – I wanted to know.

Leonora   I loved somebody once – very much – never so much before – and never so much since.

Christian   I see.

Leonora   I'm tired. Let's go home now, shall we?

Christian   Very well – if you like.

He signals to the **waiter** *for the bill.*

Scene 128

INT. WEST END CLUB. NIGHT.

CLOSE SHOT of **Christian**, *covering scene 127.*

Scene 129

INT. WEST END CLUB. NIGHT.

MEDIUM CLOSE SHOT of **Christian** *and* **Leonora** *– he signals for the* **waiter**.

DISSOLVE TO

Scene 130

EXT. LEONORA'S HOUSE. NIGHT.

Christian *and* **Leonora** *arrive in a taxi outside her house, which is on Upper Brook Street. They get out and make their way into the house,* **Leonora** *opening the front door with her keys. As* **Leonora** *goes inside,* **Christian** *follows her.*

Scene 131

INT. LENORA'S HALL. NIGHT.

He gives her a moment to shut the front door and then takes her in his arms and kisses her. **Leonora** *returns the kiss. Then she breaks away and says ...*

Leonora   You must go.

Christian   Must I?

Leonora   Of course.

Christian   Isn't that rather inconsistent?

Leonora   Yes – I suppose it is.

Christian   What's the matter?

Leonora   I didn't mean it to be like this?

Christian   Don't send me away yet.

Leonora   I must.

Christian   Do you really want to?

Leonora   No.

Christian   Well, then –

She turns and goes into the lounge. He follows her.

Scene 132

INT. LENORA'S LOUNGE. NIGHT.

Leonora *comes in, switching on the light.* **Christian** *follows her into the room. She turns to face him, looking very serious and unhappy.*

Leonora   Christ. I lied just now when I said I didn't mean it to be like this.

Christian   Does it matter?

Leonora   Yes, it matters dreadfully –

Christian   (*taking a step towards her*) My dear –

Leonora   Please stay there.

Christian   Very well.

Leonora   (*with a rush*) I did mean it to be like this, but – but not quite like this – I mean – it was all a trick. I planned it – the first day I came, you remember, when you snubbed me. I teased you about it at dinner time – I made up my mind then to make you fall in love with me. Now I wish I hadn't. I feel cheap – I feel frightened – I wish with all my heart I hadn't.

Christian   I think it was rather a gay trick. Don't be upset. There's nothing to be upset about. Let's sit down quietly and have a drink.

Scene 133

INT. LEONORA'S LOUNGE. NIGHT.

CLOSE SHOT of **Leonora**, *to cover scene 132.*

Scene 134

INT. LEONORA'S LOUNGE. NIGHT.

Christian *moves to the drinks table and pours one for himself.*

Christian   Will you have one?

Leonora   No, thank you.

Christian *moves back to her.*

Christian   Please sit down and relax.

Leonora   Now you're treating me like a patient.

Christian   (*offering her a cigarette*) Only because you're behaving like one.

Leonora   I see (*she laughs suddenly and sits on sofa*).

Christian   That's better.

Leonora   I'd like a match.

Christian   Here. (*he lights one for her*) You're a lovely creature.

He stands at the fireplace.

Leonora   I'm all right outside, but I'm not very pleased with myself inside at the moment.

Christian   Pangs of conscious are tiresome, Leonora. They're also exceedingly bad for you.

Leonora   I'm feeling better now.

Christian   I gather that the trick is on again.

Leonora   (*sharply*) That was unkind.

Christian   You're very touchy.

Leonora   What about Barbara?

Christian   She's very well, thank you. I had a letter from her this morning.

Leonora   Are you in love with her?

Christian   What on earth did you say that for?

Leonora   Are you in love with her?

Christian   You're behaving like a patient again.

Leonora   Are you?

Christian   Barbara has nothing to do with this.

Leonora   You're certainly not in love with me.

Scene 135

INT. LEONORA'S LOUNGE. NIGHT.

CLOSE SHOT of **Leonora**, *seated, to cover scene 134.*

Scene 136

INT. LEONORA'S LOUNGE. NIGHT.

CLOSE SHOT of **Christian**, *standing, to cover scene 134.*

Scene 137

INT. LEONORA'S LOUNGE. NIGHT.

Christian *sits beside* **Leonora**.

Christian   You have lovely eyes, but there's a little sadness in them, a little disappointment. I could tell your fortune by your eyes. Shall I?

Leonora   I'd rather you didn't.

Christian   And your nose –

Leonora   I'd rather you didn't mention my nose at all.

Christian   It's the most unwise nose I've ever seen.

Leonora   Do stop.

Christian   Then there's your mouth.

Leonora   You must go.

Christian   You'd be astounded if you knew how desperately I want to kiss your mouth again.

Leonora   Please, Chris.

Christian   You're so foolish up on your romantic high horse.

How often have you ridden it wildly until it went lame and you had to walk home?

Leonora   Often enough to teach me never to do it again.

Christian   That's what made the sadness in your eyes. You should never have left school – it was a great mistake.

Leonora   You win.

Christian   Do I?

Leonora   I knew you would. Quite early in the evening, I know …

He kisses her. She returns the kiss passionately …

FADE OUT.

Scene 138

INT. LEONORA'S LOUNGE. NIGHT.

CLOSE UP of **Leonora**, *to cover scene 137.*

Scene 139

INT. LEONORA'S LOUNGE. NIGHT.

CLOSE UP of **Christian**, *to cover scene 137.*

FADE IN TO

Scene 140

INT. CONSULTING ROOM. FABERS' FLAT. DAY.

Tim *is standing at the far side of* **Christian**'*s desk, sorting papers, when* **Susan** *comes in.*

Susan   Mrs. Hurst is on the line. She wants to know if she can change her time to five this afternoon. Is Chris free then?

Tim   (*swings round the diary on the desk*) I'll see.

As he runs through the appointments for the day, he finds L.V pencilled in at four o'clock and the rest of the afternoon left blank.

Tim   Looks doubtful to me. He's pencilled in L.V for four o'clock, whoever that may be – but how long for, he doesn't say.

Susan   In that case, I'd better put her off till tomorrow (*then as she turns to go*) L.V couldn't by any chance be Leonora Vail, could it?

Tim   (*thoughtfully*) Could be.

A little flash of understanding passes between them.

Scene 141

INT. CONSULTING ROOM. FABERS' FLAT. DAY. (INSERT)

INSERT of the diary.

DISSOLVE TO

Scene 142

EXT. COUNTRY ROAD. DAY.

Christian's *car travelling along the road.*

Scene 143

INT. CAR. DAY. (COUNTRY ROAD. B/P)

Christian *and* **Leonora** *are motoring along a quiet road.*
Christian *glances at her and finds she is looking very pensive.*

Christian   What's worrying you?

Leonora   Conscience.

Christian   The best treatment for an unquiet conscience is to take it out and give it an airing occasionally.

Leonora   Very well … but please, Chris, I'm being really honest now. If you and I had an – an affair – how much would it hurt Barbara?

Christian   I don't know. If she knew, I expect it would upset her a good deal. But it would upset her just as much, if not more, if she thought we wanted to and were denying ourselves on her account. Barbara's that sort of person.

Leonora   You're been married twelve years.

Christian   How naïve you are. (*he pulls the car off the road and parks on the grass verge*)

Scene 144

EXT. COUNTRY ROAD. DAY.

The car stops.

Scene 145

INT. CAR. (COUNTRY ROAD. B.P). DAY.

Christian *and* **Leonora** *in the car.*

Christian   There's a lovely view from here.

Leonora   (*paying no attention to the view*) Do you love her? You never answered me before.

Christian   Yes, I love her deeply and truly and forever.

Leonora   I see.

Christian   I don't suppose you do, but it doesn't matter.

Leonora   It matters a lot.

Christian   What do you want? Truth or lies – reality or pretence?

Leonora   How clever of you to know, without looking, what you have in your safe.

Christian   Don't be unkind to me, Leonora.

Leonora   It's you who are unkind to me.

Christian   Why, in what way?

Leonora   It's my own fault, of course –

Christian   Entirely.

Leonora   If you feel that it would make our – our flirtation any more satisfactory, I have some X-ray plates of my teeth.

Christian   You really mustn't be quarrelsome.

Leonora   I can't help it, you make me angry – horribly angry. I want to hit out at you.

Christian   Any other impulse at this particular stage of the proceedings would be abnormal.

Leonora   You're so superbly sure of yourself, aren't you?

Christian   No, the basis of everything I've ever learned is not being sure – not being sure of anyone or anything in the world – myself least of all.

They start to get out of the car.

Scene 146

INT. CAR. (COUNTRY ROAD. B/P). DAY.

CLOSE SHOT of **Leonora** *and* **Christian**, *to cover scene 145.*

DISSOLVE TO

Scene 147

INT. CORRIDOR OF FLATS. LATE AFTERNOON.

Barbara *comes from the lift and lets herself into her flat, carrying a weekend case.*

Scene 148

INT. FABERS' FLAT. HALL. LATE AFTERNOON.

Barbara *shuts the front door, puts down her case, and crosses the hall to look into the drawing room – then she goes into the office.*

Scene 149

INT. OFFICE AND CONSULTING ROOM. FABERS' FLAT. LATE AFTERNOON.

Barbara *walks through the office into the consulting room which is also empty. She rings a bell on the desk, and while she is waiting, takes off her gloves, hat, etc.*

Scene 150

INT. CONSULTING ROOM. FABERS' FLAT. LATE AFTERNOON.

In a moment, **Ernest***, the butler, enters the room.*

Note. **Ernest** *to say he is pleased to see her home.*

Barbara   Oh, Ernest – did the doctor say whether he'd be in for dinner tonight?

Ernest   No, madam. Are you expecting him?

Scene 151

INT. CONSULTING ROOM. FABERS' FLAT. LATE AFTERNOON.

Barbara *turns to the desk.*

Barbara   I'm not sure. (*picking up* **Christian***'s appointment diary*) Just a minute. This may give us a clue.

Scene 152

INT. CONSULTING ROOM. FABERS' FLAT. LATE AFTERNOON.

CLOSE SHOT of **Barbara***. She looks at the list, then says quietly ...*

Barbara   No, Ernest, I'll have a tray in the library by the fire.

Ernest   Very good, madam.

He leaves her still staring down thoughtfully at the appointment diary.

Scene 153

EXT. COUNTRY ROAD. EVENING.

It is getting dark as **Christian** *and* **Leonora** *walk back across the fields to the parked car.* **Christian** *opens the door of the car for* **Leonora***, and she sits down.*

Scene 154

EXT. CAR. EVENING.

Leonora *gets into the car –* **Christian** *outside.*

Leonora   Can you put a light on?

Christian   What for?

Leonora   I want to powder my – unwise nose.

Christian   There (*as he switches on the car light*).

Leonora   Thank you.

She begins to powder. **Christian** *watches her.*

Christian   There's a bit of fluff on the left.

Leonora   I can see it.

Christian   Allow me.

He tweaks the offending piece of fluff from her cheek. Then he kisses her full on the lips.

Leonora   Don't – please, Chris. Don't.

She struggles and tries to push him away. She stands up.

Christian   Don't be unkind – I want you. You must know that. It wasn't all a trick. It may have started as a trick, but it isn't that now, is it?

Leonora   (*trying to turn him away*) Yes – yes it is.

Christian   Liar. Look at me.

Leonora   No.

Christian   Please.

He turns her face slowly round and looks into her eyes.

Leonora   (*in a whisper*) Well – what's my fortune?

Christian   You're going to love me a little?

Leonora   (*shaking her head*) That's not enough.

Christian   Oh, yes – yes – more than enough.

Leonora   Are you sure?

Christian   Oh, my dear.

He kisses her once more, and on their embrace, we slowly fade out.

Scene 155

EXT. CAR. EVENING

CLOSE SHOT of **Leonora**, *covering scene 154, before she rises.*

Scene 156

EXT. CAR. EVENING.

CLOSE SHOT of **Christian**, *covering scene 154, before* **Leonora** *rises.*

FADE OUT.

FADE IN

Scene 157

INT. OFFICE. FABERS' FLAT. DAY.

Susan *is sitting at her desk in the office as* **Miss Harper**, *the odd looking patient we saw earlier on, comes from the consulting room and over to the desk.* **Susan** *consults her engagement book.*

Susan   Same time next month, Miss Harper?

Miss Harper   Oh no, Miss Birch. Dr. Faber says I'm finished.

Susan   Finished?

Miss Harper   Yes, my rehabilitation is complete. He doesn't think there's any need for me to come again. Unless, of course, that horrid dream comes back again.

Susan   You must be very pleased.

Miss Harper   I don't know – I shall miss my visits. You get used to a thing after six months.

Susan   It doesn't seem as long as that.

Miss Harper   As a matter of fact, I'm thinking of going to some of the doctor's lectures. I've got really interested in psychology. I feel that anyone who has helped me as much as Dr. Faber has is a real saviour of mankind. Yes, I think I shall definitely take it up. We shouldn't leave the field only open to the men, should we, Miss Birch?

Susan   No, of course not. But I'm afraid Dr. Faber's not giving any more lectures this season.

Miss Harper   Oh dear, what a pity. I was so looking forward to them.

Susan   Perhaps he'll be starting again in the autumn.

Miss Harper   Then you must let me know. I should hate to miss them. Well, goodbye Miss Birch. It's been a wonderful experience.

Susan   Goodbye.

Susan *shakes hands with her and sees her out. As she returns to the room,* **Christian** *comes from the consulting room and meets her. He hesitates a second and then goes out into the hall.*

Scene 158

INT. DRAWING ROOM. FABERS' FLAT. DAY.

Barbara *is playing the piano, softly. She looks up as* **Christian** *comes in at the door.*

Christian   I just thought I'd warn you – I may not be in to dinner tonight, so don't wait, will you?

Barbara   Of course not, darling. What time do you think you'll be back?

Christian   I don't know. It all depends.

Barbara   All right.

He smiles and goes. The moment he has shut the door, **Barbara** *rises. She takes a turn or two about the room restlessly, and then finds herself at the window. She looks down as she goes on to the balcony.*

Scene 159

INT. DRAWING ROOM. DAY.

From over **Barbara***'s shoulder, we see* **Christian** *get into his car and drive away.*

Scene 160

INT. DRAWING ROOM. FABERS' FLAT. DAY.

Barbara *is still staring with a strained look in her eyes down into the street below as we ...*

DISSOLVE TO

Scene 161

INT. BEDROOM. FABERS' FLAT. NIGHT.

Barbara *is reading in bed by the light of a table lamp. She stubs out a cigarette and picks up the little travelling clock from the small table beside her. It says nearly two o'clock.*

Scene 162

INT. BEDROOM. FABERS' FLAT. NIGHT.

She throws off the bedclothes, puts on her dressing gown and goes out of the room.

Scene 163

INT. HALL. FABERS' FLAT. NIGHT.

Barbara *comes down the corridor into the drawing room.*

Scene 164

INT. DRAWING ROOM. FABERS' FLAT. NIGHT.

Barbara *switches on a lamp by the fireplace. The room is empty and she shivers slightly. She goes to the window and looks down, then turns away restlessly, takes a drink and sits in a chair.*

Scene 165

INT. DRAWING ROOM. FABERS' FLAT. NIGHT.

Barbara *is sitting in a chair. She closes her eyes wearily. The click of the front door shutting rouses her, and she bites her lip as though she were trying to gather courage.*

Scene 166

INT. DRAWING ROOM. FABERS' FLAT. NIGHT.

Christian, *passing the open door, sees the light and comes into the doorway. His face looks tired and strained.*

Barbara   (*in as ordinary a voice as she can manage*) Hello, darling.

Christian   (*startled*) Barbara!

Barbara   I'm sorry if I made you jump.

Christian   What on earth … ?

Barbara   I couldn't sleep.

Christian   Oh, I see …

Scene 167

INT. DRAWING ROOM. FABERS' FLAT. NIGHT.

CLOSE SHOT of **Barbara** *from* **Christian***'s eyeline.*

Scene 168

INT. DRAWING ROOM. FABERS' FLAT. NIGHT.

Christian *walks into the room and switches on the light behind the sofa – facing* **Barbara***.*

Barbara   Not all the lights, Chris, it's so glarey.

Christian *switches the light off again.*

Christian   That better?

Barbara   Would you like a drink?

Christian   No – no, thanks. I think I'll get to bed.

Barbara   (*getting up*) Yes, it's a bit chilly in here.

Christian *goes out.* **Barbara** *switches off the lamp and walks out.*

Scene 169

INT. BEDROOM. FABERS' FLAT. NIGHT.

Christian *comes in and, sitting down wearily, begins to take off his shoes.* **Barbara** *follows him in with her drink and sits down* *on the edge of the bed. She sips her brandy and then lights a cigarette. She throws the empty packet into the wastepaper basket.* **Christian** *watches her in silence and then notices the ashtray piled with cigarette ends.*

Christian   Have you smoked all these tonight?

Barbara   Yes – it looks awfully unattractive, doesn't it – like after a party.

Christian   I'm awfully sorry, darling.

Barbara   There isn't anything to be sorry for – I mean this isn't a scene, really it isn't. Only I do want to talk to you. I've wanted to for a long while.

Christian   I know.

Barbara   It's probably a bad moment, but – but during the day it's difficult – there never seems to be any time.

Christian   I meant it when I said I was sorry – I am – desperately sorry.

Barbara   Of course you are. I'm sorry too – that's the worst of the whole business, nobody's having a good time. How is Leonora?

Christian *rises nervously and moves away from her towards the dressing table mirror.*

Christian   She's all right, I've just left her.

Barbara   I didn't imagine you'd been to a Masonic dinner, darling.

Christian   (*smiling wryly*) No, I didn't think you did.

Barbara   I hate her quite normally with all my feminine instincts. Sometimes I get almost violent, all by myself. It's funny, isn't it? After so many years – I've got over wishing to strangle her now. I just wish she'd never been born.

Christian   I think I do, too.

Scene 170

INT. BEDROOM. FABERS' FLAT. NIGHT.

Christian *at the dressing table and* **Barbara** *sitting on the bed.*

Barbara   I don't see how we can go on like this, quite, do you? It really is too uncomfortable. That's why I sat up for you. I'm dreadfully worried. The personal, loving you part of the affair I could manage, I think. Painful as it is, but it's everything else too. We are all in a state, Tim and Susan – I think even Ernest's getting a bit agitated.

Christian *stands looking into the mirror of the dressing table as he mechanically undoes his collar and tie.* **Barbara** *pauses for a moment and then goes on ...*

Barbara   You're working under such tremendous pressure, and you're so terribly strained and tired. We're all frightened that you'll crack up or something.

Christian   Don't worry, I shan't crack up. And let's not talk about it any more just now –

Barbara   But ...

Christian   Please, Barbara. You've said I'm tired – I am, and so are you. It wouldn't do any good.

Barbara   All right, darling, just as you say.

She moves away and leaves his staring into the mirror.

Scene 171

INT. BEDROOM. FABERS' FLAT. NIGHT.

CLOSE SHOT of **Christian**, *to cover scene 169, when he is seated.*

Scene 172

INT. BEDROOM. FABERS' FLAT. NIGHT.

CLOSE SHOT of **Barbara**, *to cover scene 169, when seated.*

Scene 173

INT. BEDROOM. FABERS' FLAT. NIGHT.

CLOSE SHOT of **Christian**, *to cover scene 170 – at mirror.*

Scene 174

INT. BEDROOM. FABERS' FLAT. NIGHT.

CLOSE SHOT of **Barbara**, *covering scene 170 – she looks over her shoulder to him at mirror.*

DISSOLVE TO

Scene 175

INT. WEST END. CLUB. NIGHT.

Christian *is waiting for* **Leonora**. (*This should be the same club as before.*) *In a moment she comes hurrying towards him and arrives a little breathless.*

Leonora   Oh, Christ! (*they walk to table*) I'm terribly sorry to be so late. I got held up at the Grangers'.

They sit down.

Scene 176

INT. WEST END CLUB. NIGHT

Christian *and* **Leonora** *at the table.*

Christian   You're very dishevelled. Your eyes are shining and your brooch is undone. It's all highly suspicious.

Leonora *quickly adjusts it.*

Leonora   It's always doing that, I must have it mended. Thank you, darling, I'd hate to lose it.

Christian   Why – isn't it insured?

Leonora   Of course. It's not that – it's the sentimental value.

Christian   (*looking at it more closely*) It's very pretty. Who gave it to you?

Leonora   (*airily*) Oh, no one you know.

Christian   (*banteringly*) How can I be sure of that?

Leonora   That's the fun of it! You can never be sure with me, can you?

Christian *looks up to* **waiter**.

Christian   Two dry Martinis, please.

Waiter   Two dry Martinis – yes, sir.

Scene 177

INT. WEST END CLUB. NIGHT.

We follow the **waiter** *as he crosses to the bar and calls for the drinks. The* **barman** *shakes and pours them and the* **waiter** *puts them on his try and exits. We hold the cocktail shaker.*

Scene 178

INT. WEST END CLUB. NIGHT.

In this brief interval, the mood of **Christian** *and* **Leonora** *has changed completely. Now they are tight-lipped and quarrelling. (Note: If necessary, we must give the* **barman** *and* **waiter** *a couple of lines to cover the time occupied by shaking the cocktails – a couple of rather Rabelaisian comments on* **Christian** *and* **Leonora** *perhaps?)*

Christian   I can't understand you. Why make a secret of it?

Leonora   I'm not.

They stop talking as the **waiter** *puts down the drinks.*

Christian   A little brooch with emeralds and sapphires – and you won't say who gave it to you.

Leonora   (*slightly exasperated*) Oh, well, since you're so persistent, it was Ronnie Hughes.

Christian   How long ago?

Leonora   A long time – during the war.

Christian   What did he do?

Leonora   He was in the R.A.F.

Christian   Were you fond of him?

Leonora   Yes, very.

Christian   Do you ever see him now?

Leonora   He was shot down in flames over Cologne on May 15th, 1945 Is there anything else you wish to know?

Christian   I'm so sorry.

He tries to take her hand in his, but she snatches it away. She is very angry.

DISSOLVE TO

Scene 179

INT. BEDROOM. FABERS' FLAT. NIGHT.

Christian *is asleep in bed. We TRACK IN to hold his head in a large CLOSE UP. From the movement of his eyelids, we can see that he is very restless. He is muttering something but the words are inaudible to us. The CAMERA continues TRACKING IN – and as it does so – we ...*

DISSOLVE

DREAM SEQUENCE.

Scene 180

INT. BEDROOM. FABERS' FLAT. NIGHT.

Barbara *is bending over* **Christian** *and shaking him gently.*

Barbara   All right, Chris, it's all right. I'm coming. Wake up.

Christian   (*opening his eyes suddenly*) Yes – what is it? (*he sees her bending over him*) Oh, Barbara!

Barbara   Bad dreams?

Christian   Horrible. I was drowning. I'm glad you woke me.

Barbara   You seemed terribly upset.

Christian   Did I?

Barbara   Yes. You kept calling for me.

Christian   You were so far away. I thought I'd never get back. I seemed to be submerged. (*wryly*) It looks as though I shall have to start analysing my own dreams, doesn't it?

Barbara   There's no need for that. I can tell you what's wrong with you.

Christian   Can you?

Barbara   Yes. Unless you put a stop to this agonising battle between your emotions and your intelligence, you'll break down completely.

Christian   How can I put a stop to it? It's there – it's there all the time – every moment of the day and night. It started so easily, so gaily – a little more than a joke. There were no danger signals whatever. Then suddenly I felt myself being swept away and I started to struggle.

Barbara   Stop struggling.

Christian   I can't. If I stopped struggling, I should be lost forever.

Barbara   You know, Chris, you've neglected your emotions for years, and now you're paying for it. It's nothing to be ashamed of – with your sort of temperament it was inevitable. It had to happen. I've been waiting for it.

Christian   It isn't Leonora, it's nothing to do with Leonora any more. It's the thing itself – her face and her body and her charm make a frame, but the picture's in me, before my eyes constantly, and I can't get it out.

Barbara   Do you want to marry her?

Christian   No, it isn't anything to do with marriage.

Barbara   Does she want you to marry her?

Christian   No, I don't think so – no, I'm sure she doesn't.

Barbara   I can't see why that should make me feel a bit better, but it does. How clearly do you see the situation – in your more detached moments, I mean?

Christian   Quite clearly, but my detached moments are getting rare, I'm afraid.

Barbara   Look, Chris, I have a plan – but I'm not going to worry you with it now. We're both too tired and upset to tackle it properly – it must wait till the morning. Meanwhile, will you try and get a little sleep?

Christian   I'll try.

Barbara   Goodnight then, darling.

She goes back to bed.

Christian   Goodnight, Barbara.

She smiles at him and switches off the light.

Scene 181

INT. BEDROOM. NIGHT.

CLOSE SHOT of **Barbara**, *to cover scene 180.*

Scene 182

INT. BEDROOM. FABERS' FLAT. NIGHT.

CLOSE SHOT of **Christian**, *to cover scene 180.*

Scene 183

INT. BEDROOM. FABERS' FLAT. NIGHT.

BIG CLOSE UP of **Christian**, *to cover scene 180.*

Scene 184

INT. BEDROOM. FABERS' FLAT. NIGHT.

BIG CLOSE UP of **Barbara**, *to cover scene 180.*

DISSOLVE TO

Scene 185

INT. DINING ROOM. FABERS' FLAT. DAY.

Christian *and* **Barbara** *are having breakfast – at least they are making pretence of eating.* **Barbara** *is talking as the scene opens.*

Barbara   … but first I want you to promise that you won't worry about me.

Christian   I'll try not to.

Barbara   Well – this is how I see the situation. It would be different if I were still in love with you, but I'm not, any more than you are with me. That was all settled years ago. We are tremendously necessary to each other, though, and I hope we always shall be, but I must know – you must tell me how long.

Christian   I'm in too deep now – I can't tell.

Barbara   Very well then, you must go away.

Christian   Go away! How can I?

Barbara   You must.

Christian   I've thought of it. I want to, but it's quite impossible. Even if there wasn't work or anything to prevent me, it wouldn't be any use – running away is never any use.

Barbara   I didn't mean you to go away alone, it's too late for that now. I meant you to go away with her – take two months, three months if necessary – and relax utterly. Don't think about work or me or any of the things that are standing in the way.

Christian   I can't, Babs, you know I can't.

He rises from the table and moves to the window, lighting a cigarette.

Barbara   I don't know anything of the sort. It's clear, cold sense. I'm not thinking only of your happiness. I'm thinking of my happiness too and, more important still, of your job. (*she goes over to him and faces him squarely*) You can't deal wisely and successfully with twisted and nerve-strained people if you're twisted and nerve-strained yourself. You must see that. It isn't your passion for Leonora alone that's undermining you, it's the fight you're putting up. You're being torn in half.

Christian   Darling, you're making me so dreadfully ashamed.

Barbara   That's idiotic – unreasonable and idiotic. You said just now that you were submerged, that's true, you are. You'll go under altogether unless you try this way out. Will you ask Leonora?

Christian   Very well. If you wish it.

Barbara   I do.

He comes to her and takes her by the arms as though to kiss her. But he doesn't kiss her. He just turns and goes out. She is left watching him go, as we ...

DISSOLVE.

Scene 186

INT. DINING ROOM. FABERS' FLAT. DAY.

CLOSE SHOT of **Christian** *seated, to cover scene 185.*

Scene 187

INT. DINING ROOM. FABERS' FLAT. DAY.

CLOSE SHOT of **Barbara**, *seated, to cover scene 185.*

Scene 188

INT. DINING ROOM. FABERS' FLAT. DAY.

CLOSE SHOT of **Christian** *at the window, to cover scene 185.*

Scene 189

INT. DINING ROOM. FABERS' FLAT. DAY.

CLOSE SHOT of **Barbara** *turning to look at* **Christian** *at the window, covering scene 185.*

DISSOLVE TO

Scene 190

EXT. HYDE PARK. DAY.

Christian *and* **Leonora** *walk beside the Serpentine.*

Scene 191

EXT. HYDE PARK. DAY.

Christian *and* **Leonora** *walk to the balustrade overlooking the river.*

Scene 192

EXT. SERPENTINE TERRACE. DAY.

They lean over the balustrade and look down.

Leonora   I'm not arguing, darling – and I don't mean to be difficult – it's just that I don't understand.

Christian   You don't know Barbara.

Leonora   I know women. No woman would suggest that – not if she really loved you.

Christian   Barbara would. She doesn't in the least approve of our relationship but she completely understands what she is doing.

That's her way of loving. She loves with her reason and mind as well as her heart.

Leonora   A very admirable character.

Christian   Don't sneer at Barbara, Leonora – it's pitifully unworthy of you.

Leonora   (*putting her hand on his arm*) I know – I'm sorry – I don't mean to really – but it is difficult for me – you do see, don't you?

Christian   It's difficult for us all.

Leonora   Does she hate me?

Christian   No – I don't think so.

Leonora   Perhaps it would be easier if she did. We're all trying so desperately to be wise and well-behaved and reasonable – it's a dreadful strain.

Christian   Leonora …

Leonora   (*near tears*) Oh, Chris!

Christian   (*gently – putting his arm round her*) Are we to do as she says? Shall we accept her gesture and profit by her wisdom? Are you prepared to take the chance?

Leonora   I don't know – I really don't know.

Christian   I want you so dreadfully – it's too late to go back now – too late to run away.

Leonora   (*wistfully*) I wonder.

Scene 193

EXT. SERPENTINE TERRACE. DAY.

CLOSE UP of **Leonora**, *covering scene 192.*

Scene 194

EXT. SERPENTINE TERRACE. DAY.

CLOSE UP of **Christian**, *covering scene 192.*

Scene 195

EXT. SERPENTINE TERRACE. DAY.

CLOSE SHOT of **Christian** *and* **Leonora**, *covering scene 192.*

DISSOLVE TO

Scene 196

INT. OFFICE. FABERS' FLAT. DAY.

Barbara *at* **Tim**'s *desk, and* **Susan** *are settling* **Christian**'s *affairs before he goes away.*

Susan   But what on earth will happen to the work while he's away?

Barbara   It's all settled, Tim's agreed to take over everything for three months.

Susan   Oh, Barbara …

Barbara   What's the matter?

Susan   I hate it all so.

Barbara   Do you, Susan?

Susan   Don't be angry with me – I must say what's on my mind, what I feel about the whole business. I think you're hopelessly wrong to let him go like this and no good will ever come of it. It's not only the moral aspect of the situation that's worrying me – in the sort of work I do with Chris, moral attitudes are both trivial and irrelevant, but I do feel most desperately that what you are doing is bad for him and for you and for all of us.

Barbara   Please Susan – please don't.

Susan   I'm sorry.

Barbara   Dear Susan – I'm trying to be sensible, more sensible than I have ever been in my life. It's rather difficult so please help me all you can even though you do disapprove.

Susan   It's nothing to do with approval or disapproval – it's deeper than that.

Barbara   I know it is. But I have thought it all over interminably and there isn't anything else to do, really there isn't.

Susan   Very well.

Scene 197

INT. OFFICE. FABERS' FLAT. DAY.

CLOSE SHOT of **Susan**, *to cover scene 196.*

Scene 198

INT. OFFICE. FABERS' FLAT. DAY.

Barbara *moves to* **Susan***'s desk.*

Barbara   I shall go away somewhere myself, of course … Laura's in Paris, I can stay with her – or with Mary – she's taken the Birrels' house in Kent for six months. It's absolutely lovely. I shall be much happier there than I am here.

Susan   Well, you know best, of course. But it's a mystery to me how you can let him go away like that. Aren't you jealous?

Barbara   Not of her – but of his work and our happiness. I'm jealous of the time he's wasting now and will go on wasting – until he gets her out of his system. I sense the futility of it all, and I must help him, help him back –

Susan   To you?

Barbara   No – to sanity.

Scene 199

INT. OFFICE. FABERS' FLAT. DAY.

CLOSE UP of **Barbara**, *to cover scene 198.*

Scene 200

INT. OFFICE. FABERS' FLAT. DAY.

CLOSE UP of **Susan**, *to cover scene 198.*

DISSOLVE TO

Scene 201

EXT. CHESTER HOUSE. DAY.

The Fabers' car is drawn up at the curb. A **porter** *comes out of the building with some luggage which he puts in the boot. A moment later, he is followed by* **Christian** *and* **Tim**, *who get into the car and drive away.*

DISSOLVE TO

Scene 202

INT. CAR. B/P. DAY.

Christian *and* **Tim** *in the car.*

Scene 203

INT. CAR. B.P. DAY.

Christian *is driving and, at the same time, giving last minute instructions to* **Tim**.

Christian   … and you'll send me the proofs of the book as soon as they come from Chatham's?

Tim   Where shall I send them?

Christian   Cairo, if they come before the end of the month. After that, I'll let you know … My plans are a bit uncertain.

Tim   As long as you keep me posted …

Christian   Of course. There's just one other thing, Tim (*he pauses a little diffidently*) …

Tim   (*a grunt supplying a question mark*) Huh?

Christian   Barbara – I'd be grateful if you would see that she has everything she wants while I'm away.

Tim   Don't worry. I'll do all I can.

Christian   Thank, Tim.

Tim   Please don't thank me. I'd do anything for Barbara – always.

Christian   I know.

Tim   Good.

Christian   I've had all this out with Barbara, you know, and myself.

Tim   (*bleakly*) I'm sure you have.

Christian   You disapprove very strongly, don't you?

Tim   I neither approve nor disapprove – it's deeper than that.

Christian   I see.

Tim   I'm afraid you don't, but perhaps some day you will.

Christian   I'm sorry, Tim.

Tim   So am I. I'm sorry for you and I'm sorry for Barbara – as you know, I am deeply fond of you both – (*with a slight, ironic smile*) … I believe I can also find it in my heart to be a little sorry for Mrs. Leonora Vail.

Scene 204

INT. CAR. B/P. DAY.

SHOT of **Christian** *and* **Tim**, *covering scene 203.*

Scene 205

EXT. AIRPORT. DAY.

A trans-continental 'plane is taking off. **Tim**, *standing by the outside barrier on the tarmac, waves as it rises into the air. The camera holds the 'plane.*

FADE OUT.

FADE IN

Scene 206

INT. HALL. FABERS' FLAT. DAY.

The postman's ring is heard as some letters are slipped into the box on the door. In a moment, **Ernest** *collects them. He drops one on to the hall tray, and then returns to the kitchen.*

Scene 207

INT. KITCHEN. FABERS' FLAT. DAY.

*The cook (**Mrs. Smith**) is sitting at the breakfast table reading the paper, and **Ernest** comes in with the letters.*

Mrs. Smith   (*looking up*) Any for me?

Ernest   Only a card. The postmark's Portsmouth and it's signed 'Sid'.

Mrs. Smith   Some people aren't half nosey! (*she takes the card that **Ernest** passes over to her*) You didn't catch a glimpse of what it said, of course.

Ernest   (*sitting down and getting on with his breakfast*) Yes. He's on leave for a week, but it's not much cop as he's got a boil on the back of his neck and Ada's had the sack from Peterson's. Edie's expecting a happy event in August, so they've got to change their digs. 'What a lark! Yours Sid'.

Mrs. Smith   (*looking at the card*) Edie! Fancy! Wonders'll never cease.

*There is the sound of the front door shutting outside. **Ernest** looks up at the clock.*

Ernest   She's late this morning.

Mrs. Smith   Why does she trouble to come in at all? – that's what I'd like to know. Three months' holiday, that's what she had. I'd like to be some people!

Ernest   It's lucky for some people you aren't. (*he hands over his cup*) Is there another cuppa in the pot?

Mrs. Smith   No. And if you want any more – you can make it yourself.

Ernest   (*angrily*) Come off it. What are you here for?

Mrs. Smith   Not to wait on you, Mr. Sarcastic.

She gets up in high dudgeon and walks away.

Scene 208

INT. OFFICE. FABERS' FLAT. DAY.

Susan *is standing at the desk, reading her letter, when* **Tim** *comes out of the consulting room.*

Tim   I thought I heard you come in. Is that from Chris?

Susan   No, Barbara.

Tim   How is she?

Susan   Sounds cheerful enough – but you can never tell with her. She wouldn't say if she was dying.

Tim   No, I suppose not.

Susan   As usual, the only item of importance is in the P.S.

Tim   What's that?

Susan   Have we heard from Chris?

Tim   (*grimly*) There isn't any answer to that one, is there?

Susan   No. I just wish one didn't feel so utterly helpless, though.

Tim   (*shrugging his shoulders*) Well, let's hope he's having a good time, that's all. Nobody else is.

He turns away and returns to the consulting room, slamming the door behind him.

Scene 209

INT. OFFICE. FABERS' FLAT. DAY.

MEDIUM CLOSE SHOT of **Susan**, *to cover scene 208.*

Scene 210

INT. OFFICE. FABERS' FLAT. DAY.

MEDIUM CLOSE SHOT of **Tim**, *to cover scene 208.*

DISSOLVE TO

Scene 211

INT. APARTMENT. VENICE. NIGHT.

This is an attractive room with a balcony overlooking the canal.
Christian *is sitting in an armchair correcting some proofs and
making odd notes. An old Italian clock in the room chimes the
hour. He puts aside his papers and walks out on to the balcony. He
looks out and over the moonlit canal. There is no sign of* **Leonora**
*returning, so, after a moment or two, he comes back and goes to
the telephone. He dials a number and waits.*

Christian   (*into telephone*) Hello, can I speak to –? Oh, is that
you, Mrs. Gore? Christian Faber here … No, not in the least. I was
just wondering if Leonora was still with you … . When? Oh. I see.
You, yes, we certainly must – it's very good of you, Mrs Gore … .
Many thanks. Til tomorrow then … .

*He replaces the receiver and goes thoughtfully back to his chair.
Picking up his papers, he tries to concentrate on his work again.*

Scene 212

INT. APARTMENT. VENICE. NIGHT.

Christian *is seated.* **Leonora** *comes in. She is in evening dress
and looks very lovely.*

Leonora   Oh, Chris. You're not *still* working?

Christian   I'm nearly finished. Did you have a good time?

Leonora   So – so.

*She yawns, takes off her cloak and throws it down on a chair, then
comes to the table beside him to pour a drink.*

Christian   That sounds ominously as though you were bored.

Leonora   My dear, what can you expect? Gore rhymes with bore.

Christian   (*laughing*) And Faber with labour, it seems.

Leonora   What's the matter? Tired?

Christian   No. Why did you stay so long if the Gores were such bores?

Leonora   You know how difficult it is to get away.

Christian   Yes – I know. Was the dinner good?

Leonora   Yes, darling. Do you want me to itemise the courses? I can see you're in your best quiz mood.

Christian   Why do you try to deceive me? You dined with David Hartley tonight, didn't you?

Leonora   Oh, don't be absurd, Chris.

Christian   It's true, isn't it?

Leonora   Yes.

She walks away from the table.

Christian   Then why did you have to make a secret of it?

Leonora   Because I knew you'd make a dreadful scene if I didn't.

Christian   Our love inspires great confidence, apparently.

Leonora   It's not my fault that you imagine things and torture yourself.

Christian   I was under the impression that you loved me.

Leonora   Darling – don't –

Christian   More than anyone or anything in the world. How long ago was it you said that to me ...

Leonora   Please, Chris, I can't bear it when you go on like this.

Christian   (*rises*) You love me so much that you have to lie to me – you love me so much that you must play tricks on me – you twist me and torture me until I'm driven beyond endurance – then you cry and say I'm cruel.

Leonora   (*frantically*) Don't look at me like that – you're mad –

Christian   (*grimly*) Answer me one question – why didn't you stay the night with him – you wanted to, didn't you? What held you back? Your love for me. Or was it fear …?

Leonora   (*turns away from him*) Oh, what's the use – what's the use?

Christian   (*brokenly*) Do you think I like the situation? You not loving me any more, and me wanting you so –

Leonora   Why do you say that? You've worked it all up in your imagination. None of it's true – none of it's real.

Christian   Don't lie any more.

Leonora   I'm not – I'm not.

Christian   How do I know? You've lied before – I've caught you out. Trivial though they were, I grant you, but they were lies all the same – little lies and big lies – what's the difference? Perhaps you forget that charming little episode in Cairo?

Leonora   (*turning to face him*) Chris.

Christian   All right – all right. I know I'm dragging things up from the past – why shouldn't I?

The sound of her slamming the door in his face brings him to his senses with a painful jerk. He is still staring at the door as we dissolve.

Scene 213

INT. APARTMENT. VENICE. NIGHT.

MEDIUM SHOT of **Leonora,** *covering scene 213, as she is standing with her drink.*

Scene 214

INT. APARTMENT. VENICE. NIGHT.

MEDIUM CLOSE SHOT of **Christian** *seated, to cover scene 212.*

Scene 215

INT. APARTMENT. VENICE. NIGHT.

MEDIUM CLOSE SHOT as **Christian** *rises and comes to*
Leonora, *to cover scene 212.*

Scene 216

INT. APARTMENT. VENICE. NIGHT.

MEDIUM SHOT of **Leonora** *– she exits, to cover scene 212.*

DISSOLVE TO

Scene 217

EXT. COUNTRY HOUSE 'B'. DAY.

Barbara *is cycling up the drive of* **Mary**'s *country house in Kent.
She dismounts as* **Mary** *comes out of the front door and calls to
her.*

Mary   Oh, Barbara. I'm glad you're back.

Barbara   Why – anything wrong?

Mary   No. They came through on the telephone just now, asking
if you'd take a call from Venice.

Barbara   Chris?

Mary   Yes. I told them you'd take it between eight and nine
tonight. Was that all right?

Barbara   Perfectly. Thanks, Mary.

Mary   Tea's ready, dear.

Barbara   I'll just go and put this away. I won't be a minute.

As she wheels away her machine, we ...

DISSOLVE TO

Scene 218

INT. HALL. COUNTRY HOUSE 'B'. NIGHT.

*This is a small corner of the hall in **Mary**'s house. The telephone is ringing. **Barbara** comes in and picks up the receiver.*

Barbara   Hello? Yes, this is Maidstone 54. Mrs. Faber speaking ... Yes, I'll hold the line ... .

She sits down and patiently prepares to wait.

Scene 219

INT. APARTMENT. VENICE. NIGHT.

to

INT. HALL. COUNTRY HOUSE 'B'. NIGHT.

Scene 224

(*These six scene numbers to cover cross outs*)

Christian *is alone in the room, as he speaks to* **Barbara**.

(*For smooth reading this scene has not been split up into separate shots, but it will of course be a series of cross cuts*).

Christian   (*into telephone*) ... Is that you, Barbara?

Barbara   Yes, it's me, darling.

Christian   It doesn't sound like your voice a bit.

Barbara   You sound very far away, Chris.

Christian   (*nervously*) How – how are you?

Barbara   Better, thanks. I had a wretched cold last week, but it's gone now, thank goodness. How are you, Chris?

Christian   I'm all right.

Barbara   That's good.

Christian   How's Mary?

Barbara   Oh, Mary's fine.

Christian   Have you seen Tim?

Barbara   Not lately, no.

Christian   When you do see him, tell him I've sent the proofs back to Chatham's.

Barbara   I don't think I shall be seeing him for a few weeks, dear.

Christian   Oh.

Barbara   Frank and Laura have invited me up to Scotland for a fortnight – so I think I'll go.

Christian   Yes, of course. It'll do you good.

Barbara   (*after a strained pause*) How – how is Leonora?

Christian   Oh – she's just the same … Barbara –

Barbara   Yes?

Christian   I was going to say – I was going to ask you …

Barbara   I can't hear you. You've gone very faint all of a sudden –

Christian   (*knocking the receiver*) Is that better?

Barbara   Yes, that's better. What did you say?

Christian   I was – (*he breaks off*) Oh, nothing of importance.

Barbara   Will you be back soon?

Christian   I don't know – it's difficult to tell. (*then in a rush*) Barbara, there are a thousand things I wanted to say and now I just can't say one of them.

Barbara   Never mind, Chris – I understand. They'll have to wait till you come back. (*there is an interruption on the wire*) Oh. That means our time's up, doesn't it?

Christian   Yes. Barbara – just a moment.

Barbara   We'd better say goodbye quickly or they'll cut us off, won't they?

Christian   Yes.

Barbara   Goodbye, then, darling.

Christian   Goodbye Barbara – dear Barbara.

The operator cuts them off. As he hangs up the receiver, **Christian** *is on the verge of tears.*

FADE OUT.

FADE IN.

Scene 225

INT. HALL AND OFFICE. FABERS' FLAT. DAY.

Tim *lets himself in with a key and goes into the office, throws down his hat and coat and goes into the consulting room.*

Scene 226

INT. CONSULTING ROOM. FABERS' FLAT. DAY.

Tim *opens the door, makes for the desk and then stops short.*
Christian *is sitting there.*

Tim   Oh! (*not very cordially*) Welcome home.

Christian   It's good to see you, Tim.

Tim   When did you get back?

Christian   Seven-thirty this morning.

Tim   You should have let me know.

Christian   I didn't have time. It was all rather a rush.

Tim   You look pretty tired.

Christian   I didn't sleep much last night. It was a bumpy flight.

Tim   Have you eaten?

Christian   Oh, yes. Ernest rallied round splendidly – I had a
huge breakfast.

Tim   Want to run over the records with me?

Christian   Not just yet. Don't rush me.

Tim   All right. I'll bring them in later on, shall I?

Christian   Yes, do.

Tim *is just going out when he thinks of something and turns back.*

Tim   Shall I get Susan to telephone Barbara? – She has her
number.

Christian   (*a little agitated*) No – no, I don't think I'd do that,
Tim. As a matter of fact, I'd rather not let her know I'm back just
yet – not for a few days at any rate.

Tim   Oh. All right.

Christian   I feel I ought to let myself get acclimatised first. It's a bit more difficult than you imagine – when one's been away for so long. Once I've settled down to the normal routine here again, I'll call her myself.

Tim   Anything you say.

He goes out into the office, closing the door behind him.

Scene 227

INT. CONSULTING ROOM. FABERS' FLAT. DAY.

CLOSE SHOT of **Christian**, *to cover scene 226, when he is first seen by* **Tim**.

Scene 228

INT. CONSULTING ROOM. FABERS' FLAT. DAY.

CLOSE SHOT of **Tim**, *the camera PANS as he goes out, to cover scene 226.*

Scene 229

INT. CONSULTING ROOM. FABERS' FLAT. DAY.

CLOSE SHOT of **Christian** *at the desk* (*when* **Tim** *is at the door*), *to cover scene 226.*

Scene 230

INT. OFFICE. FABERS' FLAT. DAY.

Susan *has come in and starts to take off her things, preparatory to settling down to work as* **Tim** *comes to his desk.*

Susan   Good morning, Tim.

Tim   Hello.

Susan   Have you got a patient in there already?

Tim   No.

Susan   Oh. I just thought I heard voices.

Tim   It's Chris.

Susan   (*dropping her bag on the desk in surprise*) Chris!

Tim   Yes – arrived early this morning.

Susan   He might have let us know.

She moves to the coat rack.

Tim   That's what I told him.

Susan   What did he say?

Tim   Oh, something about being too rushed.

Susan   What's he like?

Tim   I don't know quite. But there's something strange about him. He's changed, Susan. Changed in an intangible sort of way. I don't like it.

Susan   You mean he's ill?

Tim   Not exactly ill – but there's something wrong.

Susan   Can I do anything?

Tim   No – just give me the records. We're going over them.

Scene 231

INT. OFFICE. FABERS' FLAT. DAY.

CLOSE SHOT of **Tim**, *to cover scene 230.*

Scene 232

INT. OFFICE. FABERS' FLAT. DAY.

Susan *crosses to her filing cabinet and extracts several folders.*

Tim   By the way, he doesn't want Barbara to know he's back.

Susan   Why not?

Tim   Some poppycock about settling in first.

Susan   How odd.

Tim   (*gives a grunt that means 'yes'*)

He takes the records and disappears into the consulting room. **Susan** *sits down at the desk and automatically removes the typewriter cover. A thoughtful frown wrinkles her forehead as we ...*

FADE OUT.

Scene 233

EXT. WATERLOO STATION. NIGHT.

Susan *is waiting under the large clock for the arrival of* **Barbara**. *The clock says ten-thirty. She shivers a little as she paces to and fro. The loudspeaker announces that the train, due at ten-fifteen, now running fifteen minutes late, will arrive on number ten platform, not eight, as scheduled* (*check for correct details*). **Susan** *hurries over to number ten platform.*

Scene 234

EXT. WATERLOO STATION. NIGHT.

CLOSE SHOT of scene 233.

Scene 235

EXT. WATERLOO STATION. NIGHT.

Susan *is waiting at the barrier to one of the platforms as the train comes in. In a moment,* **Barbara** *comes through with a* **porter** *following, carrying her bags.* **Susan** *hurries towards her.*

Barbara   Susan! How good of you to meet me.

Susan   It's the least I could do. (*to Porter*) I've a taxi waiting.

As they go off towards it ...

DISSOLVE TO

Scene 236

INT. TAXI. B/P. NIGHT.

Barbara *and* **Susan** *in the taxi going home.*

Barbara   Your letter sounded so cryptic I thought I'd better come at once – just in case there was more behind it.

Susan   There was.

Barbara   Tell me.

Susan   When I told you Chris was back, I didn't say he'd been home for the past ten days.

Barbara   Why not?

Susan   Tim and I thought it would only worry you. Besides he said he'd let you know the moment he really felt settled in.

Barbara   He didn't.

Susan   No, we guessed that.

Barbara   Well?

Susan   Oh, Barbara – it's been awful this last week. He's changed so completely, you'd hardly know him – he's quite unaccountable. One minute he makes an appointment – the next he breaks it and forgets to tell me. It's quite impossible to know how to deal with him. So we thought we ought to send for you.

Barbara   Quite right.

Susan   His work's going to pieces. He just can't pick up the threads. (*she decides she's saying too much*) Don't worry. He'll be different now you're back.

Barbara   I hope I can be of some use, that's all.

Susan   You'll have him right in no time.

Barbara   If it's not too late.

They start to get out as we dissolve.

Scene 237

INT. TAXI. B/P. NIGHT.

CLOSE SHOT of **Susan**, *to cover scene 236.*

Scene 238

INT. TAXI. B/P. NIGHT.

CLOSE SHOT of **Barbara**, *to cover scene 236.*

DISSOLVE TO

Scene 239

INT. HALL. FABERS' FLAT. NIGHT.

Ernest *opens the front door and* **Barbara** *and* **Susan** *come in to the flat, followed by the* **porter** *with the bags, which he stacks in the hall.*

Ernest   Good evening, madam. Welcome home.

Barbara   Thank you, Ernest.

Ernest   I hope you had a good journey, madam.

Barbara   Yes, not too bad, but I'm rather tired.

Ernest   Can I get you anything, madam?

Barbara   No, thank you Ernest. Is Dr. Faber in?

Ernest   No, madam. He went out early this evening and didn't say when he'd be back.

Barbara   Oh, I see. That'll be all, then, Ernest.

Ernest   Very good, madam.

He starts to pick up the bags as **Barbara** *follows* **Susan** *into the drawing room.*

Scene 240

INT. LEONORA'S LOUNGE. NIGHT.

We come to a big head of **Leonora**. *She is lying face downwards on the sofa, sobbing. We DRAW BACK to reveal* **Christian**, *standing nearby, with his back to her.*

Christian   For the love of heaven, stop crying. (*she continues to sob*) I'm sorry – I've said I was sorry.

Leonora   I can't bear any more.

Christian   (*coming over to her*) Darling, please –

Leonora   Don't, don't come near me.

Christian   (*kneeling beside her*) You must forgive me – you must.

Leonora   (*slowly sitting up*) It isn't forgiving – it's that I can't bear any more. I mean it this time – I really can't.

Christian   (*rising – bitterly*) I should like to know what you propose to do then.

Leonora   I'm going – I'm going away for good.

Christian   I see.

Leonora   I'll go tomorrow –

Scene 241

INT. LEONORA'S LOUNGE. NIGHT.

Christian *comes round the sofa to* **Leonora**.

Christian   No, you can't. (*he takes her in his arms*) You can't possibly.

Leonora   Please, Chris. I've got to go away, I must – I've told you – I really can't bear any more.

Christian   You can't bear any more. What about me?

Leonora   It's not my fault you create these fearful scenes that make our lives a dreary misery.

Christian   Tell me one thing – without lying or evading – tell me one thing honestly –

Leonora   (*wearily*) What is it?

Christian   Do you still – love me?

Leonora   Oh, Christ.

She turns away hopelessly.

Christian   Do you?

Leonora   Yes.

Scene 242

INT. LEONORA'S LOUNGE. NIGHT.

CLOSE SHOT of **Leonora**, *to cover scene 241.*

Scene 243

INT. LEONORA'S LOUNGE. NIGHT.

BIG CLOSE UP of **Leonora**, *to cover scene 241.*

Scene 244

INT. LEONORA'S LOUNGE. NIGHT.

BIG CLOSE UP of **Christian**, *to cover scene 241.*

Scene 245

INT. LEONORA'S LOUNGE. NIGHT.

Leonora *rises and walks towards the fire, leaving* **Christian** *on the sofa.*

Christian   As much as you did in the beginning?

Leonora   Differently, Chris, things have changed – a year has gone by since the beginning.

Christian   That's an evasion.

Leonora   It's the truth – nothing stays the same.

Christian *starts to come to her.*

Christian   You wanted me in the beginning, didn't you? Whenever I came near you – whenever I touched you – it was more important than anything else in the world, wasn't it?

Leonora   Yes – it was.

Christian   And now it isn't any more?

Leonora   Chris – what's the use of –

Christian   Answer me. Do you love me as much as you did in the beginning?

Leonora   (*violently – as she turns to him*) No – no – no!

Christian   At last.

Leonora   That's what you wanted, isn't it? The truth – that's the truth.

Christian   Then you have been lying – for weeks – for months probably …

Leonora   Yes, I have – I have –

Christian   When did it die, this poor shabby love of yours?

Leonora   (*wildly*) A long while ago – you killed it yourself with your insane jealousies and cruelties. You never trusted me – never for a minute – you've spoiled hours that could have been perfect by making scenes out of nothing. You've dug up things that were once dear to me and made them look cheap and horrible. I can't even go back into my own memory now without finding you there jeering on every threshold – walking with me through the empty rooms – making them tawdry – shutting them off from me for ever. I hate you for that – bitterly.

She turns away and he stares at her sardonically.

Christian   Sentiment for the dead at the expense of the living – very interesting – quite magnificent.

Leonora   The dead at least have the sense to be quiet.

Christian   Long live the dead.

Leonora   (*with bitterness*) You are one of them now.

Scene 246

INT. LEONORA'S LOUNGE. NIGHT.

CLOSE SHOT of **Leonora**, *to cover scene 245.*

Scene 247

INT. LEONORA'S LOUNGE. NIGHT.

CLOSE UP of **Christian**, *to cover scene 245.*

Scene 248

INT. LEONORA'S LOUNGE. NIGHT.

CLOSE UP of **Leonora**, *to cover scene 245.*

Scene 249

INT. LEONORA'S LOUNGE. NIGHT.

There is a dreadful silence for a moment. They stand quite still looking at each other. The silence is eventually broken by the telephone ringing. They ignore it.

Christian   (*quietly*) Did you mean that?

Leonora   (*hesitantly*) Yes – I think I did.

The telephone continues to ring. **Leonora** *crosses to the door and goes out into the hall, closing the door behind her.*

Scene 250

INT. LEONORA'S HALL. NIGHT.

Leonora *picks up the telephone.*

Leonora   (*into telephone*) Yes? Speaking.

(*hold this for dialogue in scene 251*)

Scene 251

INT. FABERS' FLAT. DRAWING ROOM. NIGHT.

Barbara *is on the other end of the wire, with* **Susan** *sitting nearby.*

(*Dialogue to be crossed out where necessary, with shot of* **Leonora** *in the hall of her house*)

Barbara   I'm so sorry to ring up at this horribly late hour, but I was worried. Chris went out early this evening and nobody seems to know where. If he's with you, it'll relieve my mind a bit. Is he?

Leonora   Yes. Do you want to talk to him?

Barbara   No. I was frightened that something had happened to him. Please don't say I've rung, will you?

Leonora   Not if you don't want me to.

Barbara   He'll only think I'm checking up on him, and I'd hate that.

Leonora   Very well – just as you like. Is there anything else?

Barbara   No, nothing else – except that I'm sorry I disturbed you.

Leonora   Goodnight.

She hangs up the receiver and moves away.

Scene 252

INT. LEONORA'S LOUNGE. NIGHT.

Leonora *comes slowly from the hall back into the lounge.*

Christian *is standing by the fire and turns round as she moves towards him.*

Christian   I know it's over now – I really do. I won't make any more scenes. I promise.

Leonora   Goodbye, Chris.

She takes both his hands in hers and he grips them.

Christian   (*hoarsely*) It is quite dead – quite dead?

Leonora   (*struggling to release her hands*) Don't Chris – please.

Christian   All passion spent – everything tied up and put back in the box.

Leonora   (*trying to twist away from him*) Chris – let me go.

He kisses her again violently and throws her away from him. She staggers and falls on to the sofa.

Scene 253

INT. LENORA'S LOUNGE. NIGHT.

Christian *stands looking down to LEONORA on the sofa.*

Christian   How does it feel to be so desirable – to be wanted so much? Tell me, please. I want to know – I want to know what your heart's doing now, your loving female heart. How enviable to be able to walk away into the future, free of love, free of longing, a new life before you and the dead behind you – not quite the dead, though. Let's say the dying. The dying aren't as sensibly quiet as the dead – they can't help crying a little. You must walk swiftly out of earshot and don't – don't, I implore you, look back. There's little charm in dying – it's only clinically interesting – but your viewpoint is far from clinical, my dear – you're a sane, thrilling animal without complications, and the fact that my life has been broken on your loveliness isn't your fault. I don't believe it's even mine …

Scene 254

INT. LENORA'S LOUNGE. NIGHT.

CLOSE UP of **Christian**, *to cover scene 253.*

Scene 255

INT. LENORA'S LOUNGE. NIGHT.

As **Christian** *continues to talk, turning his back to her,* **Leonora** *slips quietly out of the room without his noticing.*

Christian   (*continuing*) You're in on a grand tragedy, the best tragedy of all, the best joke, the triumphant, inevitable defeat of mind by matter. Just for a minute, I'm seeing it all clearly, myself, you and the world around us. You see, I had a life to live and work to do and people to love and now I haven't any more. They're eager to help, those people I love and who love me. I can see them still straining to get to me – but they can't reach me – any more. (*he realises that he is quite alone, and that Leonora has left him*) It's too late.

He walks out into the hall.

Scene 256

INT. LEONORA'S LOUNGE. NIGHT.

CLOSE SHOT of **Leonora** *on the sofa, covering scene 255.*

Scene 257

INT. LEONORA'S LOUNGE. NIGHT.

MEDIUM close shot of **Leonora**, *as she exits in scene 255.*

Scene 258

INT. LEONORA'S LOUNGE. NIGHT.

MEDIUM SHOT of **Christian**, *from* **Leonora***'s eye line in scene 255.*

Scene 259

INT. LEONORA'S LOUNGE. NIGHT.

CLOSE SHOT of **Christian**, *as he realises he is alone, in scene 255*

Scene 260

INT. LEONORA'S HALL. NIGHT.

Christian *lets himself out of the house, leaving his hat and coat behind.*

Scene 261

INT. LEONORA'S HOUSE. NIGHT.

Christian *leaves the house and walks away up the street.*

DISSOLVE TO

Scene 262

EXT. PARK. NIGHT.

Christian *crosses Park Lane and goes through the entrance into Hyde Park.*

Scene 263

EXT. HYDE PARK. NIGHT.

Christian *walking across the park.*

Scene 264

EXT. HYDE PARK. NIGHT.

Christian *arrives at the Serpentine balustrade.*

Scene 265

EXT. SERPENTINE TERRACE. NIGHT.

Christian *leans over the balustrade.*

Scene 266

EXT. SERPENTINE TERRACE. NIGHT.

CLOSE UP of **Christian** *as he leans over the balustrade.*

Scene 267

INT. DRAWING ROOM. FABERS' FLAT. NIGHT.

Barbara *and* **Susan** *are still waiting for* **Christian**.

Barbara   There's no point in staying any longer, Susan. He's bound to be in soon.

Susan   It's nearly three.

Barbara   Yes – and I shall get really angry with you if you persist in coddling me.

Susan   (*rising and putting down her glass*) Oh, very well – have it your own way.

Barbara   Would you like another drink before you go?

Susan   No, thanks. I've got to get up in the morning.

She starts to move towards the hall.

Barbara   (*getting up*) If he wants anything early, I can easily see to it.

Susan   Thanks. But I'll be here just the same.

She vanishes into the hall, leaving **Barbara**.

DISSOLVE TO

Scene 268

EXT. HYDE PARK. DAWN

Dawn is just breaking. **Christian** *is still leaning over the balustrade gazing down the length of the Serpentine. He is quite motionless for several moments. Then he suddenly straightens up and moves away with a certain determination in his walk.*

Scene 269

EXT. HYDE PARK. DAWN.

CLOSE SHOT of **Christian** *leaning over the balustrade, to cover scene 268.*

Scene 270

EXT. HYDE PARK. DAWN.

Christian *walks through the park and out of the gates.*

DISSOLVE TO

Scene 271

INT. DRAWING ROOM. FABERS' FLAT. NIGHT.

Barbara, *her nerves now on edge by the effort of waiting, is walking up and down. She comes face to face with the telephone, picks up the receiver and dials a number. She waits.*

Scene 272

INT. HALL. LEONORA's HOUSE. NIGHT.

The telephone in **Leonora***'s hall begins to ring. No one comes to answer it. It goes on ringing.*

Scene 273

INT. DRAWING ROOM. FABERS' FLAT. NIGHT/DAWN.

Barbara*, still waiting. As there is no reply to her ringing, she finally puts the receiver down and goes to the window and draws the curtains. She looks at her watch. She turns out the electric lights and exits to the hall.*

Scene 274

EXT. CHESTER HOUSE. DAY.

Christian *arrives at the building and makes his way inside. His face wears a dead, set expression.*

Scene 275

INT. FOYER. CHESTER HOUSE. DAY.

The **porter** *is asleep in his cubby-hole.* **Christian** *walks over to* *the lift and pushes the button. In a moment it arrives and he gets inside.*

Scene 276

INT. LIFT. DAY.

Christian *coming up in the lift.*

Scene 277

INT. HALL. FABERS' FLAT. DAY.

Barbara *finishes scribbling a note on the hall pad and stands it up for* **Christian** *to see. 'Back in half an hour – Barbara'. She puts on her coat and goes out of the front door.*

Scene 278

INT. LANDING. DAY.

Christian *gets out of the lift and mounts a narrow staircase which leads to the roof.*

Scene 279

INT. LANDING. DAY.

Barbara *crosses to the lift – the doors are open – she enters it and closes the gates. The lift descends.*

Scene 280

INT. STAIRCASE. DAY.

Christian *goes up the stairs and then through a door on to the roof.*

Scene 281

EXT. ROOF. CHESTER HOUSE. DAY.

Christian *walks to the parapet.*

Scene 282

EXT. ROOF. CHESTER HOUSE. DAY.

Christian *is on the flat roof of the block of flats staring down over the parapet. The street below seems miles away and every object in it looks very small and remote. He straightens up and climbs on to the parapet. Shielding his eyes with one hand, he leaps over the side.*

Scene 283

EXT. ROOF. CHESTER HOUSE. DAY.

CLOSE SHOT of **Christian**, *to cover scene 282.*

Scene 284

EXT. ROOF. CHESTER HOUSE. DAY.

LONG SHOT of the street from **Christian***'s eye line to cut into scene 282*

Scene 285

EXT. ROOF. CHESTER HOUSE. DAY.

Shooting on to the puddles on the roof. **Christian***'s shadow passes across as he falls.*

Scene 286

INT. LIFT. DAY.

Barbara *descending.*

Scene 287

INT. FOYER. CHESTER HOUSE. DAY.

Barbara *comes out of the lift and walks out through the door.*

Scene 288

EXT. CHESTER HOUSE. DAY.

Barbara *comes out of the building. She turns as she hears voices from the corner of the street.*

Scene 289

EXT. CHESTER HOUSE. DAY.

A small knot of people – a **policeman**, *a* **roadman** *and a nondescript man or two – is gathered round something on the pavement. Someone breaks away and runs into the building.*

Scene 290

EXT. CHESTER HOUSE. DAY.

She walks over towards the group. As **Barbara** *reaches the knot of people, she hears murmurs of 'Accident, I suppose'. 'Accident, my foot', etc. She glances over a* **taxi driver**'s *shoulder and looks down. We do not see what is on the pavement, but* **Barbara**'s *agonised look is enough to tell the story.*

DISSOLVE TO

Scene 291

INT. DRAWING ROOM. FABERS' FLAT. DAY.

It is still raining, as we come back to **Barbara** *staring out of the window with unseeing eyes.*

Barbara   How extraordinary.

Tim   What?

Barbara   I've just remembered. It was exactly like this the day I met her again – and it's exactly a year ago. I was standing looking out of the window at the rain – only it wasn't this window. It was Darlington's in Fulham Road and …

Ernest*'s voice breaks in over the scene.*

Ernest   (*announcing*) Mrs. Vail, madam.

Scene 292

INT. DRAWING ROOM. FABERS' FLAT. DAY.

Barbara *turns to meet her.* **Leonora** *comes in. Her eyes are red from crying and she is obviously trying with all her will to control herself.* **Tim** *and* **Susan** *can scarcely look at her.*

Barbara   Leonora – at last!

Leonora   I should have been sooner but I got held up in the traffic. It was awful.

Barbara   Never mind. You're here now.

Tim   Hadn't you better go in right away? He's been asking for you.

Leonora *looks at* **Barbara**, *who goes to pour her a brandy.*

Barbara   She'll need this first – (*she brings the glass to* **Leonora**) Here – it's important that you don't break down.

Leonora *still cannot bring herself to take it.*

Leonora   I'll be all right.

Barbara   Please drink it.

Leonora   Very well.

She gulps it down.

Barbara   Tim, will you please take her?

Tim   Of course.

Tim *goes into the corridor and* **Leonora** *follows him.*

Scene 293

INT. DRAWING ROOM. FABERS' FLAT. DAY.

CLOSE TWO SHOT of **Leonora** *and* **Barbara**, *to cover scene 292.*

Scene 294

INT. HALL. FABERS' FLAT. DAY.

Leonora *and* **Tim** *reach the bedroom door.* **Tim** *knocks gently and then opens it.*

Leonora   (*whispering*) Thank you.

She goes through into the room and **Tim** *closes the door.*

SLOW DISSOLVE TO

Scene 295

INT. DRAWING ROOM. FABERS' FLAT. DAY.

We HOLD on a tray of coffee things and then PULL BACK to show **Tim** *filling one of the cups.*

Tim   Do you want some more, Barbara?

Barbara   No.

Tim   Susan?

Susan   No, thank you.

Barbara *is wandering around the room.*

Tim   (*gently to* **Barbara**) Do sit down, my dear.

Barbara   No, I'm all right. I like wandering.

Tim *strolls over to the window and looks out.*

Tim   (*to make conversation*) I believe it's stopped raining at last.

Barbara   It's too much of a good thing – it is, really.

She breaks off and turns her hand away. **Tim** *and* **Susan** *look at each other miserably.* **Barbara** *recovers herself quickly.*

Barbara   I have a dreadful feeling that I'm making it all much harder for you –

Tim   Don't be so foolish.

Susan   (*looking towards the door*) I wonder if –

Tim   (*quickly*) Don't wonder anything, it's better not.

Barbara   You mustn't snap at Susan, Tim, it's beastly of you.

Tim   Sorry, Susan, I didn't mean to snap.

Susan   (*trying to smile at him*) I didn't even hear.

Barbara   I wish she'd come out now – I wish to God she'd come out now.

Tim   She will in a minute …

Barbara   A minute! Don't you realise she's been in there an hour (*then suddenly she decides she can bear it no longer*). It's no use – I must find out what's happening …

She hurries out of the room into the hall.

Scene 296

INT. DRAWING ROOM. FABERS' FLAT. DAY.

Barbara *exits, to cover scene 293 at the end.*

Scene 297

INT. DRAWING ROOM. FABERS' FLAT. DAY.

Tim *and* **Susan**, *to cover scene 295.*

Scene 298

INT. HALL. FABERS' FLAT. DAY.

As **Barbara** comes into the hall, she meets **Leonora** coming from the direction of the bedroom. **Barbara** stops dead and stares at her.

Barbara   (*whispering*) Is he? … Is he? …

Leonora   Yes.

Barbara   Oh – oh, dear …

She stands there, stricken, unable to move.

Leonora   He didn't know me, he thought it was you, he said … 'Babs – I'm not submerged any more …' and then he said 'Babs' again – and then – then he died.

Scene 299

INT. HALL. FABERS' FLAT. DAY.

CLOSE UP of **Barbara**, *to cover scene 298.*

Scene 300

INT. HALL. FABERS' FLAT. DAY.

A second or two later, **Barbara**, *hearing the door shut, draws a deep breath and moves away along the hall. She is completely composed now and there is a clear light in her eyes. She opens the bedroom door and goes inside, then closes it softly behind her.*

FADE OUT.

THE END

Scene 301[1]

INT. BEDROOM. FABERS' FLAT. NIGHT.

Christian *is asleep in bed. From the movement of his eyelids, we can see that he is very restless. He is muttering something but the words are inaudible to us.*

CAMERA TRACKS up to high shot and we ...

DISSOLVE.

Scene 302

INT. OFFICE. FABERS' FLAT. NIGHT. (DREAM)

Tim *and* **Susan** *are in the office.* **Christian**, *looking more haggard than at any other time in the film, glides up towards them.*

Scene 303

INT. OFFICE. FABERS' FLAT. NIGHT. (DREAM)

Christian *comes to* **Tim** *and* **Susan**.

Christian   I want to see Dr. Faber please.

Susan   I'm afraid that is out of the question – so many people want to see Dr. Faber. They have been waiting to see him for days, for weeks, for months. They want him to help them, to smooth out their minds, to cure their dreadful sadness, their fear, their despair – but he can't help them any more because he is so very, very busy.

Tim   That's what they all say.

---

[1] The script contains a dream sequence – Scenes 301–21 – that was not used in the final film. It has been restored to its relevant place in the plot, while retaining its later scene numbers.

Christian   But it's urgent – you don't understand – it's tremendously urgent.

Susan   It always is.

Christian   Please, please ask him to see me. He knew me well when I was young, when my mind was untroubled, when I could see clearly – I know he'd see me if he knew.

Tim   That's what they all say.

Christian   I implore you to let me see him just for a little – just for one brief minute.

Susan   What name please?

Christian   Dr. Faber. Dr. Christian Faber.

Susan *switches a switch on her desk and speaks – her voice becomes more and more amplified as the scene DISSOLVES.*

Susan   Dr. Faber to see Dr. Faber – Dr. Christian Faber to see Dr. Christian Faber. Dr. Faber to see Dr. Faber – Doctor Faber – Doctor Faber, DOCTOR FABER, DOCTOR FABER, DOCTOR FABER …

Scene 304

INT. OFFICE. FABERS' FLAT. NIGHT. (DREAM)
CLOSE SHOT, covering scene 303.

Scene 305

INT. OFFICE. FABERS' FLAT. NIGHT. (DREAM)
CLOSE SHOT, **Christian,** *covering scene 303.*

Scene 306

INT. CONSULTING ROOM. FABERS' FLAT. NIGHT.
(DREAM)

To distinguish between the two **Christian**s *in this scene, the one
behind the desk is referred to as* **Faber**.

Faber   Come in – come in – sit down.

Tim   This is Doctor Faber, sir. His mind is troubled. He cannot
see clearly any more. His heart is tortured by love, and he is mad.

Faber   Mad?

Tim   Mad.

Faber   Mad.

Christian   No, no – not yet – that's why I want you to cure me –
I'm not mad – not quite – but you see …

Faber   What makes you think that I can cure you?

Christian   You're Doctor Faber, the great psychiatrist, aren't you?

Faber   I was – I was – when I was younger, when my mind was
untroubled – when I could see clearly.

Christian   Then you must be able to cure. You must. I can't go
on like this. I'm sick – I want to be well.

Tim   (*to* **Faber**, *mockingly*) Well, maestro, what's the answer to
that? Are you going to cure him, or aren't you?

Faber   (*to* **Christian**) I'm sorry. I'm afraid I can't help you.

Christian   Why not?

Faber   Because of this. (*he holds out a little brooch of emeralds
and sapphires, which* **Leonora** *was wearing in the scene in
the club.*) Do you know what this is? It's a little brooch with
emeralds and sapphires. Someone gave it to Leonora years ago –
a handsome young man, burnt to death in a plane – the one she
really loved – the only one she ever really loved.

Tim   (*holding out his hand*) Let me see that.

Faber   (*holding it away from* **Tim**) Oh no, you think you're going to steal her away from me, don't you? Well, you're not. Nobody's going to have her, but me.

Tim   (*to* **Christian**) You'd better go – you'll get no help from him.

Christian   (*to* **Faber**) You must help. You must.

Tim   You're wasting your time.

Scene 307

INT. CONSULTING ROOM. FABERS' FLAT. NIGHT. (DREAM).

M.C.S. over **Dr. Faber**'s *shoulder onto* **Christian** *and* **Tim**, *covering scene 306.*

Scene 308

INT. CONSULTING ROOM. FABERS' FLAT. NIGHT. (DREAM).

M.C.S. to C.S. **Tim** *and* **Christian**, *covering scene 306.*

Scene 309

INT. CONSULTING ROOM. FABERS' FLAT. NIGHT. (DREAM).

M.C.S. **Faber**, **Christian** *and* **Tim**, *covering scene 306*

Scene 310

INT. CONSULTING ROOM. FABERS' FLAT. NIGHT.
(DREAM)

C.S. **Tim** *and* **Dr. Faber**, *covering scene 306.*

Scene 311

INT. CONSULTING ROOM. FABERS' FLAT. NIGHT.
(DREAM).

Faber *has put his head in his hands. He doesn't look up as*
Christian *speaks. In a moment,* **Christian** *gets up and goes out.*
When he has gone, **Tim** *begins to shake* **Faber** *by the shoulder.*
Faber *looks up.*

Tim   You know what your motto should be?

Faber *shakes his head and* **Tim** *says, sarcastically*

Tim   Physician, heal thyself! Physician, heal thyself!

Scene 312

INT. RESTAURANT. NIGHT. (DREAM)

Start on Big Close Up of **Christian**, *with his head in his hands,*
then camera TRACKS BACK to reveal **Leonora**, *and the b.g. plate*
changes to restaurant, with band in b.g.

Leonora   I made up my mind to make you fall in love with me –
it was a trick – now I wish I hadn't. I feel cheap – I feel frightened
– I wish with all my heart that I hadn't.

Christian   I think it was rather a gay trick. Don't be upset –
there's nothing to be upset about. What do you want? Truth or lies
– reality or pretence?

Leonora   I loved somebody once – very much – never so much before and never so much since.

Christian   Liar – liar! I'm the one you love – you swore it – more than all the others – more than anyone in the world – I must be sure of that.

Leonora   (*laughing*) That's the fun of it – you can never be sure with me, can you?

Scene 313

EXT. GONDOLA. VENICE. NIGHT. (DREAM)

The scene DISSOLVES to Venice. **Leonora** *and* **Christian** *are in a gondola.*

Christian   That's the fun of it – the whole fun of it – seeing Venice with someone you love – No – No – I mean someone you're in love with.

Leonora   Is there such a difference?

Christian   Yes – yes – of course there is – being in love doesn't last but loving lasts forever.

Leonora   (*mockingly*) That's the fun of it.

Christian   He gave you the brooch because he was in love with you –

Leonora   Tell the gondolier to let us drift out into the lagoon.

Christian   No – the lagoon is dangerous – the wind springs up suddenly and people are drowned.

Leonora   Don't be silly – the gondolier would know – gondoliers know a great deal.

Christian   (*savagely*) Does he know about other men having loved you? About you lying in their arms?

Leonora   Be quiet – be quiet – you're spoiling the magic – why must your love for me make such a noise? Let's be at peace – let's drift.

Christian   No – we mustn't do that. We mustn't drift.

Leonora   Why not?

Christian   We might hurt Barbara.

Leonora   (*mockingly*) Oh we mustn't hurt Barbara! That would never do!

Christian   You know I wouldn't want to hurt her.

Leonora   Turn back then, if you can – we're drifting faster and faster – tell the gondolier to take us back to the beginning.

Scene 314

EXT. GONDOLA. VENICE. NIGHT. (DREAM)

CLOSE SHOT **Leonora** – *over* **Christian**'s *right shoulder, covering scene 313.*

Scene 315

EXT. GONDOLA. VENICE. NIGHT. (DREAM)

CLOSE SHOT of **Christian** *over* **Leonora**'s *left shoulder, covering scene 313.*

Scene 316

EXT. GONDOLA. VENICE. NIGHT. (DREAM)

CLOSE SHOT of **Christian**, *covering scene 313.*

Scene 317

EXT. GONDOLA. VENICE. NIGHT. (DREAM)

CLOSE UP, **Leonora***, covering scene 313.*

Scene 318

EXT. GONDOLA. VENICE. NIGHT. (DREAM)

Christian *kneels on seat and talks to* **Gondolier***.*

Christian   (*to* **Gondolier**) Go back. Go back – he can't hear me. We can't turn back.

Leonora   I told you so. It can't be done.

Christian   Is that a challenge?

Leonora   Yes.

Christian   Then I accept it.

He rises to his feet. She starts to rock the gondola.

Scene 319

EXT. GONDOLA. VENICE. NIGHT. (DREAM)

CLOSE SHOT of **Leonora** *over* **Christian***'s shoulder as he kneels on seat. He tries to keep his balance, covering scene 318.*

Scene 320

EXT. WHIRLPOOL. VENICE. NIGHT. (DREAM)

Christian *loses his balance and falls in the water.* **Leonora** *starts to laugh at him.*

Leonora   What did I tell you?

He tries to laugh back but suddenly finds that he is in difficulty.
He cannot get back into the gondola. It recedes from him with
alarming rapidity.

Christian   Don't go away from me. Help me! Please Leonora –
help me – I can't get back.

He struggles frantically and the disturbed waters begin to spin him
round as though he were in a whirlpool.

Christian   (*calling desperately*) Where are you? I'll never reach
you – I'll never get back.

Christian *is sucked down into the swirling waters, but struggles*
to the surface and cries out once more.

Christian   Help! Barbara! Help! I'm drowning. Barbara, help
me …………..

Scene 321

INT. BEDROOM. FABERS' FLAT. NIGHT.

Christian in bed (*match frame from end of scene 310*). **Barbara**
appears top left of frame as camera TRACKS BACK.

Barbara   (*voice a long way off*) All right, Chris. All right. I'm
coming.

DISSOLVE

END OF DREAM SEQUENCE.